Penguin Handbooks
The Penguin Book of Playgr[...]

Joyce Lucas was trained as a nursery and infant teacher
and taught for seven years before taking a child care
officer's course. She was for three years in Southampton
Children's Department and subsequently ran a playgroup
in her own house, combining this with an appointment
as a J.P. She has tutored courses for playgroup staff,
and was founder member and area organizer for the
Southampton branch of the Pre-School Playgroup
Association. She is now a part-time lecturer at La Sainte
Union College of Education and gives a monthly broadcast
on playgroup matters for BBC Radio Solent. She is
married and has three children, Caroline, Debbie and Ben.

Vivienne McKennell trained as a nursery and infant
teacher at Didsbury, Manchester. She has taught in a
variety of local authority nursery and infant schools and
has also worked with educationally sub-normal children
for the ILEA in Brixton. When her own son and
daughter, Magnus and Stephanie, were small she helped
run a hall playgroup and became an active chairman
of the Southampton Pre-School Playgroup Association. She
then went on to tutor playgroup courses at Fareham
Technical College, where she was also a lecturer in
residential child care. She is married to a social psychologist
and is currently studying for an M.A. in Educational
Research and Innovation.

The Penguin Book of Playgroups

Joyce Lucas and
Vivienne McKennell

PENGUIN BOOKS

Penguin Books Ltd, Harmondsworth,
Middlesex, England
Penguin Books Inc., 7110 Ambassador Road,
Baltimore, Maryland 21207, U.S.A.
Penguin Books Australia Ltd, Ringwood,
Victoria, Australia
Penguin Books Canada Ltd, 41 Steelcase Road West,
Markham, Ontario, Canada
Penguin Books (N.Z.) Ltd, 182–190 Wairau Road,
Auckland 10, New Zealand

First published 1974
Reprinted 1974
Copyright © Joyce Lucas and Vivienne McKennell, 1974

Made and printed in Great Britain by
Richard Clay (The Chaucer Press) Ltd, Bungay, Suffolk
Set in Linotype Pilgrim

This book is
dedicated to the people
who work in playgroups

Contents

Foreword

In the past decade public opinion has at last grasped what the great pioneers of pre-school education – Rachel MacMillan, Audemars Lafandel, Montessori, DeCroly, Froebel and others – had been saying for more than half a century. We have come to agree that early education is the most important education; and that the mother is the first and most critical of all the child's teachers. We are beginning to see that the whole ideal of equality of opportunity – for education and later for life itself – is not ensured by mere equality of access to schools; inequalities begin in differences in the intellectual, emotional and social qualities of the child's earliest environment. And this is true whether we look closely at our own society; or regard the great differences which exist between Europe and North America on the one hand and the developing countries across Africa, Asia and Latin America on the other. We become aware too that it is not only human intelligence which may be warped or wasted by inadequate, deprived or distorted early learning. The pre-school experiences of children are the bases of socialization and the birth of the broad patterns of ideas of the self and others, the foundations of the emotional life. They are the determinants of mental health not merely of the individual but of the community of which he is part.

These considerations may seem a far cry from the group of mothers banding together to provide enriched experiences for their children, but they are the context of this eminently practical book. Perhaps the pioneers of parent-cooperative pre-school education and, particularly those who founded the Pre-School Playgroup Association, were not fully aware that they had hit upon a major and most creative educational development – not so much because a few children would be happily and creatively occupied, but because, through involvement with their children, mothers and fathers would be led to improve their own nurturing skills and find support and reassurance in their roles.

The writers of this book have a long and well thought-out experience of playgroups. They are themselves mothers; they have tutored mothers in child development and in the practical business of running playgroups. They have brought together and reflected upon their experience. The result is something more than a 'how to do it'. It is in its own right a contribution to our knowledge of the way our society is changing, of how this affects children and their families and by what means we can intervene constructively to raise the whole quality of life for the family. It is simply but perspicaciously written and through it all breathes the spirit of PPA, a deep caring for children and for the parents who are the custodians of all our future.

W. D. WALL
University of London Institute of Education

Introduction

The last decade has seen an enormous expansion in the play-group movement: the number of children in Pre-School Play-group Association playgroups rose from a few hundred in 1961 to a quarter of a million in 1973. Because the movement is still a relatively recent one, and perhaps because those involved in it have been too busy to write about their experiences, there is a shortage of reading material for people working in playgroups. We feel there is a need for a book which gives basic guidelines about child care and development, and practical help in setting up, organizing and maintaining a playgroup. We hope that it will also be of interest to students in Colleges of Education.

Since the writing of this book was completed, the playgroup movement in general and the Pre-School Playgroup Association (PPA) in particular, has had official recognition from the Government. Not only has a substantial grant been made by the Department of Health and Social Security to the PPA, but the Government White Paper on Education, 'Framework for Expansion', says that 'Playgroups will continue to have a distinct and valuable role to play alongside an expanding system of nursery education.' As one education authority expresses it, 'playgroups might be "translated" into regular nursery classes'. If these suggestions are carried out, it could mean that the *community* value of playgroups, which is emphasized throughout this book, will not be eroded by traditional nursery school practice. This joining together of two differing approaches to pre-school education will not be easy, but it is only by the marriage of the best in playgroups with the best in nursery schools that the interests of families with young children will be served.

It is of paramount importance that any unit dealing with the education of young children should actively involve their parents, offering them support and guidance *as well as* a respite from child-rearing. A good playgroup does just this, partly because it answers local needs, and partly because it invites parents to become partners with the playgroup staff, thus educating them in their children's needs.

Because of the newness of playgroups, there are as yet no official titles for the people who work in them. For the purposes of this book we have referred to the person in charge, with responsibility for day-to-day running, as the 'supervisor'. Her assistants who, like her, are paid a nominal sum and work on a regular basis, are referred to as 'helpers'. A helper may, or may not, have her own child in the playgroup. A 'mother-helper' is a mother who helps occasionally, on a rota basis, perhaps two or three times a term, and has a child attending the group. She receives no pay, but contributes only a nominal sum for her child on the day she helps. Since the experienced worker and the mother-helper work together in playgroups, we hope that this book will be read by both.

The prices of books and equipment given are as far as possible correct at time of going to press but are likely to increase and are intended as a general guide to costs.

We have collaborated closely on the writing of this book. Since the work had to be divided, Parts 1 and 2 were mainly the responsibility of Joyce Lucas, Parts 3 and 4 of Vivienne McKennell. However, the ideas expressed throughout reflect the thinking of both authors.

From practical experience working in and visiting playgroups, from discussions and meetings with mothers, playgroup workers, and our students on courses, from the many professionals who have given time and expertise to advise us, we have learned a great deal; we would like to thank them all most sincerely for their ideas and comments. We should also like to pay tribute to the Pre-School Playgroup Association to whom we are giving 10 per cent of the royalties.

Most of all we should like to thank our husbands and children, whose understanding and tolerance were so supportive during the writing of this book.

JOYCE LUCAS, VIVIENNE MCKENNELL, 1973

Part 1
Playgroups and Society

1
Urban Living and Lonely Children

Playgroups are very much the phenomenon of the sixties. By any standards their growth rate is amazing: figures obtained from the Department of Health and Social Security, for instance, show that in 1967 there were 4,252 premises registered for playgroup purposes, offering 106,115 places – but by 1972 the number had much more than doubled, to 11,469 registered premises providing 285,579 places. Many additional places were provided in private homes although it is impossible to get a clear estimate of how many. The Pre-School Playgroup Association has played an active role in the development of playgroups and has shown its strength in a membership which has mushroomed from nil in 1961 to over 8,500 in 1973.

Why have playgroups sprung up in almost every suitable hall and in private homes? Why have so many busy mothers and housewives taken it upon themselves to learn the administrative skills to organize pre-school education for their children? Consider the difficulties: a suitable hall must be found; sometimes a reluctant hall committee must be convinced of the value of having a playgroup on their premises; funds must be raised; local authority officials have to be contacted and registration of the playgroup negotiated; equipment must be bought and the expertise developed to work out the daily running of the group.

Why do mothers bother? Why do they think the requirements of their children are not being met at home? We believe that the answer to these questions is that modern ways of living fail to provide a satisfactory environment for young children and that playgroups fill a deep-seated need in our communities.

Ours is very largely a town-dwelling society, with eighty per

cent of the population living in urban areas. Towns are spreading – half a million acres of countryside has been built on in
the last ten years – so that land has become very expensive and
space is at a premium. Because of this, architects have had to
find ingenious ways of housing more and more families in less
and less space. One solution has been to build tower blocks of
flats. These blocks – which have been compared to warehouses
where families are stacked like so many goods awaiting delivery
– have created certain social and health problems for both
parents and young children. A family living in a house is more
privileged. Even so, a modern housing estate often consists
merely of a series of small units, set out in neat-and-tidy garden
plots with very little provision for children's play.

It is an interesting comment on our social priorities that
although architects usually make some provision for car parks
when planning a new housing area, they rarely remember to
make adequate provision for safe, accessible play space that
children can use in either good or bad weather. Planning
authorities should remember that children are more important
than cars, and insist that both private and public building pro-
jects include suitable play areas adjacent to housing units. The
important word here is *adjacent*. Play areas lose much of their
value for mothers and young children if busy roads must be
crossed to reach them.

Once the street itself was the traditional play space for urban
children. Today the number of vehicles on the roads has increased from nearly five million in 1950 to about fifteen and a
half million in 1971 and few mothers dare let their children
past their own front doors because of the danger of traffic.
Modern life has robbed children of a place to play. It seems sad
that our Child Welfare Clinics help us to rear babies bouncing
with energy and then at a later stage when they are older and
need vigorous, adventurous movement, we have to coop them
up in tiny living spaces.

To such children, coming to playgroup can be a relief and an
adventure. We remember one small girl saying to her mother
after her first morning at playgroup: 'You are allowed to go
right over to that wall if you like.' Until then her only play

space had been a very small flat with a cramped balcony. Some children, too, are ferried everywhere in cars, and coming to the playgroup is their one chance to be in an open space where they can run and leap about without restrictions. Movement is life to the young child, and it is essential for his health that we give him room for physical play.

Because we have cut down trees, dammed up streams and covered large areas of earth with concrete and asphalt, many town-dwelling children have little chance of playing with natural materials – earth and water, the very stuff our world is made of. Children need to explore these basic substances and discover their natural laws. Although we cannot provide streams and mud in our playgroups, we do offer water, sand and clay as substitutes, giving the children a chance to learn about and enjoy these basic unsophisticated materials.

Because of cramped housing conditions, it is often difficult for parents to allow children to keep pets; indeed some housing committees ban pets in council properties. This means that large groups of children are growing up without any contact with animals and their lives are that much poorer. Children gain from handling animals: not the least of the lessons they may learn is how to be gentle and care for something which is dependent upon them. Many playgroups will beg, borrow or steal a gerbil or guinea-pig so that perhaps for the first time in his life a child will be able to touch a small, living creature.

These days, too, fewer people stay in the area where they were born. Many families move across the country two or three times during a child's young life. Sometimes this is because a man may seek promotion which entails moving the family to another region, or perhaps some boardroom decision results in moving his firm. As evidence of this social movement the sample Census done in 1966 showed that thirty per cent of people questioned had moved home in the last five years. This means that many children today grow up far from their extended family of grandparents, aunts and uncles and cousins.

If you have had this experience yourself, you may have been glad to escape from the interference and domination of an older generation and perhaps do not see this separation as a loss to your children. But for a child it is valuable to have a variety of relationships with different adults, and not be limited to intimate knowledge of just two grown-ups – his mother and father. The relationship with understanding grandparents can enrich a young child's life immeasurably: with them he can experience loving and giving on a less intense and demanding level than with his parents.

A child in touch with an extended family also begins to understand something of the ladder of growth which he has to climb to become an adult. He sees his cousins allowed to cross the road on their own on their way to school, the older child who cycles to cub meetings, the adolescents who have even greater freedom. The child in the ordinary small family sees just his parents, all-powerful adults, with no stepping-stones of development in between.

It is more than blood relationships which are lost when families become mobile. We lose touch with our school friends and those with whom we first started work, the very people who might have provided 'honorary aunts and uncles' for our children. As our own lives are enriched by having friends, so are our children's: they need casual, friendly contact with a variety of different people of all ages. To know only one female adult, your mother, or one male adult, your father, no matter how warm and loving they are, is limiting. The child whose parent is depressed, anxious or withdrawn is even more handicapped.

Another disadvantage of having a social circle confined to the family is that a child must always play the role assigned to him by his birth position. He can never experiment with different roles, different relationships, as he could if he had a wide circle of friends and relatives. He is also less likely to be familiar with the personal world outside his immediate home.

In a small village, a child is part of the community from the moment his mother lets it be known that she is pregnant. Neighbours and shopkeepers will watch his progress from pram to pushchair, from trike to bicycle. His expeditions from home will be observed by the same group of friendly, caring adults, who would not let him stray into danger Settled urban com-

munities may also consist of 'villages within towns', so that
children may progress with the same support of interested
adults.

But what of new housing estates with less stable populations?
The very size of these units makes it more difficult to get to
know people. Contrast the corner shop atmosphere and its
give-and-take of gossip with the supermarket where there is
little time for talk. In these surroundings, once children are
outside their own front gate they find themselves in an impersonal environment in which a parent dare not allow them to
make gradual experiments in independence. Such an impersonal
world may even appear a hostile one, where a child fears to
leave his mother's protective presence. To understand something
of the insecurity a child might feel when away from his home
and garden, remember how you feel if you are in an unfamiliar
building such as a large block of offices, full of strangers – and
the relief you feel on returning to a place and people you know.
If as a mature adult you have ever felt threatened by unknown
surroundings, you can sympathize with the feelings of a child
who is not 'at home', in the fullest sense, in his environment.

Social isolation has always been a problem for children living
in lonely country cottages, but it is only now that this is
being recognized as a hazard to normal development on a growing scale. Good playgroups are of immense value to children
from socially isolated families. Here they will meet warm and
friendly adults who give them an undemanding but concerned
sort of care, and they will be able to build up a relationship
with someone other than their parents. Because playgroup
helpers often live in the neighbourhood, children may meet
them, not only in the playgroup but on the way to the launder-
ette or supermarket. Seeing them, greeting them, the community outside a child's immediate home takes on a more personal
meaning for him. So he is able to build up a picture of a socially
coherent world into which he can fit.

Another effect of social mobility and the isolation of families
is that a child may grow up without playmates. There is a
pattern to children's play, a sequence of social interaction. At
first they play parallel one with the other, separately yet stim-

ulated by and enjoying each other's presence. Then they begin to play with another child for brief periods. Then follows a third stage when they play as a group. If a child is to have a satisfactory play experience at these different stages, he needs the company of other children, more or less the same age as himself. He also needs it at the right stage of his development. Some play activity, especially imaginative play, needs the presence of another child to enrich it. A child may have an understanding adult who tries to enter his fantasy world, but a grown-up rarely achieves the same quality of involvement which another child can so quickly offer.

As an adult you will be aware of the rapport – the feeling of ease – which can quickly grow up between you and another person of your age group, compared with the slight reserve you feel in contact with those a good deal older or younger than yourself. Is it surprising that children too should recognize in others of their age group a common experience and a common need which they themselves can answer? Many children, however, lead isolated lives, hemmed in by adults, seeing their own age group only in shops or in other public places where there is no time or space to play. 'The child who cannot play,' warns Dr W. D. Wall, 'is as severely threatened as the child who is deprived of nourishment.' No-one in his right mind would deprive a child of food. Yet it seems that, in accepting our modern urban way of life, we unhesitatingly risk depriving our children of an equally important necessity – play with children of their own age.

It is generally accepted that a child will suffer from emotional deprivation if he is parted from his mother. What is not so well known is that he can also suffer from deprivation if he is kept apart from his own age group. In an interesting experiment a group of baby monkeys were kept with their mothers but away from other young monkeys. When this group reached maturity they were found to display certain anti-social tendencies: they could not become successful members of the monkey colony and at a later stage failed to make good parents. These behaviour defects were thought to originate from the lack of group experience at a critical stage.

You may argue that we are not monkeys. Nevertheless, many similarities have been discovered between the social development of monkeys and human beings and it would be unwise to ignore the implications of this experiment. We know that a child needs to be introduced to his first group experience (outside the family) between the age of four and four-and-a-half. If he misses the chance at this critical period, he may find it difficult to become part of a group later on. Many young children, because of the socially isolated lives their families lead, do not have a chance to become part of a group until they go to school. There the sometimes abrupt introduction into a large class may prove an unhappy experience.

Attending a playgroup gives a child a chance to become part of a group at the stage in his development when such social contact is a necessity. In a good playgroup, his first group experience will be a happy one. From this he can go on to meet new groups, strengthened by the success of his first encounter with others. Just as important, he can be gently weaned from dependence on his mother, while still supported by her presence as he adjusts to the company of other children. This is in great contrast to the experience of some children, who one day are with their mother full-time, and the next find themselves in a large primary-school class.

In a playgroup a child has the opportunity to play a variety of roles, not merely that assigned to him by his family position. For instance, a child who is being forced into too early independence by a harassed mother can quite easily at playgroup lapse back into babyhood, and be 'mothered' – or 'fathered' – by a capable four-and-a-half-year-old child, himself perhaps escaping from an over-protective mother. A child from a one-sex family will meet the opposite sex, he will learn to adjust to various personalities, the dominant and the submissive, the boisterous and the shy. If shy and inhibited himself, he may lose these traits by watching other children, having so to speak a 'proxy' play experience until he finds courage to join the play himself. Above all he will find the precious gift of companionship – someone to challenge and fight, someone to love and forgive, someone to share his discoveries in the new world around him.

Most children learn to talk within their family circle, by listening and imitating. Up to a point, therefore, the more a child is talked to, the more advanced his language development will be. A child who is in contact with a large circle of people should have a rich social life, which will then be reflected in his language development. A child who is living isolated from other children and adults other than his own parents may however get little practice in talking, which will adversely affect his language development. The number of otherwise normal children starting school with poor speech is in fact increasing. We heard of a little boy who at the age of three, when the average child knows about a thousand words, had a vocabulary of less than a dozen words – *drink, toilet, biscuit, more, telly, chair, no* and *down*. He was of normal intelligence, but his only social contact was with his mother, a withdrawn person and separated from her husband, who lived in a high-rise block of flats. Apart from visits to the supermarket and post office, this mother and child could go for days 'without speaking to a soul'. She had kept him more or less pram-bound until he was twelve months old, then transferred him to a high chair placed in front of a television set. This was his main window into the outside world, and the only factor in his language learning.

Certainly this is an extreme case – but it is not so exceptional. Many children lead drab, lonely lives, each day as uneventful as the day before. So they have little incentive to talk. To hold a conversation, after all, you need something to talk about and someone to talk to. Most children, you may think, at least have their mothers. But mothers can be very 'switched off' to the conversational needs of their children, so bored with the child's limited level of communication that they fail to make any but the most superficial response. A caring mother with mental energy to spare will lead her child on to learn new language skills, not only by talking with him but by singing, telling stories and looking at books. Any mother can fail in this teaching role. Exposed to so many domestic pressures, and run down by the demands of a lively pre-school child, she may sometimes want to shout, 'For heaven's sake! ... Leave me alone to think my own thoughts for a while.'

At a playgroup a child can meet adults whose job it is to listen and talk to him in a relaxed way, who can afford to wait for the child to express his thoughts in words. The adults will first of all try to build up a relationship with him. Once that is achieved, they will try to strengthen and improve his language skills by giving him clear speech to copy and by introducing him to new words and ideas. Sometimes a child who has difficulty in talking to adults finds it easier to talk to children in playgroup; the spontaneous conversation of other children often sparks off speech in a non-talking child. In a good playgroup, too, there will be a succession of 'happenings' to talk about. Perhaps a guinea-pig will be brought for a morning, or the black specks of frogspawn in the jam jar will start to wriggle into tadpoles. Others will comment on these happenings and in the relaxed and busy atmosphere a child is encouraged to join in.

The general value of play as a form of therapy must be emphasized, not only for children with speech problems, but also for those with other behaviour difficulties. The treatment prescribed by a Child and Family Guidance Clinic will sometimes include play with the same sort of materials found in a good playgroup. If the disturbance is not severe, a child may even be sent to a playgroup as the main part of his treatment. A further advantage a playgroup has to offer is that the staff are often the only persons outside the family to notice a child with a handicap. They can sound an early warning by consulting the Health Visitor if they think a child needs special help. This is important, as often a disability has a greater chance of being successfully treated if discovered early enough, (see p. 206).

2
The Problems of Modern Mothers

Before the second world war, the life of the average married woman with children was usually confined to her home and family. Working mothers were unusual, unless they had no financial support from their husbands. (One exception was to be found in the north country, where mill work had been undertaken since the nineteenth century by part-time working mothers.)

Popular public opinion considered the working wife as a slur on her man's ability as breadwinner, and thus on his masculinity. Because it was socially unacceptable in most strata of society for the mother to be the wage-earner, the standard of living provided by the husband's earnings had to suffice for all the household needs.

A married woman's life was geared to the demands of her family, governed often by a seasonal pattern, particularly in rural areas – marmalade-making in January, spring-cleaning followed by fruit preservation and jam-making, finishing with the grand finale of Christmas preparation. All these specialist jobs were carried out against a constant background of cleaning, cooking and child-rearing, interspersed with occasional family outings. It was a full-time job which, though dull and repetitive, was justified by the emotional satisfactions of caring for husband and children. The housewife and mother was regarded as the sheet-anchor of her family and was valued as such.

The picture of a modern housewife is different in several ways. Labour-saving machines take some of the drudgery out of house work; the seasonal pattern of food preparation has almost disappeared. The modern housewife bakes less, relying on ready-made cakes and bread; instead of bottling her own fruit she is more likely to load up her refrigerator from the supermarket.

Perhaps because of increasing mechanization, it seems that women today take less pride in housework for its own sake, and feel unsatisfied with their domestic role. The housewife in a modern society is a person of little status and this lack of status has unfortunately extended to include motherhood. Hannah Gavron in her book *The Captive Wife* seems to have expressed the feelings of many women when she said 'Being at home all day is terribly boring, frustrating and to my mind *inferior*'. Child-rearing, involving as it often does interrupted sleep and constant exhaustion from young children's demands, can appear to many women exacting, wearing and intellectually enervating.

Because there is now a trend towards earlier marriages, young couples often start with no savings and their household expenses may outstrip a husband's earnings, leaving little to spare for the wife's 'pin money'. Strong pressures from advertising persuade us to seek a higher standard of furnishing and equipment in the home than that of housewives even a generation ago; higher standards apply also in matters of dress and general appearance. Small wonder that some mothers of young children, bored and lonely at home and continually short of money, see returning to work as a solution to their financial problems as well as an escape route from boredom. If they go back to a job they achieve status in society's eyes by making use of their work skills and supplement the family income. Instead of remaining isolated at home – and remember that with growing numbers of working wives, a mother of young children can be left throughout the day without neighbours – returning to work can also be seen as a way of gaining companionship and adult stimulation.

All these are telling arguments and acceptable when the children are older. More women these days are also receiving higher education. For them, work is not regarded simply as an interim activity between school and marriage, but a satisfying life experience which they are reluctant to forego. Of course every woman has the right to interests beyond her home and family and should be allowed to follow her chosen career. But young children also have rights. We feel concerned that the increasing trend for mothers of pre-school children to go out to work is creating problems rather than solving them.

It is now also recognized that some women, while biologically able to bear children, are psychologically unwilling to accept all the demands of motherhood. They find full-time care of their young children so difficult that for the children's sake it is probably better that a mother substitute is found. There are also numbers of unsupported mothers – divorced, separated or unmarried – who cannot accept the low standard of living offered by Social Security allowances and must work for economic reasons. Another voice raised loud and strong is that of the Women's Liberation Movement, which with its demand for 24-hour-a-day nurseries, seems to imply that if women are to enjoy equal status and opportunities with men, they should have the choice of opting out of child-care in favour of another job.

We are concerned not so much with these women as with the average mother responding to the social pressures we have described. We think it extremely likely that if a mother of a pre-school child returns to full-time work *without providing adequate substitute care*, she may damage her young child's mental growth.

In order to understand this, consider some of the problems facing a child with a working mother. Apart from weekends, he will mainly be in contact with her in the early morning, when everyone has to be out of the house in a hurry, or when she returns from work, probably tired, to prepare the evening meal. Against this background of rush and fatigue, mother and child will have difficulty in building up a comfortable, accepting relationship with each other. This seems hard on the child – if you can't feel comfortable with your own mother, who else can give you a sense of ease and content? The mother too may feel guilty and anxious about the situation.

Who is the best person to care for a child when its mother is at work? The grandmother perhaps? She may live many miles away; these days she is increasingly likely to be at work herself. To whom should the working mother then turn for help? A professional child-minder or day nursery? An au pair girl or a mother's help? A neighbour or a friend? There is no guarantee that these substitutes, some untrained and none with an emotional tie with the child, can give an adequate quality of mothering. And how long will these arrangements last? What if the child is unwell and needs his mother urgently – will he grieve if she is not there with him?

The work of the eminent child psychologist, John Bowlby, has shown the effect of maternal deprivation when an adequate mother substitute is not found. He believes that it is the mother who interprets the world to the child, who organizes the manifold impressions he receives in such a way that they make sense. Other researchers believe the acquisition of language best occurs when there is 'a continuous, undisrupted and affectionate relationship between mother and child'. If we accept these findings, then it is not surprising that the child whose mother is absent for most of his waking hours and who perhaps has to adjust to a succession of mother substitutes, may become confused and show behaviour problems.

In fact, if the mother's daily absence is sufficiently prolonged there is a risk that the child may suffer partial deprivation and it is not surprising that he may then show similar tensions and anxieties as the child who is emotionally deprived by the total loss or inadequacy of his parents. Mental illness in adults is widely believed to have its source in early childhood, so it seems reasonable to suppose that the more children are exposed to stress in the vital pre-school years, the more their future mental health is likely to be endangered.

It is, however, vital that the effects of our present way of life should be considered not only on the young child as an isolated individual but on the family as a unit. A welcome tendency in recent research has been to analyse the adverse effects on parents, especially mothers, of modern family life.

Because so many people have broken away from the extended family network, they are less likely to serve any kind of apprenticeship for parenthood. If adolescents are in touch with aunts and cousins, or on close terms with neighbours, the chances are that at some time during their growing up they will look after younger children. They will be able to take them for walks, play with them, read them stories, and generally become familiar with the characteristics of childhood. They will gradually become aware of the needs of children and of how these are best answered. They can also watch other people mothering children, an experience of value to them when they become parents themselves.

But the modern mother from a small family, who probably grew up with little contact with children, may find that the first child she has a chance to handle is her own first baby – as one midwife called it, 'the try-out baby'. This can be frightening, and make the initial experience of mothering a tense and anxious one. The tension may be transmitted to the baby, who may react by being difficult.

The grandmother, the traditional source of knowledge and support, may be hundreds of miles away. Although the mother may have books and magazine articles to consult, these are all impersonal, and may not answer her specific needs. Health Visitors and doctors do offer advice, but mothers are often reluctant to consult these experts on matters which seem trivial, especially if the problem is not mainly physical. They may also have difficulty in expressing just what is bothering them to someone who is not known personally, and may lack the technical vocabulary to use with a professional advisor.

As well as geographical mobility, there is another sort of movement in society. We do not necessarily remain in the same social class in which we were born. A couple of generations ago, we could cheerfully say 'God bless the squire and his relations, and keep us in our proper stations'. The social order was constant and established; a child could usually be expected to repeat the working pattern of his parents in greater or lesser detail. But now, with greater educational opportunity, a talented person with a working-class background can enter the professions and by so doing greatly alter his life style. A young couple, with an expectation of income very different from that of their parents, could become the first people in their family to buy their own house, use a cheque book, or run an account at a department store. Their choice of food may change; their forms of entertainment and holiday, newspapers and magazines, may be very different from those of their parents. These are superficialities; more fundamental changes often take place. The young couple may adopt a very different political outlook, have changed attitudes towards relationships within marriage, and decide to try other methods of child-rearing from those used by their parents.

Partly because of the generation gap, but also because of this change in life style, the sound advice, based on the accumulated wisdom of generations, that a mother could pass on to her daughter or daughter-in-law in child-rearing matters may be quite discredited. Many young couples have become 'unhooked' from their family background and yet have not discovered satisfactory new patterns of behaviour. This lack of certainty, this searching for new standards, is an added difficulty for parents who are having to work through child-rearing problems in isolation.

Because the good playgroup involves mothers, it works to break down this feeling of aloneness and helps them improve their skills as parents. They stay with their children until they are settled, and later may come to work in the playgroup. They see their children being dealt with by experienced people and discover how different sorts of behaviour problems are handled. They will notice the sort of activities being offered and what toys are used. Without knowing it, they will be learning how to be better mothers.

For some people parenthood is the most difficult task they are asked to perform – and one for which they are given no formal training. Yet unless they have problems severe enough to warrant professional treatment by some specialist social service, such as a Child and Family Guidance Clinic, the modern community offers them very little guidance or help.

In a playgroup situation, the supervisor is often the first person able to offer advice if it is sought – and she is in a very good position to do so. She is neither a representative of authority, nor a 'do-gooder' from outside the neighbourhood.

She usually comes from a district near the playgroup, and thus is a person with whom mothers can identify. By her active care for the child, she will have demonstrated her concern for his welfare and possibly for his parents too, so that mothers will have learnt to trust her. She is usually a mother herself and may have experienced the same difficulties which worry mothers. Because she is seen frequently, it is easy for her to build up a relationship with the mothers and this, together with her accessibility, means that she can give some of the same sort of support which used to come from the extended family.

A mother who has moved away from her own family may feel desperately lonely. The playgroup can provide a natural meeting place for her to make contact with other mothers. Sometimes a mother's need for companionship is very obvious. even though a bright social manner may conceal this need. We remember Mrs W., a young attractive mother, whose husband worked long hours and was frequently away from home. Her house was filled with every labour-saving device and she had her own car. Noticing that Mrs W. often lingered in the playgroup after bringing her son and invariably arrived ten minutes early to collect him, the supervisor asked her if she would help in the playgroup during an emergency. Mrs W. was delighted to come and it was revealing to see with what enthusiasm she worked. Talking to Mrs W., the playgroup supervisor became aware of her loneliness and of her desperate need to talk with people of her own age and interests. This playgroup then started a weekly coffee club, which began an hour or so before the children were due to go home. From the response of the mothers it obviously answered a need : 'It's my lifeline,' 'It keeps me sane,' 'It's my safety valve,' were some of their comments. A good playgroup should try and generate such a 'club' atmosphere, to provide a place where mothers can come for a cup of coffee or a chat, somewhere for lonely people to meet and talk with others without too much effort.

A good playgroup can also offer a mother continuous and practical support when she is under personal stress. The case of Mrs J. is a good example. Twenty-three years old, divorced and mother of two, Mrs J. lived on a council estate. Her children used to come to playgroup unaccompanied, until one was knocked down by a car. The young playgroup helper who lived in the same area called to talk to Mrs J.; she began to deliver and collect her children and often stayed to chat. When these prolonged visits suddenly ceased the playgroup helper naturally went to find out why. She heard that Mrs J. had been put on probation for shop-lifting and the neighbours had ostracized her – had been, in the words of the playgroup helper, 'cool and unkind'. The playgroup supervisor thought that she could perhaps overcome Mrs J.'s feelings of rejection by asking her to help once a week in the playgroup. This weekly contact, which allows Mrs J. to feel that she has something to give to her community, has done much to help her. Her relationship with her children improved, she is accepted by her neighbours again and is now engaged to be married.

We can think of no other social agency which would have given this mother such understanding and practical help. And even though this case may seem extreme, it is by no means isolated. In our experience there are many instances where the playgroup provides the only meaningful social contact for mothers outside their own home.

3
The Case for Playgroups

The arguments for providing pre-school education for children, and a parallel supportive service for their parents, have been accepted by educationalists for many decades. Even at the beginning of the century, two sisters, Margaret and Rachel Mac-Millan, were campaigning for nursery schools. Partly as a result of their efforts, the 1918 Education Act empowered local authorities to supply and aid nursery schools. Successive Acts have continued to give local authorities power to build nursery schools though considering how long ago permissive powers were given it is surprising how few have been built. Politicians, and the officials who advise them, have consistently ignored the research evidence which emphasizes the importance of the pre-school years; instead of investing money in nursery schools they have preferred to use public resources for secondary and tertiary education and, more recently, for improvements to the primary schools.

Thanks to pressure groups such as the National Campaign for Nursery Education, started in 1965, this policy has, however, now changed: in 1973 the White Paper, 'Framework for Expansion' gave local authorities the go-ahead to provide nursery education for which government would supply capital costs.

Here now is a brief guide to current provision for pre-school education.

Nursery schools are run by local education authorities. Children between two and five years may attend free of charge but in practice few children go before they are three. Classes are staffed by a trained nursery teacher who has completed a three-year teacher-training course and has specialized in teaching under-fives. She is assisted by nursery nurses who have completed a two-year training. Due to the fact that small classes are necessary and therefore more staff needed, nursery schools are expensive establishments -- the cost per head equals that of an old-style grammar school place. In 1970 only approximately four per cent of under-fives were enjoying the privilege of a place in a state nursery school; this figure, issued by the Department of Education and Science, does not tell us whether a child has experienced a full six terms (from his third to his fifth birthday) or only one term before starting infant school. Nor are figures available to clarify the numbers of children attending full-time or part-time.

The 1944 Education Act gave permissive powers to local authorities to provide nursery education, but few took advantage of this legislation. In 1960 a circular was issued (Circular 8/60) in which it was stated that the Minister of Education 'values the excellent work being done in existing nursery schools and classes, but cannot encourage authorities to propose any new nursery schools ... or any enlargement of nursery schools which would require additional staff'. The only exception to this ruling was if the establishment of a nursery unit would free teachers with pre-school children to return to their profession. It should be noted that the reasoning behind this decision was economic, not educational. This circular has now been withdrawn and money is available for the building of nursery units, priority being given to areas of special need.

Nursery classes are run as far as possible on nursery school lines, but attached to infant schools. They use a room in the school building and are the responsibility of the infant-school head. They are staffed by either a nursery or infant teacher with N.N.E.B. or untrained auxiliary help. Such classes, although a useful attempt to supplement the over-subscribed nursery schools, may represent a far from satisfactory arrangement in that the needs of the under-fives sometimes have to be sacrificed to the physical limitations and routines imposed by the infant school and its building.

Day nurseries are the responsibility of the social services departments. They were started as a war-time measure to allow mothers to work. After the war most were closed down, but a few remained to accommodate the children of one-parent families: unsupported mothers, widows, divorcees, etc. The waiting lists are again very long, sometimes involving a twelve to eighteen months' delay. A charge is made for a place, usually somewhere between 25p and 50p per day, according to a means test. Day nurseries are open from 7.30 a.m. to 5 or 6 p.m. – a working mother's day. Children are taken from between six weeks to five years.

The staff consists of a matron, with a nursing or nursery nurse training, assisted by nursery nurses. The staff wear uniforms and the bias in many day nurseries is still towards the physical care of children, often at the expense of social and intellectual development. Little can be done to involve and educate parents.

Private nursery schools, kindergartens, and preparatory schools are always run on a commercial basis and so their fees are often beyond most people's means. If there are more than five children over five years of age on the roll, then they must be registered with the Department of Education and Science. Note: if you intend to open a playgroup, it avoids adding to the confusion if you do not call your group a nursery school.

Crèches are attached to factories or other places of work and financed by the management with mothers making a nominal contribution. Their primary concern is to free mothers to go to work; the needs of the children are at best secondary. As there is some evidence to show that the number of crèches is increasing rapidly, legislation is needed to ensure that children have adequate standards of care, and that staff receive the right training.

A child-minder is, officially, a woman who accepts payment for looking after, in her own home for two hours or more, one or more children under five, not related to her. She has to be registered with her local social services department. Many 'minders' offer a high standard of care and are valuable alternatives to day nurseries, providing a constant, caring mother-substitute figure for the young child. However, there are still many others, often unregistered, who offer little more than a roof over the children's heads. Health visitors, in many areas, attempt to guide child-minders towards a deeper understanding of children's needs, particularly the value of play, and they suggest courses which 'minders' may follow in their area. It is a good idea for Pre-School Playgroup Association branches to try to attract child-minders to their meetings – a list of 'minders' in your area can be obtained from the local social services department.

Playgroups. Under the Nurseries and Child-Minders Regulation Act, 1948, as amended by Health Services and Public Health Act, 1968, the local department of social services is required to register :

a) 'premises not wholly or mainly used as private dwellings, where children are looked after for the day or a part or parts thereof of a duration, or an aggregate duration, of two hours or longer or for any longer period not exceeding six days;
and
b) persons who for reward receive into their home a child under five years of age, of whom they are not a relative, for any period not exceeding six days'.

In accordance with these regulations, all people responsible for a playgroup are registered as either a child-minder (home-based playgroups) or a day nursery (hall-based playgroups).

The Pre-School Playgroups Association, developed after a letter to the *Guardian* in 1961, stimulated a petition with 3,000 signatures from mothers of under-fives demanding the withdrawal of Circular 8/60 (see p. 33). As no change of policy was promised by the Ministry of Education, parents began to organize themselves into voluntary cooperative nursery schools or 'playgroups', as they came to be called. The New Zealand Federation of Nursery Play Centres Association provided a precedent. In 1965 there were approximately 600 playgroups affiliated to the organization and 950 members. By 1973, there were 8,500 members. In 1966 the Department of Education and Science made a grant of £3,000 for three years to enable the Association to appoint and pay the salary and expenses of a national advisor. In 1970, the D.E.S. grant was increased to £7,000 to include the appointment of a second national advisor. Then in 1972 the Department of Health and Social Services gave a grant of £9,500 for capital work, and up to £45,000 in a year for revenue costs. This money is to pay for the establishment of three regional centres, and for the appointment of eight full-time Training and Development officers, based on different parts of the country.

At a local level, area organizers (AO's) have been appointed by the PPA National Executive and they work on a voluntary basis to serve an area and act as a link with the National Executive. AO's visit playgroups in an advisory capacity and are concerned with raising standards of care in playgroups. They liaise with appropriate local authority services and generally act as spokeswomen for the PPA in their area. AO's are often the instigators of courses which they encourage members to attend. They also initiate local PPA branches which draw together members of the Association to hear speakers and have discussions. These meetings provide opportunities for a necessary exchange of ideas for playgroup workers who often feel isolated and undervalued. A few enlightened authorities have appointed playgroup advisors who carry out virtually the same functions as an AO but with a rightful recognition and a realistic salary.

Mother and Toddler Clubs are a new development whose existence recognizes two important points. First, that children under about three years old should not be separated for long periods from their mothers. Second, that the third year of a child's life can impose enormous strains on mothers, especially if another baby arrives during this period. These clubs may be started as an offshoot of a playgroup by a keen committee or by a Young Wives group or a sympathetic Social Worker or Health Visitor. Sometimes the clubs are held in a small room attached to a playgroup which caters for the over-threes. There are comparatively few of these clubs, but numbers are growing, partly thanks to the encouragement given by the Pre-School Playgroup Association. Mother and Toddler Clubs can use the same equipment and staff as the playgroups; with watchful adults to keep an eye on the children, the mothers can relax and enjoy a chat and a cup of coffee with one another – a much-needed break in the often demanding routine of looking after a child of this age.

This brief account of our Association and its attempts to provide for the needs of mothers with young children should serve to show the social as well as the educational value of playgroups and may help anyone with the intention of starting a playgroup to marshal arguments to use in persuading those in authority to support them. Here is a 12-point checklist:

1. There is no evidence to show that any one type of pre-school provision is superior to another. It seems reasonable, therefore, to consider with respect a movement which has developed in sensitive response to the demands of a new and changing social order, and to realize the value to the community of a form of pre-school education which also involves parents. Playgroups should be seen not as second-rate nursery schools nor as a stop-gap measure, but as something unique and worthwhile in their own right.

2. Misconceptions which tend to confuse 'separation' with 'deprivation' should be ironed out. Bowlby's work* on children in institutions suffering from lack of maternal love has been grossly misinterpreted in many quarters – conclusions originally referring to children in institutions have been applied to children living at home with their parents, leading to the belief that a child under five should never leave his mother's side, whereas a short separation can supply stimulus for the child and breathing space for his mother. This has provided the rationale for a mistakenly laissez-faire policy on pre-school education in most local authorities.

3. There is, however, evidence that women who for a variety of reasons do go out to work, often leave their small children with highly unsuitable people because of the lack of better alternatives.

4. Local authorities should appoint playgroup advisors whose training and understanding enable them to be sensitive to the needs of young children and their families. It is wise to use the experience of voluntary PPA area organizers when

* *Child Care and the Growth of Love*, John Bowlby, Pelican

appointing an advisor; the PPA issues a useful pamphlet 'Playgroup Advisors' to help local authorities make suitable appointments.

5. Local education authorities should also set up courses for playgroup staff. There is, as yet, no national qualification or syllabus. Some courses need to be much less theoretical than others in their content, depending on the educational backgrounds of the participants. In large cities, it may be necessary to provide a few short courses simultaneously in different districts, so avoiding high travelling costs, and at times convenient to the participants if they are to be well attended. In lower-income areas costs should be borne by the local authority.

6. There is a dearth of suitable tutors for playgroup courses. Immediate priority should be given by local authorities to schemes for finding and training tutors. Practising heads and teachers in nursery schools and experienced supervisors of good playgroups are a valuable source of supply.

7. Often playgroups are opened on a shoe-string; we know many playgroups where the staff have taken no salary for the whole of the first year. Because the initial choice of equipment affects the quality of the environment provided for the children, it is essential for enough money to be available at the outset to provide a well-balanced set of good equipment (see p. 127). Loans or grants from social services or education departments to new playgroups would be of value to get them off to a good start. Playgroups receiving local authority grants or loans should first satisfy criteria laid down by that authority, such as training or willingness to be trained of supervisors, positive efforts towards parent involvement, and registration as a charity.

8. In some areas the supervisor's salary could be paid by the local authority so as to avoid a rapid turnover of supervisors; 65p per morning, often all the playgroup can offer, is not a realistic sum to encourage women who may have acquired a great deal of skill with young children and parents to stay rather than moving on to more financially rewarding work.

9. Local authorities should provide free places for children recommended as needing playgroup experience, but whose parents cannot afford to pay.

10. Chief education officers should alert infant school heads to their responsibilities as on-the-spot advisors to the play-groups in their catchment areas. A healthy liaison between playgroups and infant school is vital for the wellbeing of the children involved.

11. In planning new buildings for general community use, architects should bear in mind the practical needs of playgroups. Safe outdoor play space, with access by french windows; floor surfaces suitable for sand and water play; ease of access to storage areas – these should not be expensive requirements if considered early in the planning stage.

12. Education departments should allow playgroups to order equipment through educational suppliers and thus benefit from discounts available. Bulk buying of paper and paint is particularly valuable, as are bulk loans of books from public libraries.

The most cogent and persuasive arguments are the ones which should kindle enthusiasm among those who stand to gain most from the playgroup idea – the thoughtful, concerned, up-to-date mothers who, although bored and lonely with their house-bound condition, have an intuitive understanding of their children's need for loving, personal care. A playgroup offers mothers the chance to share responsibility for the care of their children with other experienced adults, so that they are not forced into a twenty-four-hour-a-day, seven-day-a-week duty. For two or three hours they are free to follow their own interests – perhaps just to relax with a cup of coffee and a magazine, or if they need some intellectual stimulus, to take part in some organized activity, such as an adult educational class. (The Workers Educational Association sometimes runs morning classes in conjunction with playgroups.)

The strain of continuously caring for two or three young children under present housing conditions can only be appreciated by those who have undergone this experience and may be one of the factors resulting in the number of women – one out of every nine of our female population – who receive psychiatric treatment. The value of giving a mother a 'breathing space' must not be underestimated; it could be a positive contribution to her mental health and so to the well-being of her family and ultimately her community.

We have already suggested that a good playgroup should create a club atmosphere, thus serving the social needs of parents of the over-threes who attend. The growth of Mother and Toddler Clubs is also an indication of the need of mothers to escape now and again from the constricting atmosphere of their own home, while not forcing them into too early separation from their children. Ideally these clubs should be equipped with facilities such as for ironing and sewing, and should have a library of books on child-rearing and regular visits from the Health Clinic staff. They could then become centres of parent education, a place where the constructive forces of family life could be preserved and revitalized.

Lastly, we described earlier how domestic appliances have freed women from many time-consuming chores, so that if their children are past the toddler stage, they may have a great deal of creative energy for which active involvement in the running of a playgroup can provide a very satisfying outlet. There are many jobs connected with running a large playgroup, not only the daily caring for children but organizing jumble sales, looking after the equipment, or typing a newsletter. If an association of playgroups is formed, usually a branch of the Pre-School Playgroup Association, jobs proliferate. Women may find themselves arranging meetings, contacting officials in local government, negotiating bulk purchases from toy manufacturers and generally becoming involved in the outside world. Almost by accident, a good playgroup often finds that it flourishes best and achieves the greatest good when it is family-centred as opposed to being solely concerned with children.

Part 2
Playgroups and Child Development

4

The Growth of the Child
from Birth to Five Years

Anyone thinking of setting up a playgroup probably feels that
their energies are better spent in solving the many practical
problems – finding suitable premises, staff, equipment – than
trying to supplement their existing understanding of parents
and children with the acquisition of new theoretical knowledge.
Manning book stalls at conferences for playgroup supervisors,
we have found that for every one book sold on child development, ten are sold giving advice on practical matters. This is a
pity. The reason may be that the average playgroup worker is
discouraged from reading books on child development because
they are mostly written by psychologists whose language is
too technical.

With these facts in mind, this section of the book is written
from the basis of our practical experience both as mothers and
playgroup supervisors. As far as possible we have used everyday language. Because we believe so strongly that playgroups
should be concerned with parent *and* child, we have traced a
normal child's development against the background of his relationship with his mother and father.

The first five years of a child's life are the most crucial to
his future emotional and intellectual development. During
this period of rapid growth a child is particularly vulnerable
to damage, for it is in these early years that behaviour patterns
are established which influence all later personality development. As parents and as playgroup workers it is surely our
duty to learn all we can about young children.

Where should we start our study? The obvious time might
seem to be at the three-years-old when the children first come to
a playgroup. But a child's three-year-old self is the result of the

experiences he has had since the beginning of his life. So we must start at the beginning, too. Another reason for studying the first three years is that playgroup workers are often asked for advice about the younger children in a family. A mother may find it easier to discuss a problem with the supervisor first, rather than go to her doctor or clinic for help.

Our western civilization places great emphasis in a child's first years on a warm, continuous relationship with his mother or mother substitute.* This relationship starts even before a child's birth. As soon as a woman knows she is pregnant, she begins to form some sort of idea of her baby-to-be, to build up a relationship with the expected child in her imagination.

Some children are conceived in love, borne with pride and welcomed with joy. Others are conceived by accident, borne with resentment and accepted only grudgingly. The commonly used phrase 'I've fallen for another' implies bad luck, one doesn't fall deliberately! An unsupported mother, possibly with financial and emotional worries, might feel differently towards her unborn child than would a securely married woman. Similarly the harassed mother of a large family, inadvertently pregnant again after several years free of child-bearing, may have a different attitute towards this later pregnancy. Happily, the majority of parents come to terms with their babies once born, but it must be accepted that some perhaps do not.

The first year

Although we know little of the effect on the unborn baby of the mother's state of mind, we do know that the actual birth process can colour the early mother-and-child relationship. A prolonged and painful birth can cause a mother to resent the baby who was the cause of her pain. The mother whose baby refuses to feed may herself feel rejected and in turn find it difficult to feel warmly towards him.

* From now on we shall use the word 'mother' to mean 'mother figure', rather than keep on repeating the words 'mother' or 'mother substitute'.

The first three or four weeks of a new baby's life are spent adjusting to his new environment. By the same token his mother is adapting her life to his needs. Mothers of first babies often feel anxious in their new role, an uncertainty which can affect the child. Handled with calm assurance, the new baby feels secure, able to get on with the business of feeding, digesting, excreting and sleeping. Clumsy handling, however, can disturb his delicate physical mechanism, causing upset digestion, crying or sleeplessness; this in turn can increase the inexperienced mother's feelings of anxiety and inadequacy. In these early weeks mothers with first babies need the support and comfort of an experienced person, such as a grandmother; she can not only reassure the mother, but also help with household chores and give her much-needed rest. Unfortunately, however, a mother is often left to soldier on alone.

By the age of sixteen weeks, a normal baby is most responsive to his environment and especially to his mother. His face brightens at her approach, his frantic crying stops when she picks him up, though it might increase in volume if someone else does. He responds particularly to her voice – it is thought by some researchers that a baby can hear its mother's voice in the womb. During the first months the mother is the main source of love and comfort for the baby and she therefore answers his deepest needs.

It is in the way that a baby's needs are answered, especially in the way he is fed, that his first ideas of the world will be formed. The baby safely held in his mother's arms, aware of the rhythm of her breathing and warmth of her body, allowed to suck at his own rate, sometimes dropping the nipple to softly mouth it or to explore the breast or bottle with his hands, is being allowed to come to terms with the world outside himself in a pleasurable way. He will begin to feel the world as a good place, and to associate this goodness with the personal relationship he is developing with his mother. Each feeding time will enrich him not merely physically, but, equally important, psychologically.

It may sound strange to say a young baby can have a relationship with an adult, and of course it only occurs within the limits of the baby's immaturity. Like any other one-to-one relationship, it is based on the interaction between the two concerned. Bowlby, who has written a good deal about the attachment between mother and child, refers to the mother as the child's 'psychic organizer'. She is the person who guides the child in his understanding of the world and helps him to make sense of his inner life. This is why a young child needs an uninterrupted relationship with his mother if he is to grow up with a well-organized personality. The baby is born knowing very little, and is dependent on the adult in charge to teach him, even though this teaching may not take place in any formal sense.

Because of his extreme immaturity, the young baby needs the same person repeatedly interpreting the world to him so that each new lesson can reinforce previous ones without wasting psychic energy adjusting to a strange 'interpreter'. It is accepted by most educationalists that all the best learning takes place within a good relationship – you learn more from a teacher you like than from one you do not. Remember how distressed an older child can be if he loses a familiar school teacher, or how too many changes in a school staff can hamper children's learning.

Of course it doesn't matter if some other person occasionally feeds the baby as long as, in the main, the child has the same person caring for him. But some babies, such as those in institutions, may have a succession of adults feeding them, or be left with a bottle propped in their mouths. The baby fed in this way will be getting physical nourishment, but in an impersonal and therefore impoverished way, because the experience of feeding does not take place within the context of a developing relationship with another human being. He will have difficulty learning one of the most important lessons of his life: that he is a person who needs to relate to others.

Very early in his life, a child experiences powerful feelings of anger if his needs are not answered promptly and effectively. Consider the red-faced screaming baby, arms impotently punching the air, legs kicking like pistons as he is bathed before his feed. Who could doubt that he is consumed with anger, directed against the author of his frustration – his mother? Yet a few minutes later, cradled in her arms and sucking contentedly, he will be filled with loving feelings for her. He has to come to terms with these mixed feelings towards his mother throughout their growing relationship. The good mother helps him to adjust to this by ensuring that he is not left without comfort and especially food, for too long, so that the amount of frustration he has to bear is tolerable.

During this first year, a baby is a sensuous being and takes great pleasure in discovering his body and all its functions – even, it has been suggested, in crying. Far and away his deepest satisfaction is derived from his mouth, especially from sucking. A young baby sucking, eyes closed, breathing rhythmically, is obviously concentrating his whole being on this act. He needs to have this experience repeated again and again over a long period. Yet many mothers often completely wean their babies from breast or bottle at an early age, boasting that the child used only a cup and spoon from three months onwards. As children have the next sixty or seventy years ahead of them to drink from a cup, it seems sad to deprive them of the satisfaction of sucking at an early age. Perhaps this is because mothers, especially of first babies, are anxious to push their children on as fast as possible in a sort of infantile 'rat race'.

When taken off the breast or bottle a baby will soon find something to suck; it may be his thumb or a piece of blanket or shawl, but suck he will, and in so doing strengthen his mouth and tongue muscles ready for the more complicated business of chewing and, eventually, talking. The sound 'mama' for instance, emerges when a baby, anticipating food, is starting to make sucking or chewing movements with his lips, at the same time as he is making sounds. The mouth also continues to be a source of comfort and pleasure in older children and in adults. Think how we play with our lips during moments of tension or boredom, and the sensuous satisfaction we gain from a cup of tea or a cigarette.

As well as providing pleasure, the mouth also plays an important part in the way the baby begins to come to terms with the world around him. Everything goes into his mouth. This is nothing to do with being hungry or even with 'feeling his

his pram or cot, which he can touch with fingers or toes. Unless he is physically uncomfortable – hungry or damp – he will be content on his own in a garden or quiet room for short periods. But he also needs and benefits from social contact with his mother. Some mothers isolate their baby during the pram-bound period and then boast how 'good' the baby is, how he never cries. These 'good' babies may be bored babies, who would benefit immeasurably from spending more time with their mothers, observing them work about the house and especially by listening to them talking.

The early responsiveness to bodily contact with the mother continues and develops with greater emphasis on play. The baby also learns to enjoy playing with his father or other members of the family – being bounced up and down, tickled under the chin and so on. He becomes increasingly aware of people talking to him. The beginnings of language development occur during the first year, and a child's ability to learn to talk depends on how much his mother, and others, talk to him.

All normal babies babble during the early months, making the same sounds, no matter what part of the world they come from. It is thought that a child enjoys the sound of his own babble and the sensation of making noises. (Deaf children do not babble to nearly the same extent as a hearing child.) He also enjoys the adult's reaction to his babble and quickly learns that some sounds, e.g. 'mama' and 'dada', evoke a particularly warm response from his parents. The child who is talked to frequently is stimulated to imitate, and learns that words are tools which give him command over situations. For instance, if he says 'more' he will probably be given extra food. If he says 'bye-bye', the adult who is leaving will respond by saying 'bye-bye' and probably wave his hand. At about the same time, usually between eleven and eighteen months, the child may take his first steps. From now on he will make more demands on his environment and thus on his mother.

The difficulties of these first months must not be underestimated. We remember our own anxieties: like many other mothers we would sometimes wake our sleeping babies to make sure they were alive. We remember our own weariness and appreciate how the constant crying of a young baby can drive a mother to despair. We are aware of the numbers of 'battered babies' reported in the newspapers and can imagine the tensions that cause some young parents to behave in this way. It is more common, however, for the young mother to be so preoccupied with her baby, so single-minded about her mothering that she neglects her husband or older children, so causing tension within the family. On the credit side, she may find relations easier with her mother or mother-in-law because they have the common interest in the baby.

To conclude, the majority of mothers manage to cope very successfully with any uncomfortable realities of babyhood and when their baby appears healthy and normal find enormous satisfaction in his growth and progress.

12–24 months

During the first half of the second year of his life, the child continues to develop quickly. He gains two or three inches in height, as many pounds in weight and cuts his back teeth. He will probably be able to walk and climb, to lift and pull. He achieves increasing skills with his hands. He has an innate drive to explore and examine everything he can reach; in fact he must be able to do so if he is to understand and master his world.

His mother has to adjust to this new stage of development, which compared with the first year of the baby's life, makes more and different demands on her. She can feel dismayed by the change between the placid, pram-bound baby of a few months ago and the determinedly curious toddler who seems bent on turning out every cupboard and emptying every bowl in sight. It is easy to see how this gives rise to conflicts between mother and child. The child has an overwhelming urge to investigate everything that excites his interest; the mother must protect him from hurting himself and safeguard the smooth running of the household. If thwarted, he may explode into angry screams bewildering her by the intensity of his anger.

Many mothers try – uselessly – to reason with a child in this situation. When this fails, they may smack him or strap him into his high chair, whereupon he yells himself into a state of exhaustion. Far better to weather this period by organizing the domestic routine as much as possible to cope with the child's demands. For instance, all fragile household goods should be removed from the child's reach, cupboards containing breakable crockery should be securely fastened and a gate should be fitted at the bottom of dangerous stairs. Thus the environment can be free for the child to explore, with the minimum of risk and without constant correction. The less you have to say 'No' to a child the better, and the more firm you can be with essential prohibitions.

A wise mother will allow her child to explore a cupboard holding cake tins and saucepans, will provide a wooden spoon for him to bang the saucepan lid, and may put the peg basket temptingly near so that he can empty it out. He will delight in putting the pegs in the saucepan, inexpertly jamming on the lid and then clumsily emptying them out again. He will repeat this process again and again. The mother will need tolerance to pick her way through this kitchen clutter as she goes about her chores. She will make an effort to talk to her child, praising him when he successfully accomplishes putting the lid on the saucepan, warning him with a sharp 'Hot!' if he goes too near the cooker. In a variety of subtle ways, she is teaching him important lessons in living.

This task is not made any easier by the fact that the child is physically very clumsy during most of his second year. He almost needs to wear a crash helmet, so numerous and painful are his bumps and falls! He can be very messy at meal times when his urge to feed himself outstrips his manual skills. His cup tips before it reaches his mouth, sending the contents cascading down his clothes; his heaped spoon empties itself on the newly washed rug. If this happens after a run of wet days, when the spin-dryer has broken down so that he has no more clean jerseys, is it any wonder if a mother screams 'Naughty!' and gives him a sharp slap on the hand! Yet the child of course will be only bewildered by this reaction.

Another characteristic which can cause his mother great annoyance is that he learns to do things backwards – that is to say, he can take off his shoes and socks long before he can put them on. She may dress him ready for some expedition, turn her back for a moment and find that he has thrown his shoes and socks behind a cupboard. If she is meeting a deadline – perhaps fetching a child from school, or catching a bus to town – or if she is feeling unwell, say with the start of a second pregnancy, it is all too easy to be angry. But it is a little easier to be tolerant when you remind yourself that this is the natural developmental pattern – to take off before putting on, to unpack before packing away.

During this second year, a change takes place in the child's attitude to sleeping. At about eighteen months he may show signs of distress when his mother leaves the room and refuse to settle for sleep unless she is sitting by his cot. As he learns more words, he may use a variety of devices to delay going to sleep, such as demanding drinks or food. He may become very attached to a soft toy, or some piece of shawl or blanket without which he refuses to relax. These much-needed objects are of great importance to some children, not so much as playthings but as a comfort. If they are missing at bedtime, most parents feel it is worth turning the house upside down to find them, rather than suffer the deprived child's misery. Dependence at bedtimes can prove very demanding and is another reason why mothers find this second year a trying one.

During this year many children achieve control over their bowels and bladders. The usual pattern is for the child to draw attention to his needs by the word used in the family, such as 'wee-wee' or 'poo poo', but a little after the event rather than before. Next the child calls for the pot or lavatory immediately before wetting or dirtying himself, leaving too small a time interval for the mother to cope. 'It's coming', 'It's coming', is a frequently heard cry from this age group! Then he learns to anticipate this need in time to undress and use the pot. The child realizes that his mother is invariably willing to answer this call and sometimes uses it as an attention-seeking weapon. The compelling word 'Pottie!' or whatever the accepted term is, uttered when his mother is talking to a neighbour, is sure to attract her attention even if she ignores all other attempts.

When the child starts to express this need in words, some mothers try to pressure him into being completely toilet-trained. Most children do not learn until the end of this second year how to organize their mental and physical resources to anticipate and answer this need. Too much pressurizing can lead to total refusal and the child should be allowed to develop at his own pace.

During the second year conflicts may arise between mother and child over meal times. The child begins to realize that he is a separate person with the power to accept or refuse food. If a mother insists that the child sits at the table and finishes up every scrap, he tends to rebel at the enforced confinement and food becomes associated for him with this negative attitude. On the whole, it is better for a mother to say in effect, 'Take it or leave it'. If meal times become a contest, this is a battle she might lose. She should not be tempted into offering an alternative menu: the child will quickly learn that he has a powerful weapon in his hand, which he is not slow to use. He knows if he makes enough fuss about the minced meat and cabbage it will go in the dustbin and a tin of baked beans be opened just for him. All sorts of rituals may grow up around meal times – we heard of one little tyrant who would only eat if he was rocked in his toy boat by his father while his mother fed him!

At about eighteen months the child is beginning to have a sense of his own identity, to be aware of his separate existence. If you are on a bus and stare at a baby of twelve months, he will give you stare for stare back, without any signs of self-consciousness. Try the same experiment with an eighteen-month-old: soon after he is aware that your eyes are in contact with his, he will take fright and duck his head on to his mother's shoulder, reappearing for shy peeps at you from time to time.

This increasing maturity makes for difficulties for his mother. Before he began to have this fragmentary sense of himself as a person, he was quite content to sit outside a shop while his mother went inside. Now his growing sense of his own existence intensifies his feelings of aloneness and he sets up a wail of protest when he sees her disappear from sight. She usually reacts by unstrapping him from his pram or pushchair, and enduring a harassed few minutes while she buys goods with one hand and prevents him pulling down the shop displays with the other.

For the same developmental reason, the child who would go to anyone for a cuddle in his first year, may even refuse to go to people he knows. If he is left with some person with whom he is not very familiar, when he does return to his mother he may become irritating in his dependence, wailing outside the lavatory door if she dares to shut it, following her, shadow-like, from room to room. Yet he may show great swings in behaviour, some days clinging to his mother and resisting any attempt to put him down and other days, sweating with exertion as he tries to move an adult-sized wheelbarrow, refusing all offers of help as he asserts his independence.

This is the age when the child may begin to show that particularly disruptive behaviour which we loosely term temper tantrums. Red with anger, he screams and stamps his feet or throws his body on the floor, contorted with fury. A few children will even make their bodies rigid and hold their breath until they become blue in the face and actually lose consciousness. This is alarming for a mother who may fear that her child might permanently damage himself. The whole experience may be very distressing to the child, but will not harm him physically; breathing is a reflex action – it happens automatically so that if a child does become unconscious, he relaxes, allowing breathing to start again.

Almost all children have tantrums. At this age they find it difficult to express their needs in words, and this inability to verbalize causes frustrations which overflow into temper tantrums. If you have ever been in a foreign country and attempted to buy something the name of which you did not know, you may sympathize with the frustrations of the twenty-month-old.

If temper tantrums are frequent, it would be as well to look at the way a child is managed to see if too many strains are being imposed on him. At this stage children are very physical beings; movement is their life. Yet how much of an under-two's life is spent in a small living space in the morning, with the afternoon in a push chair? Have you ever thought how limiting it must be for a boisterous twenty-month-old to be trailed around the shops in a push chair on a fine afternoon, seeing little but legs and counter supports? Whenever possible the mother should arrange her day so that the child is not forced to sit still for too long and is not allowed to get over-tired, for it is then that he cannot tolerate too much strain. She must also try to provide him with the right sort of toys and space in which to play with them.

When a tantrum does occur, the child's anger is usually directed at his mother, who is invariably the agent of his frustration. It is vital, therefore, that she tries to maintain an image of calm, loving security, so that he is aware of her controlling influence as a sort of safety net into which he can drop. Words mean little at this stage and it is pointless to try to reason with so young a child; even more so to resort to physical violence, matching temper with temper, which only increases the child's anger and insecurity. He may need holding physically, possibly tucked under the adult's arm so that he can kick and punch but still be aware of her body comfort. When the violence has subsided, he may also need to sit on her lap, until he gains control of himself and is able to once more be 'his own master'. The child who experiences loving control will emerge safely from the tantrum, his relationship with his mother intact and even strengthened.

In short, the second year of a child's life is one which makes heavy demands on his mother. He becomes mobile and thus more physically independent. At the same time he can seem so emotionally dependent on his mother that she feels trapped by his demands. Unless she has an understanding husband who will give her a rest, she may be worn down by the twenty-four-hour-a-day service expected of her. She may find it difficult to pursue a social life of her own and long for adult company; it is during this second and following year that a Mother and Toddler Club can be so beneficial.

On the other hand, children during this stage of development can be very endearing. The mother is rewarded by watching her child's personality develop and his skills improve.

Two to three years

The healthy two- or three-year-old is an attractive being and life for his mother becomes rather less demanding as he develops more physical and mental skills. Most children are fully toilet-trained by the end of their third year; this in itself is a relief. Physically they are becoming much less clumsy and can show surprising competence with their hands, especially compared with a year ago; they can thread beads, cut with blunt-ended scissors and do simple jigsaws. They begin to undress and dress themselves.

Language progresses by leaps and bounds during the second year. At two a child has an average vocabulary of 200 words; by three this has increased to 1,000. This is most rewarding for his mother, although his constant chatter as he practises his newly acquired vocabulary can be wearing. He loves sound patterns and needs to learn a variety of nursery rhymes and jingles, as well as simple, repetitive stories, especially about himself. He often refers to himself by name – 'Michael push it', 'Janie have a sweetie' – although he will be substituting pronouns – me, you and I – by the end of this year. He will cooperate over simple domestic demands: 'Fetch the dustpan, please', or 'Open the door for Mummy'.

A child of this age is a great mimic and will imitate with accuracy, say, his mother putting on her lipstick. He likes to join in household chores, helping with the washing up or with the cooking. He is beginning to play imaginatively often pretending that he is an adult. He will stagger in with the milk bottles, for instance, claiming to be the milkman. In particular, he will act out mother-and-child roles, using his teddy bears or dolls. It seems as if he is striving to understand his relationship with his mother objectively, ready to begin freeing himself from his dependence on her.

During this year, the child usually drops his daytime nap; this can mean that by tea-time he is tired and liable to whine or have a temper tantrum. Sometimes it is useful to give a child a bath before his evening meal. Playing in the water soothes and rests him and tea-time, which may coincide with father's home-coming, is then a much happier affair. Bedtime may become something of a ritual too. Perhaps all the members of the family, some of his toys and even the lamp-post outside his house must have a kiss blown to them. He may need an array of teddy bears tucked up with him. He may suck his thumb or rock before he goes to sleep.

Children in this age group are very self-centred and continue to play mainly by themselves, although perhaps *alongside* other children. During the first half of this year, unless they have been brought up in a group, they still find it difficult to accept other children as people. They may embarrass and distress their mother by pinching or biting other children, or grasping them by the hair. This should be seen more as a social experiment than aggressive behaviour: it is as if he has to find out what will happen when he grabs another child's hair and the other child's subsequent screams may amaze and frighten him. His inability to predict the consequence of his actions is an indication of his immaturity.

He may show great swings of behaviour, being sometimes assertive and possessive, holding on to a toy with grim determination, and at other times withdrawn or clinging, pressing against his mother's body as he did a year ago. He is still very dependent on his mother's presence, he seems to need her to interpret his world to him. For example, two little girls of nearly three were playing in a park with their mothers near by. One little girl looked at the other and asked, quite clearly, 'What is your name?' The other girl went to her mother and said, 'What did she say?' 'She asked your name,' replied her mother. The second child returned and said, 'I'm called Mary', whereupon the first child asked *her* mother, 'What did she say?' Both children spoke well and heard distinctly. But they still needed their mothers to interpret this simple social exchange.

A two-to-three-year-old may be a great dawdler. How often have you seen a mother twenty yards or more in front of her two-year-old, entreating him to hurry up? The child takes time to examine every gatepost, every drain, ignoring his mother's pleas until he hears her say, 'Bye bye, I'm going'. Then, panic-stricken at the thought of being left, he races to catch her up. He lingers over meals, over dressing, over going to the lavatory. Some psychologists believe that this dawdling is a natural protective mechanism and gives the child time to come to terms with the manifold impressions of life he is absorbing. The average mother often failing to realize that the growing child needs opportunities to 'switch off', can be irritated by what seems to be awkward behaviour.

True enough, a child can be very rebellious at this stage. His favourite word seems to be 'No!' It is as if he must adopt a negative attitude to emphasize his independence, increasing but still incomplete, from his mother. He may still have temper tantrums although they should begin to diminish in number.

This is the year when many mothers try to get their children into playgroups. They notice their child's increased vocabulary, ability to copy adults, and obviously increased maturity. They may resent and fear the child's rebellious attitude, feeling it is time that someone else tried to discipline him. They may also feel that he or she needs other children to play with. Sometimes a child of two will be accepted by a playgroup, and at first appear to settle; then after a few weeks, he becomes unwilling to be separated from his mother. If the mother insists that the child stay without her, he makes heavy demands on the playgroup staff, usually clinging to one person as a mother substitute.

Such behaviour shows that he is not yet at the stage of development when he can leave his mother and become part of a group. Sometimes children over three show similar behaviour. It must be stressed that there is a vital difference between *age* and *stage*; supervisors should always consider the would-be entrant's stage of development, not just his age, when deciding whether or not he is ready for playgroup. It is usually wise to wait until a child is three before accepting him into a group; many local authorities make this age of entrance a condition of registration. If this is the rule, an exception of it can be made in rare circumstances. Ideally, a playgroup should have a Mother and Toddler club attached to it (see p. 36). The child can then begin to learn to mix with other children, and to meet other adults, while still having the support of his mother's presence.

Three to four years

It is easy to see why the age of three is a good time for a child to start playgroup. He has made great strides physically: as well as being bigger and stronger, he is more in control of his body. He can, for instance, pedal a tricycle efficiently, although he has yet to learn to go at speed and steer competently. He can go up and down stairs one foot at a time and can even stand on one foot for an instant, although he can't hop. He is much less clumsy in using his hands and needs a variety of activities to practise his new skills. He will show whether he is dominantly left- or right-handed and should be allowed to use whichever hand seems strongest.

What of his inner development? Up to this point, we have emphasized the child's dependence on his mother and fragmentary sense of his own identity. It is around his third birthday that the child starts to think of himself as a person, completely separate from everyone else. His personality is becoming organized sufficiently for him to manage away from his mother. Entering a positive phase in his development, he likes to please and copy adults, to conform instead of rebel. We no longer hear 'Don't want to', 'Won't', or 'No', but rather 'Is this right?' or 'Do I do it like dat?' Taken into a new situation, out to a meal in a restaurant perhaps, he is much more likely than he was a year ago to behave acceptably, making an active effort to copy the adults' manners and attitudes.

Although he may not play cooperatively, he seems to be stimulated by other children's presence, and enjoys playing side by side with them. During this parallel play he will talk endlessly to himself, experimenting with tenses and so on. If he doesn't know the right word to express some thought he will substitute another with a similar meaning. One three-year-old said a building was covered in 'smoke', meaning 'mist'; another, wanting his birthday candles lit, suggested we 'matched' the candle. A flat-dwelling child said to his gardening grand-father, 'Shall we lawn the mow?'

It is quite normal for this age group to misuse or mis-pro-nounce words or show amusing oddities in their way of speech. We know of one little girl who added 'a' to all nouns: 'I'va put my dollya to beda'. Sometimes, because they have so much to say, they stammer in their anxiety to express themselves. Speech difficulties are best ignored unless they are very severe. If adults keep correcting the child, they may make him over-anxious so that his normal speech development is interrupted and the bad habit becomes fixed. The most helpful attitude on the part of the adult is to be patient and make time to listen to the child, so that he can relax and explain his meaning. For despite his falterings, he is more able to express his needs and thoughts in words, responding to speech in a way that was im-possible a year ago. This improved grasp of language is import-ant, it gives him not only a boost in social development, but also a limited command of his environment. He can ask for what he needs – for more paint, a turn on the slide, to go to the lavatory.

Sometimes during this year the child may invent another self, an imaginary person to whom he talks and reacts. These imaginary people may be so real that he insists a place be laid for them at table! The 'other self' is often blamed for the child's misdemeanours, becoming the scapegoat for his real or imagined naughtiness; it may be a sort of defence mechanism the child uses to protect himself against an adult's anger. If the child becomes obsessive about his 'other self', adults in charge should ask themselves if they are demanding too high a standard of behaviour. Sometimes a child who is too much in the company of adults will invent a child character, but will discard the invention if he is introduced to the company of real children.

A three-year-old is a largely unsophisticated person. He has an incomplete picture of the world, in which there is much he doesn't understand. Where does daddy disappear to each day? Why does he go? Where does the milkman come from? Why does mummy give him money? In order to comprehend the complex world into which he must fit, to help him to make sense of it all, he acts out many real-life situations. In imaginative play he becomes mummy, daddy or the milkman; his trike becomes the car or the milk float. In a playgroup we must provide a variety of props so that the child has as much opportunity as possible to try out all sorts of adult roles and thus come to terms with the different relationships people have with one another.

Because he is still a very immature personality, the child feels with great intensity – love and hate of his mother and father, jealousy of his brothers and sisters. His imaginative play can be used to test and control these deep feelings. For instance, he may be fiercely jealous of a new baby in the family, and hate his parents for all the love and affection they are giving the new arrival. He may act out these feelings in the playgroup's 'home corner', burying the baby doll in the bottom of the cot with the mattress, sheet and blanket on top, or mercilessly smacking a teddy bear which symbolizes the mother who seems to be neglecting him.

The intensity of his inner life and fantasy world can render his grasp of reality fragile. At this age a child is often subject to irrational fears, sometimes of everyday objects – such as wellington boots or an electric cleaner. These fears may be repressed during the day yet reappear at night time. The adult in charge must accept that they are very real to the child, that he needs to be calmed and reassured and not ridiculed or ignored. The three- to four-year-old may present a mature image of himself to the world. He can not only tolerate but also enjoy a short separation from his mother and begins to make relationships with adults and children outside his family circle. Nevertheless he is still a very tender person. His equilibrium is easily upset – say, by the absence of a well-loved supervisor or more especially by some change at home. He likes the same routine to be repeated each time he comes to playgroup and thrives best when he is supported by patient adults in a secure atmosphere.

Four to five years

If we compare a four-year-old with his three-year-old self, we are again aware of what great advances are made during this year.

Children of this age seem to be very much the big boys and girls of the playgroup, confident personalities playing an active part in the group's life.

They have achieved far greater control physically: they can throw or kick a ball using just their arms and legs, instead of their whole bodies as they did a year ago. They can climb, jump and balance with ease; they pedal and steer wheeled toys with great skill around a crowded hall. They show an increasing dexterity with their hands. They enjoy all sorts of constructional toys and their drawings and paintings show how much more controlled their manual movements have become. They are able to dress and undress themselves, managing even their buttons unless these are too stiff. They can put on shoes; sometimes towards the end of this year a few children can tie bows.

A four-year-old is a great talker, and the questions he asks are seemingly endless. This is because he is gathering new information about his world and is also making sure he really understands what he already knows. By approaching the same fact from different viewpoints, he makes certain that he has grasped some new idea. For instance, if a husband visits the playgroup, the four-year-old will ask, 'Who is that man?', 'Where does he live?', 'Why is he here?', 'Is he your daddy?', in quick succession. After these questions have been fully answered, he may come back after an interval and repeat them in a different form: 'Does he live with you?', 'Are you his mummy?'

He uses his new command of language as an attention-seeking device, mainly talking about himself. 'Do you know what?' he will say compellingly to any available listener, and then will go on to tell of his own doings, mixing fact with fantasy: 'I painted a picture of my playschool as big as that wall'; 'I jumped off a climbing frame as big as this house'. These exaggerations and fabrications seem to be partly to get attention, partly because the dividing line between what happened and what he imagined is still blurred.

Sometimes you get children making claims about their home to gain attention. 'Mummy has a baby in her tummy,' said Jane, an only child, skilfully making up a story of how she was going to stay with grandma when 'my new baby sister comes.' Other children in the group had pregnant mothers and Jane had noticed that this news gave these children additional interest in the supervisor's eyes. This story might also have been an expression of her desire to have a baby sister.

Children can be very forthright in their comments. 'What an awful voice!' was one child's unfortunate comment on a visiting vicar. 'You look funny in those glasses, like someone I don't know,' said Andrew to a supervisor in new spectacles.

A four-year-old is very literal in his thinking and takes words at their face value. This is why fairy stories where people change into frogs, or witches work magical deeds, are unsuitable for this age group. His drawing shows this literal way of thinking: he will draw a human figure with a head, eyes, mouth and legs and arms, but no body. All parts which have a meaning to him are there.

His idea of numbers is still meagre. He knows what is meant by one and two, but beyond this it is best to talk in general terms – 'lots of', 'many', 'a few'. He can often count well, but this is because of the sound pattern rather than because he understands in a truly quantitative way the meaning of the words. Because of his intellectual immaturity it will confuse him to be asked to have more than this generalized idea of number. Similarly, his sense of time is very limited and his idea of the past and future incomplete. He knows terms like 'yesterday' and 'tomorrow' but 'next week' or 'next month' are meaningless.

At this age, a child's powers of concentration are beginning to expand. He will persevere with a jigsaw puzzle or a problem of construction for seven or ten minutes, longer if his interest is really caught. He will listen with keen interest to a story for the same time span, moving with his whole body as he follows the actions of the characters. He enjoys songs, finger plays and listening to music.

The four-year-old's desire to understand the world and achieve a sense of order shows in the way children of this age like to sort objects into groups – say on a peg board, with all the colours arranged into different rows. A three-year-old would be content with a more haphazard arrangement. For the same reason, the four-year-old enjoys matching games such as picture dominoes – matching satisfies his need for methodical arrangement.

On the whole, the four-year-old doesn't plan his activities. He tends to create something at the first attempt, then give a name to what he has made and adapt it to his play needs. For instance, he will nail two pieces of wood together and zoom around the room claiming to have made an aeroplane. Another day, with exactly the same basic shape, he will say he has made a sword. It is the *doing* which is important, the end product is almost incidental.

The normal four-year-old enjoys playing with his own age group. Indeed, some psychologists think it is essential for a child to be introduced to a group of other children at this age if he is to make easy social relationships. He will cooperate for brief periods over some group activity, and accept the principle of turn-taking. Girls of this age are sometimes very protective towards newcomers to the playgroup; they may even be 'bossy', smothering a younger child with their attentions. Close friendships between children spring up during this period – sometimes between a child with a dominating personality and a more timid one – but usually these liaisons are short-lived.

Children of four plus are often responsive to strange adults, in contrast to their three-year-old selves who perhaps saw strangers as something of a threat. They are preoccupied with relationships, especially within the family, and will dress up and play out different roles in the home corner. They also use dramatic play to explore other experiences, say, being injected at a clinic or going into hospital. This hospital play may have in it an element of curiosity about other peoples' bodies, especially those of the opposite sex.

During this year, the child often becomes particularly attached to the parent of the opposite sex. The little girl becomes attentive to her father and proud of being known as 'daddy's girl'. It is quite acceptable for a girl to become closely attached to her father. Indeed, the better the relationship she forms with her father at this age, the more likely she is to make good relationships with men in adult life. If she copies his actions and attitudes, we call her a 'tomboy' and there is no stigma attached to this title.

This phase usually passes easily for girls. For some reason it seems to be less easy for boys. Emotionally involved with their mothers, they are jealous of their fathers and see them as rivals, intruders. At the same time, the boy wants to copy his father, to identify with him; thus he is at the mercy of two conflicting emotions. Sometimes the father is aware of his four-year-old's improved physical skills and his developing masculinity. He may also notice his son's attachment to his mother, and may fear that the boy is growing up to be a 'sissy'. He may begin to toughen him up by playing rough-and-tumble games – mock boxing matches or ball games. He may expect too much of his son, the play becomes rough and the child runs crying to his mother for comfort. These episodes often take place when the father returns from work, possibly just before the child's bedtime, so that the situation is aggravated by tiredness. The boy's tears confirms the father's feeling that the boy lacks the supposedly male attributes of courage and strength and their relationship suffers. It is interesting that we are quite able to accept girls having boyish attitudes but we are much less tolerant of boys having feminine characteristics.

Coming to playgroup helps boys through this period. Because they meet other people, their relationship with their mother becomes less intense and clinging. It is also especially helpful to boys to involve men in the running of the playgroup. Boys at this age live in a female-dominated world, yet they know they are not expected to grow up to be female and need male figures with whom to identify.

If, in partnership with parents, we as playgroup supervisors have done our job well, our rising-fives should now be ready for the further demands of school. We have helped them to become independent of their mothers and to work as part of a group. We have introduced them to new activities, helped them to gain new skills and at all times encouraged them to learn. By caring for them, we have given their mothers breathing space, the chance to lead their own lives, even if only for a few hours a week, the offer of support and a sympathetic ear when they needed it. Now, we ask the schools to carry on the work which we have begun.

Further reading

The Child, the Family, and the Outside World, D. W. Winnicott, Pelican, 35p.

Your Baby, Your One-Year-Old, Your Two-Year-Old, Your Three-Year-Old, Your Four-Year-Old, Your Five-Year-Old, Corgi, 15p.

5

The Child's Status in the Family

Many different factors contribute to the making of a child's personality, some inherited and some environmental. One of these is his position in his family: he is, so to speak, the prisoner of his birth rank, cast in a senior or junior role simply because he happened to be the first or last born.

Many adults expect children from the same family to have similar personalities, especially if they are of the same sex. However, a first-born has different experiences of life from those of a second child, if only because he does not have someone older to act as 'trail blazer' for him. It is important, therefore, to consider how a child is affected by his family status since this may be a key to understanding his behaviour outside the home and to discovering how best to help him at play group.

The observations in this section are partly based on a study of 5,000 babies born in March 1946. These children were continuously observed through childhood and adolescence to adulthood and the facts obtained analysed in *The Home and the School* by J. W. B. Douglas (Panther). One word of warning, however: though the conclusions reached by this study reinforce many of our own experiences with children, one should be aware of the dangers of rigidly classifying children according to their position in the family.

The first child

There are both advantages and disadvantages in being the first born. He is sometimes called 'the experimental child', the unfortunate one on whom the mother makes the most mistakes. Be cause he is her first big test in her new role, a mother may be over-anxious that he should do her credit and measure up to her expectations of an ideal child. When he is a baby she may fuss over his general management, his diet and his rest times; at a later stage she may be over-concerned about manners and behaviour in a way which she will not with later children. The survey of 200 mothers and babies published under the title *Pattern of Infant Care in an Urban Community* by John and Elizabeth Newson (Pelican) says there is a 'tendency for mothers to become more flexible and less routine-conscious with second and later babies'.

With no personal standards of comparison, it is easy for mothers to be more worried about the behaviour of first children. This anxiety can be communicated to the child, who may react by becoming tense and anxious himself. At a play-group, a mother can compare her child with others of a similar age, and may be reassured to find that some behaviour which may have been worrying her is found in many children.

The arrival of a second baby can be a distressing shock to the first child, who finds himself pushed out of his unique position of being the only child in a family. No matter how carefully this situation is handled by parents, the eldest child is almost bound to feel usurped from his place on his mother's lap by the new baby, unless there is already a large age gap between them. Some elder children threaten to put the newcomer 'in the dustbin', or 'down the lavatory'. Subsequent babies are used to sharing their mother from birth with at least one other child. Nevertheless, they can still react with extreme jealousy to the arrival of a new baby.

Elder children often have difficulties in making relationships with other children. This is clearly shown in the Douglas study where it is stated that 11.3 per cent of eldest children in the manual working class showed difficulties in making relationships, in comparison with 1.9 per cent of youngest children. It could be that the jealousy felt by the eldest towards the usurping baby is projected outside the family. The isolated eldest child especially, knowing only his brothers and sisters, may see social relationships with his own age group largely as a source of rivalry and jealousy. A good playgroup can help by providing less intense relationships with other children in a secure environment.

An elder child is also the 'path finder' for the family in such new experiences as going to playgroup. This can be a strain on him. A second child may have been used to accompanying his big brother or sister so that he is at least familiar with the building and staff; even so, he too may still need time to settle in. As the eldest, a child may be given responsibilities beyond his years; sent on an errand to a neighbour perhaps, or told to look after the baby while his mother goes into a shop. If a sibling is born soon after him, there is a danger that his mother will ask too much of him, because the baby in the family needs so much of her attention. How often do you see a harassed mother with baby and shopping bag in one hand, folded pushchair in the other, urging a two-year-old to mount the high bus step by telling him 'You're a big boy, you can do it.' He is not really big enough and needs a supporting arm.

There are also undoubted advantages in being the first-born and in some ways the position is a privileged one. Perhaps the chief advantage is that if he is the eldest child with normally caring parents he has the stimulus of two adults' undivided attention. He is more likely to do well academically than a youngest child of the same measured ability: because of this early attention and spurred on also by rivalry with his younger siblings, he is more geared to personal achievement as a means of gaining parental approval. He will also be the most likely one in the family to have new clothes and toys and this can produce a type of personality with a high expectation of himself and his surroundings – second best will not do.

Because he is the first of the family to be thrust into new and possibly challenging situations and may have responsibilities beyond his years, the eldest child *tends* to have a tense, reserved personality, unlike his more happy-go-lucky younger siblings. He may feel glad to come to the playgroup and find himself among the youngest members, perhaps even petted by the older children and able to assume a babyish role for a change.

The middle child

The role of the middle child is not so clearly defined as that of the eldest and seems to have attracted less attention from writers on child development. Our remarks therefore are based more on discussion with playgroup supervisors and our own observation rather than research.

When there is a small age gap between three children, the middle child is often in competition with both eldest and youngest. The eldest child has privileges and the youngest may be the pet of the family; the middle child, enjoying neither privilege nor petting, may be too young to realize that with the privilege goes responsibility and that petting belongs to babyhood. With the greater age gap there is usually less rivalry between the youngest and eldest, who may combine to form a partnership which excludes the middle child, so that he is odd man out.

If the eldest child is of the same sex, life can prove specially difficult. How annoying to be overshadowed by a rival who, because he is older than you, is bigger, stronger and more proficient at all the skills you long to master. If the first two children are of different sexes the middle child's position is easier. Parents often have different expectations of each sex and some rivalry is thus removed.

The middle child may react to his family position by being attention-seeking. He may behave aggressively, demonstrating his jealousy of his siblings by being over-assertive of his rights, refusing to share his belongings, constantly whining 'It isn't fair!' On the other hand he may suppress his feelings and react by being meek, gaining praise by his good behaviour.

If the age gap between three children is small, it is difficult for the middle child to have time alone with his mother. If there is such a child in a playgroup who is showing behaviour difficulties, suggest to the mother that she tries to have him on his own sometimes. If this is difficult to arrange, a partial answer may be for an adult in the playgroup to give this child extra attention. On the other hand, middle children who are very difficult at home are often easy to manage in a playgroup, probably because they are away from the intense sibling rivalry of home. Sometimes other children who are not 'middle ones' show these characteristics. In a family of five, for example, there may be three children born close together, then a gap followed by two more. All things being equal, the most likely child to suffer from his position is the second child of the first three.

Unless a middle child shows a preference for being near his siblings, he should be encouraged to play independently at playgroup, perhaps in a different 'family' group. Playgroup staff must be trained to see him – as they should of course see every other child – as a person in his own right. Emphasis on his individuality together with attention from one adult can often result in a great improvement in the middle child's personality.

The youngest child

One mother, commenting on the easy-going personality of her third child, said, 'I got the hang of this mothering business by the time number three came along.' She was probably expressing the feelings of many women when she went on to say, 'I learned some painful lessons with my first two children and applied what I had learnt to my third.' It is reasonable to suppose that the youngest child benefits from the parents' greater experience and that the mother has a more relaxed and less demanding attitude towards him. Perhaps because his parents' early expectations of him are lower, the youngest child, according to the Douglas study, tends to do less well at school than his older siblings. On the other hand, youngest children talk earlier than the first-born, stimulated perhaps by contact with older brothers and sisters.

Some mothers tend to cling to their last-born, feeling that once he is independent, the main reason for their existence will be gone. This may be particularly marked in the case of mothers of large families: conditioned to having a baby about the place, they continue to treat the youngest child as a baby to satisfy their own needs. Such a mother can hamper a child's normal development by dressing and undressing him, or taking him to the lavatory, long after he should be doing things for himself. She may self-indulgently pamper him, hoping to bind him even closer. He may be over-protected by his siblings, not allowed to behave appropriately for his age. This is especially true if the youngest child comes after a long gap, perhaps born during the mother's menopause; then the siblings, themselves young working adults, can become parent substitutes. Sometimes in these situations the child becomes almost a family 'mascot', spoilt and petted, his every whim indulged by the adults surrounding him.

If you have a youngest child who needs to escape from the over-safe cocoon of his family, see that he is given responsibilities, say for watering the bulbs or feeding the playgroup pet. Encourage him to be concerned for a newcomer's safety, so that he sees that he can sometimes play the part of looking after instead of always being looked after. Once again, a playgroup can thus help to free a child from the possible limitations of his family position.

Children from large families

The average family size today is 2·2 children compared with 5 in Victorian times, so that it is comparatively rare to meet children from large families. There are obvious advantages in belonging to a large family: a child is never short of playmates, relationships are less intense and more varied than in a small family. In a two-child family, rivalry between the children can be fierce; in a three-child family the middle child may be the odd one out. Perhaps this leaves four as the perfect size – if one ignores the undoubted dangers of overpopulation.

In our experience, there is a tendency for children from a large family to stay within the family unit, and to move about as a flock rather than as individuals. The child may feel a sense of security from this group life, but it can become a limitation. Children whose social needs are being met within the family do not venture out to meet other children. A child in a big family may also have less opportunity for different social experiences. Small families tend to go out to tea or on outings with other families – but it takes a brave hostess to invite seven extra for a meal! Similarly, the mother of a large family may herself be disinclined to add to her work load by inviting extra people for meals. In addition, there is evidence in the HMSO report *Circumstances of Families* that large families, as one would expect, tend to have less income per head; so these children may be further penalized by poor standards of living, including less play equipment.

The biggest disadvantage of all for a child from a large family, especially if the members are born close together, is that he may experience a poorer quality of mothering than the child from a small family, who does not have to share his mother's time and energy with so many rivals. We have found no research evidence to prove this, but common sense would seem to indicate that the average woman with a large family, tired perhaps by frequent pregnancies, provides a less effective standard of care, both on a physical and emotional level. She will have less opportunity to have a one-to-one relationship with each of her children; with so much cooking and house-work, she has less time to talk and play with them, sit and read to them or watch television together. The eldest child may have some privileges such as being last to bed; the youngest child may have his mother to himself when the others go to school, but the children in the middle may lack contact with an adult.

Much can be done in a playgroup to overcome the difficulties experienced by a child from a large family. Above all he can be treated as an individual. One adult should make it her responsibility to spend some time with him on his own, so that his sense of himself as a person of importance is strengthened. The adult concerned should make certain each day that the child has at least had a conversation with her or heard a story told specially for him. The child will also meet other children outside his family group; someone may even ask him home to tea!

Only children

There are many reasons for a child being an 'only'. Some mothers fail to conceive more than once; others feel that one experience of childbirth was enough. Couples may deliberately limit their family because they feel that they can have a freer life or a better standard of living.

Some parents of only children have told us that they have been aware of criticism, as though they had failed in their duty by having only one child. 'You don't strike me as being an only's mother, you're so sensible,' said a teacher to one such parent at the school's open evening. Such comments can be very hurtful, especially if, as in this mother's case, she had had a lot of treatment to try to aid conception.

The problems of only children are much more commonly discussed than others; is this because the difficulties of such a child are more obvious? The most common one is that he may be a 'lonely only'. Even within his own family, an only child can feel isolated. 'Mummy and Daddy have each other – I haven't even got a cat,' as one perceptive eight-year-old put it. Every child needs opportunities to make contact with a variety of other children if he is to develop happily. With a brother or sister, there is at least one person of about his own age with whom he must make a relationship; and unless he lives in a very isolated position a sibling will normally also bring friends into the family circle, thereby increasing his experience of playing with other children. No matter how hard even a sensitive adult tries, it is impossible to play on a child's level. So it is easy for an only child's play to lack spontaneity, or for him to develop into a 'sobersides' who prefers to listen to adults' conversation or tries to join in their activities. He may become precocious and achieve a false maturity beyond his years.

An only child is also on the receiving end of a great deal of feeling from adults and this can be a burden. It is possible to have too much love, too much attention. This is especially true of a mother whose marriage is unsatisfactory: she may ask from a child responses which should normally come from a husband. Parents can become over-protective, fearing that they have all their eggs in one basket. Many an only child is 'wrapped in cotton wool', not allowed to savour new experiences which might involve some quite acceptable risk. We know of one mother who had allowed her four-year-old to accept an invitation to a birthday party, yet could not stop herself asking the hostess if there was a guard in front of the fire, thereby causing offence.

An only child also has less opportunity to come to terms with his feelings of aggression. Brothers and sisters squabble and fight, say over who shall use the only free swing; the next minute they are playing together amicably, one each end of a see-saw. They learn that one can feel hatred towards a person but that these feelings will pass and be followed by ones of love and companionship. If a child is left too long without this casual give-and-take he may grow up to be a person who can have only intense relationships with others, frightening off ordinary friends by asking too much of them. An only child can also feel very isolated if he has made both parents angry. To whom does he turn? Siblings may sometimes delight in another's downfall, but will often offer comfort afterwards by word or deed.

So far we have dwelt so much on the disadvantages that parents with an only child may well feel depressed. But there are undoubted advantages. As Freud said, 'He who is the undisputed darling of his mother, wants not seldom in life that confidence of success which induces real success'. From many points of view life deals kindly with the 'only': he is never knocked off his throne by the arrival of another baby; his relationship with his mother, the most important relationship in his life, is allowed to unfold at its own rate, in all its complexity. Only children tend to have stable personalities and an assured manner. Perhaps benefiting from an abundance of adult stimulus, they initially do well at school. They also enjoy obvious material advantages such as a plentiful supply of new toys and clothes.

Coming to a playgroup, an only child enters a world largely geared to the needs of children; previously he had to fit into the world of adults. If he has had little contact with children of his own age, he may go through the main stages of play – solitary, parallel and cooperative – at an accelerated rate. Through this play he will learn that sometimes you can experience feelings of hate for a child who tries to force you off your bike, yet feel friendly affection for him when you sit together to listen to a story. He will be temporarily freed from over-attentive parents and allowed to find out on his own just what he can and cannot do. And he will meet concerned and caring adults who are content to accept him as himself without making any intense emotional demands.

Twins

There are two types of twins – identical, who develop from the same fertilized egg, and non-identical, who spring from two separate fertilized eggs. In the first case, having the same genetic makeup, the twins are bound to be of the same sex and of very similar appearance, with the same colour eyes, hair and complexion. Non-identical twins need be no more alike than any other brother or sister, being only twins by virtue of the fact that they shared their mother's womb at the same time.

Twins have the undoubted advantage of supporting each other in any new situation, such as going to a playgroup. They never lack companionship during their early years. Often they develop an understanding of each other which is not dependent on speech: they seem to communicate without words, so that their language development is sometimes below average for their age. Yet there are particular problems built in to being a twin. The main one is that the baby's early experience of his mother is less than total: there is always a rival present who has an equal claim. If both babies are crying lustily for their feed, one must be left while the other is bathed and fed. Some mothers show great skill in coping with this double burden, learning the technique of breast-feeding two babies at once so that neither shall cry while the other is being fed, putting the babies to sleep in different parts of the house so that even if one cries the other is not wakened, dressing each child differently so that each is seen as an individual and not a mirror of the other. Other mothers prefer to think of their two babies as one unit; there is actually a cult of 'twinship' which seeks to emphasize the sameness of the children rather than the differences.

It is important that each child should grow up an individual, not always seen as one half of a pair, and a playgroup can help this process. The first step may have to be to persuade the mother of twins to see her children as individuals. Even if they are physically identical, there are still some differences in personality. A mother who insists on buying identical wardrobes can be asked if it would be possible not to dress the children alike. The dangers can be tactfully explained and the twins can be given different coloured name badges. Helpers should understand the importance of calling each twin by name rather than 'twinny'; a name is a very personal possession, enhancing one's sense of individuality. Twins may well need to play near each other at first – they have almost certainly been conditioned to being within earshot of each other since birth – but once they are settled in a group, they can be encouraged to pursue different activities, so that they learn to lead separate existences. The chapter entitled 'Twins' in Winnicott's book, *The Child, the Family and the Outside World* (Pelican) has some perceptive comments on this problem.

The child's relationship with his father

So far we have written mainly about the mother–child relationship as if it happened in isolation, ignoring the fact that most children are reared within a family and will usually have a father and perhaps brothers and sisters. Let us look at the part a good father plays in bringing up a child.

Traditionally the care of children has been a female responsibility, with the father playing a minor role. Today, however, an increasing number of fathers are taking an active part in caring for their babies – it is not at all unusual for a father to feed his baby, soothe him to sleep or take him out in the pram. This occasional caring which the father gives means that another adult will talk to the child and play with him. It can be very enriching for a young child to have a play relationship with his father – the child thus has two adults presenting the world to him, each from different viewpoints, the masculine and the feminine. His mother will use the vacuum cleaner, his father will take it to pieces when it is broken and mend it. He will help his mother make the pastry, he will watch his father free the blocked-up sink. He will be learning that although much work is shared, his father and mother have different responsibilities in the running of the household – though of course these responsibilities vary from family to family; some women are more competent than their husbands at the so-called masculine skills and vice versa.

Some children have a less happy relationship with their father. Some men are hostile to the arrival of a new baby, resenting the claims made on the time and energies of their wife and jealous of the love she is giving the child, particularly if he is a boy. Others work long hours, or have interests which take them away from home, leaving them little time or energy for their children. Some fathers have to be away from home for long periods and when such an absentee father does return he may seem an interloper, intruding on the privacy of the child's relationship with his mother. The child may then react by regressing to a more infantile level of behaviour, clinging to his mother and refusing to be parted from her, or be openly hostile, shouting at his father 'I don't want you – go away'. Both boys and girls can react like this, but boys (as we saw on p. 66) may be particularly jealous of their father. This behaviour is hurtful to a returning father and sometimes this can turn to anger, so that the mother finds herself in the difficult situation of trying to placate and reconcile two angry males.

If a child in your playgroup has an absentee father, suggest to the mother that she talks about her husband and what will happen when 'Daddy comes home', so that in his imagination the child can come to terms with his father's return. Warn her of the possible difficulties and tell her that she and her husband must be patient, remembering that a child has less control over his feelings than an adult.

What about fatherless children with no male figure in their families? They may create a fantasy image, an idealized father figure and this can be dangerous. No flesh and blood man can compare with a child's ideal and any subsequent relationship with a real person may prove a disappointment. For such a child and for those who see little of their father regular male visitors are very valuable – see Starting the Playgroup, p. 142, for ways of inviting them to the playgroup.

This is only a brief introduction to child development and won't answer everybody's questions. If you want to read further, have a look at the bibliography on p. 344. Meanwhile, here are four questions which we are frequently asked by playgroup staff.

How should I deal with a child who lies?

Because young children cannot distinguish between fact and fantasy most children indulge in 'story telling' of some kind. When a three-year-old tells you, 'There's a lion at the end of my bed,' or, 'I saw an elephant in the garden today,' enter into his fantasy with him by answering in a way which also shows that you know it is a game, and then gently lead him back to reality: 'Oh, that's a funny story, now tell me what really happened.' If you have a good relationship with him, he will enjoy the game with you and not feel guilty while understanding that you prefer the truth. In a good relationship an adult can also explain to a child over four, 'If you don't tell me the truth, I won't know when to believe you.' It is essential that the adults always tell the truth to the child, even if it may be difficult. For example, in preparing a child to go to hospital it is no good promising nothing will hurt him if you know it will.

Occasionally you may have a child who spends a great deal of his time talking about imaginary friends and exploits as if he really believes in them. A child who needs to escape into a fantasy world may do so for a variety of reasons. He may have imaginary friends simply because he lacks real ones. Or his parents may ask too much of him, expecting him to conform to adult standards – a child with constantly disapproving parents may invent a wicked companion to take all the blame. Parents may be punishing a child too severely for naughtiness – this may well lead him to lie in order to protect himself. An even harsher punishment and he will make sure he tells a better lie next time! If, when he tells untruths about the fantasy world he escapes into, adults show great concern, the lies may then become an attention-seeking device. Far better to give the child sufficient attention in a more constructive way in the first instance.

Truth as an abstract idea has no meaning for under-fives, so you need to help parents not to expect too much from their children. Encourage parents of a child who is lying to relax any rigid standards they set so that the child has opportunities to play in a relaxed way at home with friends of his own age and with his parents. When these experiences are reinforced in a happy playgroup atmosphere, most children will gradually lose the need to fib.

What do you do about a child who masturbates?

It is very common for children to masturbate (or generally play with themselves) when they are listening to a story or music or sometimes if they are excited, for instance the first time they stroke a baby rabbit. They seem to touch their sex organs partly for comfort and pleasure and partly for reassurance. Many people find this habit unacceptable, however, and scold their child with a 'Take your hand away, at once!' This reaction can give a child a lasting sense of guilt about something that is perfectly natural and harmless, so make sure your helpers do not intimidate children in this way. The only point at which you might possibly be concerned about masturbation is if you have a child who plays with himself excessively, ignoring all alternative activities. Masturbation is often a way of relieving tension and may be the result of too high a standard of behaviour being expected of a child; he thus uses his body as an escape route from boredom or depression. How can you help a child who you feel is spending too much time masturbating?

First of all make quite sure not to make him feel guilty in any way. Secondly, try to establish a good relationship with him, let him see that he is important to you. Invite him to play with basic materials with you, such as wet clay; this has a strong sensual element which can be very helpful. Praise his efforts so that he can see that there are other satisfactions to be gained apart from masturbation. Sit him on your knee to look at a book, or hold his hand as you inspect the nature table together, anything which shows him that *physical contact with someone else* can give him pleasure. Encourage him to talk to you, his conversation may reveal what is causing him to need to masturbate. Try to get to know his mother, his problem probably stems from his relationship with her. Does she expect him to be too good, too quiet, too polite? Does she find it difficult to show the child physical affection? If she brings the subject up with you, you could, with great tact, tell her of some of the possible causes, and suggest that if the habit continues she might like to talk it over with someone at the Child and Family Guidance Clinic.

How do you help a child frightened by a thunderstorm?

Fears of one kind or another are normal in young children. Never ridicule a child's fears or try to laugh them off with a 'Don't be silly'. They are very real to him and must be treated with respect. It helps to be prepared for a child's fears by knowing if he is of a generally nervous disposition, or if it is only thunderstorms which terrify him. Ask mothers about this when they put their child's name down for your playgroup.

When a child is frightened he needs to be able to cling to his mother for comfort and security. He needs to see her as an all-powerful person who can protect him from all dangers. But very often, a child who is frightened of thunderstorms has a mother who is frightened of them too. So he is faced with a double threat: fear of the actual storm and, probably more important, fear that, after all, his mother is not able to protect him when he needs it most.

In playgroup you will need to reassure such children that adults are stable, strong people who can protect them. Whichever adult is most familiar to the child should take him on her knee and cuddle him closely, talking soothingly, perhaps quietly singing a familiar nursery rhyme or song. Close physical contact is very important. Give him a soft toy if he will accept it and a warm blanket to snuggle into. An older child may be calmed by your trying to explain to him the reasons for thunder and lightning, supplemented if possible with a picture book on the subject. Keep the frightened child in the same room as the other children. He will gain from seeing his friends continuing their activities unaffected by the storm, except perhaps for discussing it with the adults. If you feel, however, he is so frightened that his screams may affect some other children, carry him into another room, and calm him there. This is a time when one of the supervisor's special gimmick toys (see p. 280) can be particularly useful as a distraction.

Discuss the child's fears and the way you have dealt with them with his mother. Reassure her that such fears are normal in young children and that he will grow out of them. A mother who is herself afraid of storms may be so concerned to help her child that she will forget her own fears.

How can a playgroup help a child whose grandparent has just died?

A child who has had to experience death may be very distressed. All children are very dependent on the adults around them and if one of these disappears they may feel very threatened. If one grownup can vanish, then perhaps it can happen to others. Three-year-olds will not be able to express their worries in words, but a child of four may ask his parents, 'Are you going to die, too?', 'Will I die?', indicating his feelings of insecurity. Because of this a bereaved child may prefer to stay away from playgroup for a while, almost as if he needs to keep an eye on his mother in case she disappears too. He may regress to a very babyish stage, wanting to be carried about or sucking his thumb. He may become difficult at bedtime and start waking during the night. Try to talk to his mother about these problems, explaining why the child is behaving like this, and say that if she is able to reassure him by consistently demonstrating her love and care, the phase will pass.

The parents may have strong religious convictions, and find it easy to answer the child's question of 'Where has grandpa gone to?' with 'He's gone to live with Jesus.' Others may ask for your help over how to deal with these questions. If a person has died, it is either because they were very old, or had been ill or were involved in an accident. Death was the natural consequence of one of these conditions and it is best, therefore, to explain this to the child in everyday language, rather than use an euphemism. Death is a part of life, and the child will gradually be coming to terms with this fact. He will see bulbs planted, grow and then wither. The playgroup may have a hamster or guinea pig which dies. Adults are often too protective towards children about the subject of death – children can take a much more matter-of-fact attitude. Of course, if a dearly loved pet dies, the child will be upset and mourn, but after a comparatively short time he will come to accept it.

If a bereaved child comes to a playgroup, he may want to stay very close to the adult he knows best, ignoring all the activities. Allow him to do this, he needs a period for mourning. Show him that you understand his grief and don't attempt to jolly him along into doing something. Initially he may be glad of the basic comfort of sitting on your lap. Then you may sense, perhaps after he has drunk his milk, that he is ready for some quiet activity, say looking at a book with you and from that move on to something else. He may repeat this pattern for several days and you must be prepared to be patient with him, the initiative to resume normal play activities comes best from him. You may find that he plays a good deal in the home corner, acting out his anxieties. He may blame himself for the death, feeling guilty because of some fantasy he has had about his grandparent and he will come to terms with this through play. Be prepared to talk with him about whoever has died; he may want to keep his mental image of the person alive for some time.

Remember that the parents too may be grieving and in need of support. If they have nursed the grandparent through the last illness, they may be very weary and welcome practical help, such as the collection and delivery of the child to playgroup, or the care of the child on the day of the funeral. If you can offer both child and parents your understanding and help over their bereavement you will find that your relationship with them has been greatly strengthened.

6
Children with Special Problems

We have discussed in general terms the child's position in the family and the effects this can have on his personality. What of children who do not come from ordinary family backgrounds, or who have disabilities or other difficulties? How can they be helped by attending a playgroup?

Adopted children

Parents of adopted children may resent the implication that they are not an 'ordinary family' or that they have special problems. The relationship between adoptive parents and their children can certainly be of such quality that it appears in no way different from that between parents and natural-born children. In fact, many adoptive parents say that they have to remind themselves that the child was not born to them. Nevertheless, there can be additional tensions in a family with an adopted child which anyone running a playgroup needs to know about.

Adoption is common to all classes of our society, though less so in the highest and lowest strata and most frequent in the middle classes. Throughout the ages childless couples have brought up children who were not born to them, although the first Adoption Act was not passed until 1926. According to the Home Office statistics, the number of children adopted in 1971 was 23,399. Once a child is legally adopted the natural mother loses all rights over him; in the eyes of the law he is then in every respect the equal of a natural-born child, except that he cannot inherit a title. The best way to adopt a child is through a registered adoption society, whose trained social workers attempt to place a child in the family best suited to rear him.

Before a couple are accepted as suitable they are subjected to a screening process and rejected if the adoption society is not reasonably assured that they are fit to bring up a child. There is usually a long waiting period between acceptance and placement, giving people time to change their minds.

With the new abortion laws and more widespread use of contraception, there are far fewer babies available for adoption today than there were even five years ago, although there is not the same shortage of children from racially mixed backgrounds. It is possible for private persons to place a child for adoption, perhaps to a couple who have been rejected by a registered society. This is regrettable: placement is a skilled process, and since the future of the child is in question, it should not be left to amateurs.

Adoptive parents sometimes have unvoiced feelings of inferiority. These may be due to their own failure to have children or to doubts about their own capabilities as parents. They may feel guilty at having 'taken' a child from its natural mother. They may have built up an idealized picture of the child, and when the real one does not measure up to their expectations they may feel disappointed and even reject him. They may worry over normal behaviour difficulties, blaming these on the child's unknown heredity.

If the couple has other naturally born children the adopted one may be compared unfavourably; this is why it is often preferable for the adopted child to be of a different sex, as parents may not have the same expectations of a boy as of a girl. On the credit side, adoptive parents are usually very conscientious, cherishing the child who has become theirs by deliberate choice.

Sometimes a playgroup will not be told initially that a child is adopted. But if a good relationship is built with the parents they may be glad to have someone in whom to confide. They may appreciate reassurance on the normality of the child's behaviour. The child's temper tantrums, for example, will almost certainly not be, as the parents may fear, because 'temper is in his blood'. It is far more likely to be part of his normal development (see p. 55), or perhaps because he is spending too long cooped up in a tiny, gardenless flat and needs more opportunity for play. If, however, a child's behaviour does seem to exceed the bounds of normality, or if the parent–child relationship seems to be deteriorating, the Health Visitor can be called upon for advice.

Children with unsupported mothers

There are many fatherless children growing up in our society today. This can be due to divorce, separation or the death of the father. There are also many mothers who have never married, nor indeed had a stable union with any man. These mothers and children are sometimes supported by an extended family. More often, however, the mother is beset with financial worries and left to fight a lonely battle in which she may become very isolated. With no father in the family the mother may make excessive emotional demands on her child, perhaps becoming over-possessive and protective. If she resents the father's desertion she may allow her bitterness to affect the child, teaching him to hate his father and thus other men. Even if the grandmother can help by taking care of the child, so that the mother can go out to work, the result may be that the child becomes confused as to who his mother really is – the woman whom he calls 'mummy' or the 'gran' who is fulfilling the mothering role.

A playgroup can help a child from such a background by offering him less demanding relationships and by making efforts to see that he becomes friendly with a helpful man. It can also be of great assistance to the unsupported mother, welcoming her as a visitor or helper, listening to her if she wants to talk about her difficulties. Mothers in these circumstances may be housebound in the evening, and an occasional free baby-sitter from the playgroup circle can be a godsend. If she has no proper income she can be helped to claim her rights from the Department of Health and Social Security; filling in forms can appear an insuperable difficulty when one is emotionally distressed. She may also need support during the painful experience of a court hearing for separation or divorce.

Emotionally deprived children

The term 'deprived child' means one whose first, all-important relationship with a mother figure has been so disrupted that he has suffered emotional damage. If maternal deprivation – lack of adequate care from his mother – is severe during the first three years a child's normal development is impaired and his future mental health at risk. If a child is brought up in the kind of institution where he is unable to have a continuous relationship with any one person his deprivation is likely to be severe.

The severely deprived child is likely to be in the care of the local authority's Department of Social Services or looked after by a voluntary body such as Dr Barnardo's. According to statistics published by the Home Office, *Children in Care in England and Wales*, there were 71,210 children in care in 1970, 20,720 of whom were in institutions, and they may attend a playgroup from this base, or they may be in a foster home and come to you from there.

It is less easy to identify children who are partially deprived especially if they are living at home. The difficulty may be only temporary: the mother may not be able to look after her child properly because she is away from home for a time, perhaps in hospital. Or perhaps she goes out to work full time, and has no alternative but to leave her child in the care of a succession of mother substitutes. Even less easy to recognize is the child whose mother looks after him full time yet rejects him, perhaps because he has a physical or mental handicap, or because she has personal problems herself.

What are the effects of deprivation? It can produce a child who is physically, mentally or emotionally retarded. One researcher describes babies reared in institutions as 'unresponsive ... poor sleepers ... with an appearance of unhappiness'. Because a severely deprived child has not had the initial experience of making a relationship with one person – a mother figure – he often seems unable to learn how to make a relationship with anyone. He may withdraw from all emotional entanglements, appearing apathetic and uncaring towards others: receiving no satisfaction from relationships he 'turns in on himself'. He may wet his bed, soil himself, or show some bizarre behaviour such as compulsive rocking or head-banging. He may over-eat, especially sweets, as if seeking to compensate his emotional emptiness with food. Sometimes he will steal; delinquent children often have a history of deprivation. A child who has had some degree of mothering will quickly attach himself to anyone who appears to answer his needs – institutionalized children in particular are often superficially friendly – but this attachment is a shallow one. Sometimes a partially deprived child will appear very well-behaved, as if obeying all the rules gives him a sort of security.

A deprived child's personality may be unattractive – the less-damaged child may appear aggressive, fighting for his rights to be noticed and loved. He will need especially skilled handling. Of course it is impossible for anyone in a playgroup to act as an adequate mother substitute – the time he spends there is too short. Nevertheless, the fact that he will be asked to make a relationship with one adult, someone who greets him each time he attends, praises his work, prevents him from being disruptive and encourages him to play with basic materials – themselves a sort of therapy – will be helpful to him. If he is living at home, establishing a good relationship with his mother should also help – although once again we suggest the Health Visitor should be called in if either child or mother seems to need more assistance than the playgroup can provide. An interesting film called *John, nine days in a residential nursery*, shows the effect on a stable two-year-old of being put in residential care for nine days. It could well be shown at a parents' evening and can be hired from Concorde Film Council, Nacton, Ipswich.

Socially deprived children

This is the child who is handicapped because of the materially poor conditions of his home. He should not be confused with the emotionally deprived child described above. He is usually easy to recognize by the poor standard of his clothing; he may also be in poor physical condition – underweight, pale and with lack-lustre hair. His housing conditions and his standards of furnishing are likely to be poor enough to damage his health; his family perhaps has to sleep on the floor covered with only a couple of old blankets and drink out of jam jars. The wage-earner in the socially deprived family is likely to be unskilled, semi-skilled or unemployed.

The chief need of such a child is obviously improved physical care – warmer clothing and a better diet. But he also requires improved mental nourishment. If his father works long hours to add overtime earnings to his low basic wage and his mother is obliged to work, he has probably had little contact with adults. The first step in helping this type of child is to contact the Health Visitor to see if the family is eligible for supplementary benefits from the Department of Health and Social Security. If they are authorized by a note from a social worker, they can get clothing from the Women's Royal Voluntary Service. The family may already be known to the Department of Social Services which is empowered to spend money to keep children with their own families as opposed to being taken into the care of the local authority. If the playgroup is catering for a deprived area it could be eligible for a grant under the Urban Aid programme, either to pay for individual children or for equipment. A letter to the local Director of Social Services should elicit the necessary information.

Attending a good playgroup can be of great compensatory value to a child from a socially deprived home. If he is to hold his own on anything like equal footing with more privileged children, he must be given a wealth of verbal stimulation, encouraged to handle a wide variety of materials and taken out to places of interest. Unless he lives in the country, this type of child may rarely come into contact with anything growing and should be encouraged to plant seeds and bulbs, to examine any collections brought for the nature table and to handle pets. Socially deprived children who have a somewhat inadequate mother, often with a succession of 'uncles' floating in and out of their lives rather than a stable father figure, will draw particular comfort from the presence of the same playgroup staff at each session and will be reassured by the ongoing relationship that the group provides. If a child's attendance is irregular, an effort should be made to arrange for him to be collected. Helpers who complain that this is 'spoiling the mother' should be reminded that it is the child who will benefit. Nevertheless, it must be realized that working in an area with a high concentration of socially deprived children is very demanding; anyone who tries to be playgroup supervisor, welfare officer, and fairy godmother all at the same time risks failing at all three. The welfare services should be pressured into being efficient, not have their work done for them.

Accident-prone children

Some children seem to have what an Irish friend calls 'the unlucky hand'. They are consistently clumsy and frequently break things. This may be due to poor coordination or inadequate early training, to not being taught to concentrate on what they were doing. Or a child can have small accidents because he has grown quickly and has not yet adapted to his new size. But beyond this normal range, one occasionally comes across a child who is rarely seen without a bandage or plaster and who is such a frequent hospital out-patient that the staff there know him by name.

One explanation for this is that such a child is suffering from some sort of stress and that his preoccupation with inner worry prevents him noticing danger signals which would normally alert him to certain avoidable situations. Anyone who has ever had too much to think about and do will have probably noticed that they became absent-minded, leaving purchases in shops, forgetting some relative's birthday, or even burning themselves on the oven or cutting themselves while trimming meat. (It's an interesting fact that in the two weeks before Christmas, when female minds are preoccupied with a hundred-and-one details, the notifiable accidents for women increase substantially!)

There are a number of research documents to support the theory that an accident-prone child is, in oversimplified terms, a worried child. The World Health Organization Report *Child-*

ren in Accidents (1957) says that 'children of this type often come from broken homes or problem families'. Another piece of research, into children involved in road accidents, found that there were two significant factors in their backgrounds: either their mother was preoccupied with something which diluted the quality of care she gave her child – perhaps she was ill or working, pregnant or busy with a young baby – or the child lived in an overcrowded area with unsatisfactory play provision. Another study showed that children who were accident-prone had similar problems to children who wet their bed, often a symptom of emotional stress.

A playgroup can help a child showing this sort of behaviour by teaching him to handle things with care and attention. He should not be nagged but encouraged to look where he is putting things and to move unhurriedly from place to place, generally concentrating on what he is doing. An eye can be kept on him to make sure he is not being neglected or pressurized into being too clean or too well-mannered, or that too much is not being demanded of him, either intellectually or emotionally. Plenty of time for play will provide him with a kind of therapy, as will the friendship of some reliable adult. Praise in front of his mother will show her that he is valued as himself, not as the child she may be trying to force him to be.

Immigrant children

An immigrant child has the same needs as any other child coming to a playgroup – companionship and the opportunity to play in the right environment. But since a child should be considered within the context of his family, it is necessary to look at the problems which may face immigrants and how these may affect their children.

Throughout our history, other nationals have come to our land, either as invaders – the Romans, the Vikings or the French – or as immigrants, the Huguenots and the European Jews who sought a refuge from political or religious persecution. We have absorbed these peoples and our national life is the richer for it. In the last two decades people have come to settle here

o escape not from persecution but from poverty, to build a new
life in a land which in some cases they have been brought up to
think of as the 'mother country'. It is an ugly fact that they
have met with racial prejudice based on fear and ignorance.
Many attitudes towards people are learnt before a child is five
- all the more important that children and parents from different racial, as well as social, backgrounds should work together
in a happy playgroup.

For very young children, the change brought about by im-
migration can be quite traumatic. They may have come from
a large, extended family which was part of a stable society.
They may have only experienced life in a simple, rural setting.
After only a few hours flight, they are suddenly transferred to
a totally different world, where the customs, language and
behaviour of the people seem strange and the weather down-
right cruel. Some children show a severe reaction to this up-
heaval, clinging to their mother or refusing to eat or speak.
Ideally immigrant children need a period of adjustment to
their new surroundings before being introduced to a playgroup – otherwise they may be in a state of cultural shock and
react to the wealth of activities offered in a playgroup by being
aggressive or withdrawn.

If this is the case, the first step is to talk to the child in a
soothing voice; he will understand the tone if not the words. If
he will hold an adult's hand and sit on her lap, he can then be
shown a picture book. Every effort should be made to form a
relationship, for once this is achieved, language-learning can
begin. Specific language teaching, using slow speech and extra-
clear pronunciation, is obviously helpful, starting, say, with
naming and repeating parts of the body then after several days
moving on to some other topic – the names of furniture or
toys, for instance. A local college of education, university or
technical college, may be prepared to send students to help
give this language experience; it should however be the same
person each week, as immigrant children are especially confused by meeting too many strange adults. Each practice should
be kept very short, at the most five to seven minutes.

An immigrant child may be bewildered by the many toys

available to him and seem unable to play. He may have few toys of his own, perhaps because of poverty, perhaps because it is not the custom of his people. Going to a western-type lavatory may also frighten immigrant children, who in rural communities may have been used to running into the bushes or squatting over a basin at floor level. Some immigrant children will also be unused to western traffic dangers. All these things will have to be explained, preferably with parents present.

There is sometimes a tendency in a multiracial group for children from the same country to play together, ignoring other nationalities. This is only to be expected at first, since it is comforting to be with children who look and sound familiar. But once the children are all settled, ways should be found to encourage at least parallel play, say by placing two children of different nationalities next to each other for painting. Co-operation cannot be forced, but, in the right atmosphere, friendships will flourish. If there are only a few immigrant children, they will be accepted without comment by the rest, who often do not notice any difference in colour of skin or hair. There is a nice story of a little boy who, asked if his best friend at school was a 'coloured boy', replied, 'I dunno, I'll ask him.'

There may be aspects of the immigrant children's culture that all the group could share – such as traditional games for example. Older immigrant children from local secondary schools may be able to provide help with these. Or travel posters showing a child's home country could be put up on the walls. The dressing-up box could contain lengths of gay cloth for Asian children and others to make saris; the home corner can have dark- and light-coloured dolls and national costumes in which to dress them. Read out books in which the main character has dark skin – we like Ezra Jack Keats' *Whistle for Willie* or *A Snowy Day* (Puffin); or make up stories with characters who have 'beautiful dark brown eyes' and whatever sort of hair is most common in the group. Having straight mousy hair ourselves, we feel very sympathetic, since we have always resented the typical blond, curly haired heroines of most stories! Oxfam also sell books with a multiracial flavour.

Making contact with immigrant parents can be difficult,

especially if there is no common language. Can you learn how to say at least 'hello' and 'goodbye' in their language, a small courtesy which shows that you are trying? A good deal can be achieved with a smiling face and sign language, but some misunderstanding will be inevitable. Immigrant parents may be as bewildered as their child by the way a playgroup is organized; they may have expected a more formal approach to work, equating education with book learning and seeing both as a vehicle of escape from the trap of poverty in which they find themselves. However, they are impressed as their children learn our language. Perhaps an interpreter can be found to explain just how much the children are gaining, to teach the group helpers a few polite phrases in the immigrant's language and to help with tactful advice over suitable clothing. Newly arrived immigrant mothers who have not experienced the fickleness of British weather may send their children inadequately dressed. Parents' evenings are less difficult to arrange if the language barrier can be overcome. One 'parents'' group we remember consisted mostly of secondary-school-age sisters, with a very few non-English speaking mothers and one or two fathers. Evenings were most successful when immigrant families supplied the food and playgroup workers showed a film of the children working in the playgroup. If contact with parents is close, on the other hand, they may ask for help with such matters as sickness benefit, or how to register as voters.

The more the playgroup knows its immigrant children's background, the more it can help them, so it pays to find out as much as possible about cultural traditions, family structure, religious and food customs. One should never, for instance, take off a Muslim child's shalwar (pouched trousers) unless they are sopping wet – her parents may be outraged at this attack on her modesty in a way that would never occur to an English parent whose children's pants were removed. Similarly some Sikh sects must never have their turbans removed.

Further information

The local Community Relations Officer should be able to give useful advice; if there is no local office, write to the Community Relations Commission, 15–16 Bedford Street, London WC2. Another useful organization is Priority Area Children, 32 Trumpington Street, Cambridge.

Handicapped children

There may be those who think that a playgroup for normal children is not the place to care for a handicapped child. The supervisor and helpers have no special training, nor does an ordinary playgroup have equipment to answer all the needs of a handicapped child. But for many disabled children there are no special facilities available and it is often a choice between attending a playgroup while living at home or being sent away to an institution. So the chances are that any group is likely to be asked to accept a handicapped child at any time during its existence. What should be the basic principles behind such a decision?

The first consideration must be to safeguard the life of the playgroup as a whole: is it well established, running smoothly, without any great financial worries? We suggest that a playgroup be open for a year before accepting a handicapped child, unless the disablement is a minor one.

The local Health Visitor should be consulted, since she should also know a group well enough to judge whether it can cope with any particular child. Mothers who make a direct approach should be treated sympathetically, but any doubts should also be raised with the Health Visitor, who probably knows the family background. Mothers are often understandably defensive about their child's condition and may not reveal the full extent of his disability. Plans must also be discussed with helpers and the parents of other children in the group, to anticipate all the possible effects.

We suggest that it is best to accept only one disabled child in each group, although again this depends on the severity of the handicap. It may be a great asset to enlist an extra helper, so that another pair of hands is available in case of extra mess or a more serious crisis. Premises must be carefully examined. What hazards exist for the handicapped child which a normal child could overcome? Are there steps leading to the lavatories without a handhold? If the floor is full of splinters, what would happen to the child whose main form of locomotion is by rolling? If you decide to accept a handicapped child, this should be for a trial period at first and the mother should understand that it may take some time for the child to settle. Have him for a short period – say an hour, two sessions a week – then increase the time if all goes well.

No matter how severe a child's handicap is, he is still a child. Although he may progress at a snail's pace, he will follow the same pattern of development as a normal child, and thus have similar play needs which a playgroup can satisfy. But he may have additional special needs: his disability may have restricted his opportunities for learning; he may be immobile, or a mental handicap may have left him with less innate ability than a normal child. It should therefore be the responsibility of one adult to make a relationship with the handicapped child which is both concerned yet detached, to ensure that he has direct stimulation by conversation, songs and stories and by the right sort of equipment. (Advice and information on helping handicapped children is given later, p. 100, under the headings of specific disabilities, together with the names and addresses of appropriate organizations.)

Once a child has settled in, it is best that he should conform as nearly as possible to the rules of the playgroup. The aim is to help him to live in a normal world, so he must learn to accept authority in the same way as anyone else; it is a disservice to give him any special consideration other than that due to his disability. Tempting though it is to lift a physically disabled child down the steps, it is far better that he be allowed to move slowly down himself, thus seeing that he can do it as well as strengthening his muscles. (With some children, such as those who are mentally subnormal, discipline may pose particular problems which we discuss later (p. 102).)

Other children in a playgroup usually treat a handicapped child with a surprising absence of concern, possibly because they are not so self-aware as older children. We have never known disabled children be teased or bullied in a playgroup. They may ask, 'If he is four, why can't he walk properly?' The answer must be honest, simple and safeguard the feelings of the handicapped child. If the child has spina bifida, for example, say 'His legs haven't grown strong like yours'; if he is mentally handicapped the reply could be, 'He is a big boy outside but inside he is still like a baby and we must look after him.' One problem is that the older children sometimes treat a handicapped child as a kind of pet; older girls particularly are delighted to have a sort of 'living doll' to fuss over. This of course will not help the disabled child to be independent; on the other hand it is valuable for the other children to learn the right way to look after someone less able than themselves. The adults involved gain too.

The general rules in choosing equipment for the handicapped child are much the same as for a normal child: their play needs are the same although they may be at a less advanced stage than their chronological age would suggest. They may play for long periods with basic materials – sand, water and clay. Many handicaps involve a loss of physical dexterity, so that trays with raised edges to stop bits of equipment falling out of reach are a helpful device. Strong equipment in bright colours will best attract a handicapped child's interest. A firm which specializes in making toys for handicapped children and gives a two-year guarantee with its products is Toy and Furniture Workshop, address on p. 343.

What of the playgroup's relationship with parents of a handicapped child? Looked at from one viewpoint, of course, all children are a burden to their parents. They are a financial drain on the family purse, they create extra work and until they are old enough to attend a playgroup or school, they restrict a mother like a ball-and-chain. However, most parents can cope with the heavy demands of their young knowing that eventually they will grow up and become independent; the roles may even be reversed eventually, with the child caring for the parent. The parents of a handicapped child, on the other hand, know that for them the future holds little respite; they must continue to care for their child well beyond the normal period. Unless they live in an area which provides day care, they have the agonizing choice of looking after their child twenty-four hours a day or having him 'taken away', admitted to an institution. We believe that the community, of which a playgroup is part, should try to help shoulder some of the burden which the family of a handicapped child has to bear.

One of the biggest advantages that a playgroup has to offer is that, once the child is settled, the mother is given a few hours freedom to live her own life at her own pace rather than slowed down to that of the child. Parents with this problem can become very isolated. Many people fear the handicapped and will not offer to babysit or entertain the family. The parents, especially the mother, can become wearied with the day-and-night care that must be given; they feel different from other people, perhaps guilty because they have a disabled child, even believing that this is a retribution for some past wrong-doing. Immersed in answering the demands of the handicapped child, they may neglect their normal children. Often the strain can put the marriage at risk.

To have a child go to playgroup is so blessedly normal. One mother told us that when a neighbour asked her what had happened to her mongol daughter, she felt tremendously proud to reply, as a mother of any child might have done, 'She's gone to playgroup'. Playgroups can also prevent parents from becoming over-protective and 'fixed' in their attitudes towards their child. They may not have noticed, for example, that he is actually making progress, however slow, and seeing his achievements at playgroup can help them to put the child's disability in a better perspective and encourage them to expect more from him. Often, too, parents feel discouraged by the lack of help offered to them or bewildered by the overlapping of the appropriate services. The playgroup can be a valuable source of information and help on their rights, in particular the attendance allowance for children. (See Leaflet N1 182 obtainable from the Department of Health and Social Security.) *The Consumer's Guide to the British Social Services*, Willmott (Pelican) is also a useful guide.

Physically handicapped children

often suffer from a disability which prevents them from controlling their limbs. If you take any such child, his medical background should be known and contact maintained with anyone who is still treating him. He may have special equipment to support his disabled limbs or help him move about. The best way to become familiar with any problems involving his care is to visit the child in his own home to see how his mother manages.

If a child is completely immobile, it must be one person's special responsibility to hold his interest and to ensure that if some group activity is taking place, he is in a position to take part. A child who cannot walk can sometimes pedal a trike.

A physically handicapped child may be mentally handicapped as well, or he may give the appearance of being so, because of his lack of muscle control. He may have learning problems – this is often true of spastic children – in that he is easily distracted by sounds and movements and finds it difficult to focus his attention on any one task. His concentration can be helped by an adult joining in with his activity and, if he is confined to a wheel-chair, placing him for short periods so that he is screened off from the main body of the playroom, perhaps by the adult's own body as she talks and plays with him.

It is amazing how severely disabled children can be helped by attending a playgroup. Philip, for instance, was knocked down by a motor cycle and left paralysed, blind and deaf. Once he had learnt to trust her, the supervisor used to call for him each morning and push him to the playgroup in his bath-chair. His mother, who had been up three or four times during the night, could then get some sleep; at first this was the main reason for Philip's attendance. But the helpers played finger games with him and gradually his hearing and sight began to return on one side. Other activities were tried with him and before he left the playgroup he had abandoned his wheel-chair and, although very unsteady, had learned to walk. Philip might certainly have made the same progress at home. But the supervisor is sure that the movement and life of the playgroup was a great stimulant to him and no one can doubt the benefit to Philip's mother.

Further information

Invalid Children's Aid Association, 126 Buckingham Palace Road, London SW1

National Association for Spina Bifida and Hydrocephalus, The Don and Dearn, 43 Cutts Avenue, Rotherham, Yorks

Spastics Society, 12 Park Crescent, London W1

Mentally handicapped children

may be suffering from a genetic disorder, such as mongolism, or have sustained brain damage at birth or later. This can result in diminished responses, disordered behaviour or almost complete helplessness. Research has shown, however, that a favourable environment will help a mentally handicapped child to increase his measurable intelligence, while an unfavourable one will cause it to decrease. Because his responses are limited, it is understandable if his parents sometimes stop giving appropriate stimulation at the right time, especially in language: it is unrewarding to talk and sing to someone who seems to take little notice of you. A busy mother, her mind preoccupied with caring for all members of her household, may also find it simpler and quicker to do things for her mentally handicapped child which, given time and support, he could do for himself. Many mentally handicapped children have poor speech. (See following section on speech difficulties, p. 103.)

Being part of a playgroup will give a child a good deal of incidental language experience – he will hear more conversation than in his own home, be encouraged to listen to finger plays and rhymes, as well as having one adult with time to spend in speaking slowly and clearly to him, perhaps while looking at a simple picture book. An extra helper is particularly necessary if a mentally handicapped child is accepted; it is then easier for the playgroup staff to train themselves to be patient and allow the child time to solve problems for himself. He will be stimulated by watching other children at work and may want to copy them; he will benefit, too, from being offered a wider range of equipment than he could be given at home. Care must be taken not to confuse mentally handicapped children by giving them too many stimuli at once; give them one definite thing to do, otherwise they may drift about aimlessly, lacking the ability to choose for themselves. Your expectations of them must be realistic – give them something to do at which they are likely to succeed and don't expect too long a span of concentration.

Equipment which is aimed at stretching the normal child must be adapted to the needs of mentally handicapped children. For example, let them attempt a jig-saw with only two pieces not in place, rather than the whole puzzle at once. Devise ways of helping them to handle everyday equipment: cutting with scissors for instance is a difficult task, but gripping is made much easier if string is bound round the handles. As a general principle, let such children learn to cope with big pieces of equipment before introducing them to smaller things. Every success should be praised, with even more warmth than for a normal child.

As with all children, there are great variations in the personalities of mentally handicapped children. Some will be affectionate and easy to manage, others may be aggressive and difficult to control. No matter how handicapped a child is, care must be taken to ensure that his behaviour does not disrupt the group as a whole. He must be corrected in a firm tone of voice, and if he persists in wrongdoing, removed to another part of the room (see Disruptive children, page 182), if necessary picking him up and holding him firmly. If you and your helpers always use the same sort of discipline, he will learn what sort of behaviour is tolerated and what is not. Make sure that his level of functioning is not affected by any other factors such as poor sight or fits. The Health Visitor should be asked to call and observe the child; she will know if any further action is necessary.

We ourselves observed two severely handicapped children in different playgroups. Charlotte, nearly five, sat in a chair near the piano sucking her thumb and rocking to and fro almost all morning. Withdrawn from the life of the group, she was largely ignored by staff and children alike. When the others were having their milk and the equipment was deserted, she would venture out to play with the sand, letting it trickle through her fingers as a much younger child would do. When the other children returned to play she went back to her chair.

Tony, aged three, sat docilely in a chair in the second group, gazing aimlessly around the room. A helper led him to the dough table, sitting him next to another boy, Richard. She talked to Tony, quietly and slowly, about the way Richard was rolling and stretching the dough. Tony looked at Richard's hands but despite the helper's invitation would not touch the dough. She put a lump in his hand but still no response. So she began to press his fingers into it. Slowly Tony smiled and he began to knead the dough. He stayed at this activity, concentrating on it for several minutes.

Tony gained from his playgroup experience through being actively helped by an adult. Charlotte would have benefited more if a helper had tried to build up a relationship with her by talking to her and perhaps by bringing her sand or other materials in a small bowl. It is not enough merely to accept mentally handicapped children in a playgroup; no matter how limited their ability is, as with all children, ways must be sought of encouraging them to learn.

Children with speech difficulties

may have been born with an organic disorder, such as a cleft lip and palate, mental subnormality or deafness; or they may be suffering from the effects of emotional deprivation (children living in institutions often have retarded language development) or shock, such as being suddenly removed from the mother because she was sent to hospital. A child may be jealous of a new baby in the family and revert to baby talk as an attention-seeking device; or his parents may be hindering his normal development by being over-protective, perhaps by doing any necessary talking for him.

Whatever the reason, a playgroup can do a great deal to help a child overcome speech difficulties. Much of the equipment provided is identical to that used in speech therapy: dry and wet sand, dolls, books and jigsaws. The non-talking child should be particularly encouraged to play with water, which will help him relax – not even the most fluent of us can talk freely if we feel strained. He should play games which will strengthen the muscles used in talking, imitating everyday sounds – engines revving, clocks ticking – or games involving blowing. He should hear clear speech and plenty of it, and find enough of interest in the playgroup to tempt him to comment and ask questions.

One of the most important factors in helping a child to talk is that he should have a good relationship with an adult. We all know that speech does not come easily if one is ill at ease with a stranger. It is not unusual for children between the age of three and four to stumble over their words. A child mispronouncing a word should not be stopped, as this prevents fluency. A better tactic is to repeat the mispronounced word correctly in one's answer. For instance, if he says 'I had two goes on a woundabout,' say, 'Did you go fast on the roundabout?' A child with a severe stutter or stammer should be helped to relax; patience is needed to listen to his efforts to talk without supplying the words. If you have a child from a bi-lingual home who is having speech difficulties, suggest to his parents that only one language is used until he becomes fluent in that. If this is impossible, say that it is wisest if one adult always uses one language and not a mixture. The College of Speech Therapists, 47 St John's High Street, London NW8 produces some helpful pamphlets which you can have available for parents – for example, 'Is your child a stammerer?', 'Are you worried about your children's speech?', 'Teaching your child to talk'.

Children with epilepsy or fits

Epilepsy is a frightening label but many epileptic children can easily fit into a playgroup, largely because their condition is controlled by drugs. If you are asked to accept an epileptic child, find out about his treatment and how often he should be dosed. If he does have an attack at playgroup, there is nothing you can do to stop it. Simply clear the area around him so that he cannot damage himself. With index finger or a handkerchief, remove any vomit. Place the head with the chin jutting forward, so that the tongue will not block the air passages. If it is necessary to restrain the child's movements, on no account do this by force. The other children and some helpers may be frightened, so keep calm and talk in a soothing voice. Attacks usually pass quite soon and what happens then depends largely on the child's reaction. He may get up and go on with some normal activity, and should be allowed to do so if this is his choice. A watchful eye should be kept on him in case one attack triggers off another. On the other hand, if he seems exhausted and wants only to be cuddled, it may be better to send for his mother to take him home and put him to bed.

Further information

The British Epilepsy Association, 3 Alfred Place, London WC1.

Deaf children

Deaf children obviously suffer chiefly from difficulties in communication. During the settling-in period, the mother of a deaf or partially hearing child must be asked how much he can hear; does he make his needs known by words or signs? how in particular does he usually ask to go to the lavatory, or say that he is thirsty?

Children with hearing difficulties often speak badly also and need special patience and understanding from adults over this as well as possibly the trained guidance of a speech therapist. Because of their difficulty in communicating they may appear to be less stable than the hearing child of the same age and be quick to laugh or cry and more liable to have temper tantrums.

It doesn't necessarily help to shout to a deaf child. Speech should be slow with clear lip movements and simple sentences: 'Do you want your milk now?' or 'Find your coat, please.' Always make certain you are facing him. A deaf child deeply involved in play should not be touched to attract his attention. Unless an expert advises otherwise, use speech and not signs.

Deaf children's play needs are the same as a hearing child's, but they also require extra stimulation, missing so much learning because of their disability. They enjoy plenty of music – they love percussion instruments. Above all see that one concerned adult is responsible for trying to look after them.

It helps to find out as much as possible from people with specialist knowledge. There may be a teacher working for the local Education Department who travels around to the homes of deaf children and who should, if possible, be contacted. Some areas have special nursery classes for deaf children, which you can visit.

Further information

The National Deaf Children's Society, 31 Gloucester Place, London, W1H 4EA, is a helpful body to contact. The annual subscription is only 25p and this includes a quarterly magazine which you could pass on to parents.

Blind and partially sighted children

suffer mainly from difficulties in building up relationships with groups of people. Perhaps because it is easy to simulate their condition, merely by closing our eyes and attempting to walk across the room, it is easy to feel sympathy for them and to want to help them.

Again, it is advisable to have an extra helper who could be mainly responsible for caring for a blind child. As this handicap cuts a child off from the many sources of learning which depend on looking and imitating, he must develop his other senses to compensate, especially hearing; thus he will benefit from having an adult prepared to spend time with him, interpreting his surroundings through talking. Let him handle something, say some bricks, and then describe them. Help him to build with them, using words like 'more' and 'higher', then, when they topple, 'all fall down', to help him come to terms with ideas of quantity and heights. Give him an abundance of stories and songs and a chance to play musical instruments with very distinctive sounds.

To the child who cannot see, movement is a hazard, yet he must be encouraged to be active. Other children must be warned about the dangers this disability brings in its wake and their cooperation sought. A blind child should be introduced to any new activity, such as the climbing frame, with a watchful adult nearby. Extra praise for his efforts will be appreciated, since he cannot see the approval in the faces of those round him, only hear it in their voices. With this disability, perhaps more than any other, care must be taken not to be over-protective. A blind child has to learn to live in a seeing world.

Further information

A blind child will probably be on a Register of the Blind, and may be visited by a specially trained teacher, who should prove a valuable source of information. Also contact the Royal National Institute for the Blind, 224/6/8 Great Portland Street, London W1, for helpful leaflets and to ask whether there is any local organization.

Asthmatic children

are sometimes subject to an allergy to some substance or animal; but sometimes an attack seems to be triggered off by anxiety or emotional upset. Most researchers seem to feel that the mother-child relationship is an important factor. Certainly there is a good deal of evidence which shows that the asthmatic child is unlikely to have an attack when he is away from his own home. It seems sensible, therefore, to encourage the mother of a child with this disorder to send him to playgroup, even if he has had a mild attack in the night. (Obviously, if the attack is very severe he will not be able to come.) Sometimes a mother with an asthmatic child may be over-protective and feel that he should be kept indoors at the first sign of wheezing. However, we have sometimes noticed that once a child is at playgroup and happily occupied, his breathing becomes normal and he is discouraged from regarding himself as ill.

Everything possible should be done to improve the asthmatic child's physical health, encouraging him especially to run, jump and tackle anything that stimulates deep breathing. He should be coaxed into playing games which involve blowing bubbles or ping-pong balls. Above all efforts should be made not to treat him as an invalid. Nursing a child with an asthmatic attack can cause great anxiety in a mother; she will probably welcome the opportunity to talk over her worries with the supervisor, or, if more expert help is needed, the Health Visitor.

Autistic children

are unable to communicate with other people and thus cannot make any relationships. They live in an isolated state, either without speech or talking in a mechanical way without normal expression. Cut off from the people around them they create their own lonely world, sometimes developing strange rituals, such as running between two set points, or spinning round in a bizarre manner. They may become obsessed with one toy, and play with it continuously.

Autism is not a common condition and very little is known about its causes and treatment. The parents of such children face great problems. They may look perfectly ordinary, yet seem unable to respond to normal life. They are difficult to control, because speech and facial expressions are meaningless to them. Looking after a child with this disability is a great strain, which some playgroups are able to share – we know of two such children who were greatly helped by attending. If asked to accept a child with this condition, be certain to take advice from the doctor who is treating him.

Further information

The National Society for Autistic Children, 1a Golders Green Road, London NW11.

Part 3
Starting and Running a Playgroup

7
Starting the Playgroup

Personality and role of the supervisor

If you feel you'd like to start a playgroup, you are probably a married woman with small children of your own – most of the women working in the playgroup movement are. Before you set out on this rewarding but difficult enterprise, it is worthwhile first of all to consider your own motives and personal qualities – as well as the problems that organizing a playgroup may raise in your own life.

Do you hope running a playgroup will provide companionship for your own child? Do you regard it as a community service, perhaps part of your membership of a church? Did you want to be a teacher and see this as a way of achieving your ambition without the chore of training? Perhaps you think of running a playgroup as a business venture, a way of bringing an income into your house which fits in well with your family commitments.

Are you warm and outgoing? Are you capable of communicating both with a boisterous three-year-old and the dignified headmaster of the local school? Are you sensitive to the needs of others, mature enough to know your own weaknesses and to see another person's point of view, but strong enough to hold firm to your own beliefs against opposition? You will need to be resilient, able to accept the difficulties which inevitably crop up with good humour. Physically you must be strong, for you will be exposed to a wide variety of infections as well as having to unpack and pack away bulky pieces of equipment every day. And you will have to be mentally fit, to meet the emotional demands of the children, their parents and your helpers as well as those of your own family.

There is a good deal of job satisfaction to be found in this work: visiting a head teacher in a school, or phoning a Health Visitor to discuss a child's problems has a certain drama which is lacking in the humdrum business of running a home. It can give you a feeling of importance which being a wife and mother does not. But it is easy to over-extend yourself and neglect your family, sacrificing their wellbeing to that of the playgroup. Discussing this dual role with a group of supervisors, one told us that after a hard week in the playgroup, praising the children's paintings and junk models, she could only smile weakly when her own five-year-old bounced in from school with his work. Another supervisor remembered sadly how long it was since she had cooked her husband his favourite Cornish pasty!

You can lead this double life only if you are careful not to get overtired. Use any money you earn to buy labour-saving machines or to pay for help in the home. Can you plan a week's menu in advance and do a once-a-week gigantic shop instead of a daily dash to the shops on your way back from playgroup? If you are confident that the domestic wheels are turning smoothly at home, you will be able to be single-minded about your playgroup when you are there. Above all take heed if you find your family complaining that you seem to be spending too much time on playgroup affairs.

What do you do if one of your family is ill? If one of your school-age children is below par, you may think it right to leave him with a neighbour, but with a pre-school child or an older child who is really ill, you must be prepared to stay at home. This means that you should have at least one reliable helper who is able to step into your playgroup shoes. This is one reason why it is often a good idea to run a playgroup on a partnership basis with a friend.

If you work in a playgroup with your own child in it, you may be amazed to find that he reacts unexpectedly to the situation by becoming demanding and clinging to you. You may feel ashamed of this babyish behaviour, feeling it reflects badly on the quality of your mothering, especially as, being a supervisor, you are making some claim to knowing how to handle children. Your child may react jealously when he sees you giving your attention to other children, feeling that his bond with you is threatened. The more you tell him to 'go away and play', or that 'Mummy is busy now', the more rejected and insecure he feels. The best way of helping a child to share his mother with other children is to safeguard his privileged relationship with you. Let him be your chief helper, reassure him by your smile and tone of voice that there is a special bond between you. As of right, he should sit on your knee if he needs this and you will find that the other children will accept this as just and proper. If he is having particular difficulties, give him extra attention at home; sit down with a book or watch television together, anything which creates an intimate relationship between you and him.

A child in a home-based playgroup also has to accept that his home and garden, as well as his mother, must be shared with other children and this can be difficult. Never use your own child's toys for your playgroup unless he wants you to. Be especially careful to put away any soft toys which have a particular personal meaning to him. Unless you respect his property, how can you expect him to respect other people's? At the same time, although your child must be reassured about his relationship with you, you must be careful to see that he obeys all the rules of the playgroup, especially when they are enforced by other helpers. This can be a cause of tension – it is easy to resent hearing your child disciplined by someone else.

Some supervisors send their own child to another playgroup to avoid these difficulties. This may be a solution if you are sure that the alternative playgroup offers the same high standards as yours, and if you can stay to settle him in. If you are holding the playgroup in your own home, you should be very careful not to seem to suggest to the child that you are excluding him from where he may feel he rightly belongs, namely at home with you. The best attitude is to consider your child's particular situation. If he is an only child and you run your group at home on your own, he will miss the opportunity to make relationships with other adults and the move to school may be difficult. In these circumstances, it might be wise to send him to a good hall-based playgroup for two or three mornings a week during the term before he starts school, remaining part of your group for the rest of the week. He may enjoy the experience of being part of a larger group and benefit from meeting children who will accompany him on to the next stage of going to school. On the other hand you may find that he is confused by belonging to two groups, in which case he would be better to remain with you.

You may be feeling uncertain about whether to have the playgroup in your own home or outside it, as well as about the advisability of running it on your own or with others. This of course depends largely on your personality and your social contacts, as much as on the size and suitability of your house. On the whole hall-based groups tend to be run by a committee and home-based groups are under the control of one 'owner-driver'. We feel that the former is the better way to run a playgroup, dependent as it is on the goodwill of parents and the local community, although well-run home-based groups have much to offer shy children who may respond better to the atmosphere of a small group in familiar surroundings. 'Your house smells just like mine,' said one new entrant to a home-based group and relaxed visibly.

Some of the most successful groups of both kinds are run by two or three partners and it is not hard to see why they run smoothly. Because it is their own organization, each partner puts a good deal of time and energy into the setting-up and running of such a group. Before entering such a partnership, you should know the other people involved fairly well and appreciate how your different talents can be drawn together to form a strong team. On the other hand 'owner-driver' groups provide very stable organization : roles are established, decisions are made very largely by the supervisor and because the project is her baby she will work hard for its success. However, there are obvious dangers in such a group. Too much authority may be vested in the supervisor; if she moves, or is ill, the playgroup may fall flat on its face. She may also run the group not so much for the good of the community as for the good of her own pocket! We know of one large group of sixty which lacks most of the basic play activities, regiments the children very strictly, yet has a waiting list as long as your arm and must provide a very acceptable income to the owner – if not to her staff.

A common arrangement is to have a paid supervisor and un-paid staff, responsible to a committee; in this situation the supervisor is usually trained and the helpers untrained. This can work very well depending on the personality of the supervisor: she must be careful not to delegate all menial jobs to other workers, but take her fair share of all the work. Unpaid workers must be given rewards other than financial ones: they enjoy the contact with the children and need to be given responsibility for them.

Because you will be dealing with very young children at a most vulnerable stage of their development, you have a duty to equip yourself to the best of your ability. You should allow time to attend a course for playgroup supervisors before you begin to plan your playgroup; if such a course does not exist in your area, then work with the local branch of your Pre-School Playgroup Association to pressurize your local education author-ity into starting one. Attend any meetings and conferences deal-ing with the needs of pre-school children; read magazines and journals which will help you to see what sort of standards you ought to be achieving in your playgroup. Watch suitable TV programmes and listen to broadcasts specially directed at the pre-school child. These are often a source of new ideas and can help you develop special techniques, such as in story-telling, or in the presentation of materials to encourage con-versation. Try to tune in too to programmes that deal with health and education in a general way. If there is no hope of attending a suitable course in your own locality, perhaps be-cause you live too far from any educational centre, you should get in touch with the National Extension College, 32 Trumping-ton Street, Cambridge, CB2 1SQ, which runs a correspondence course for playgroup leaders including some weekends of prac-tical instruction.

The ten steps to opening day

It is easy to be daunted by the difficulties of setting up a playgroup. Here is a simplified outline of the ten basic steps to be followed from writing the first letter to taking the name of the first child.

1. Joining the Pre-School Playgroup Association

The address is at the end of the book, p. 342. This is the vital first step, since the Association provides a wealth of information in booklet form and should also have an area organizer in your locality. She can guide you through the network of legal, financial and other intricacies involved in setting up a playgroup and suggest good playgroups for you to visit. If you live in a district which has a playgroup advisor working for the Department of Social Services or nursery/infant advisor for the Education Department, they should also be contacted for help.

2(a). Finding a suitable place

If you are new to the area, or do not know what its facilities are, ask your Town Clerk's Department or Clerk to the Rural District Council if a list of halls for hire is available. Contact your local Health and Education Department to see if they make youth clubs, clinics, community associations or old school buildings available for playgroups. Can you hire your village hall, or Women's Institute hall? Is there a football pavilion which would be suitable? Some authorities lend such buildings free of charge to non-profit-making groups. Perhaps there is a hall used by your Scout and Guide Association (address from your local Information Centre or from their London Headquarters, 19 and 25 Buckingham Palace Road, London SW1). Sometimes a postman or milkman may know of a suitable hall; a walk around your area may lead to the discovery of a hall belonging to some little-known organization such as the Allotment Association or a masonic order. In some places such as

Liverpool and parts of London where there is no suitable accommodation at all, people have converted double-decker buses into mobile playgroup premises. This, however, is an expensive business; it might be wiser to press your local authority to renovate an old house.

When you find your hall, look at it with a critical eye. Is there sufficient storage space for bulky equipment? Are the heating arrangements safe and adequate? Will they satisfy the statutory requirements of a temperature of 58°F minimum? Are the lavatory facilities adequate? Can the kitchen be used? Is the flooring suitable for playgroup activities, especially sand and water? Is there outside playspace? Will the caretaker be helpful? If any of these requirements are lacking, is the landlord likely to be cooperative? For instance, would he allow you to bring in lock-up cupboards? Could you clear and fence an area for outside play?

If there is a shortage of halls in your area, well, beggars cannot be choosers and you may have to take what is offered. However, playgroup workers can be too humble in pressing their demands. They are often the only tenants available for a daytime letting and if an adequate rent is being paid, a fair service should be offered in return. An average rent is £1 per morning if the hall belongs to a church or charitable organization; it may be as high as £3 if the hall is privately owned. The amount of rent will largely dictate how high your fees are, so be careful not to take on too high an overhead.

Once you decide to take the hall, have a written agreement with the landlord, making quite clear whether your rent includes lighting, heating and cleaning and the use of any outside space. The Pre-School Playgroup Association print a suitable agreement which we suggest you use.

2(b). Using your own home

First, be absolutely sure that your husband and family approve! Next, try to visit other home-based groups to pick their brains. Can you have built-in cupboards standing two feet high and deep enough to form a working surface and safe space on tables? Will your floor covering be suitable for sand and water play? Is your heating safe for children? If you are planning to build an extra room, will this mean extra rates? What about the garden? Merely making your home safe for playgroup purposes may be quite expensive – for instance, safer fencing, fire guards and a fire extinguisher cost a lot – and these expenses must be taken into consideration when calculating how much money you need to start.

How much of your home do you plan to use? Initially, you may feel safer remaining in one playroom; however, apart from general wear and tear, the fabric of a house is very little damaged by a well-run playgroup and the more varied the play areas you can offer the better, as long as they can all be supervised adequately. Can you make your hall, usually the first glimpse to mother and child of your playgroup, gay and welcoming? Can you display books and magazines on child care for parents to borrow there? The kitchen usually has easy-to-clean working surfaces and floor for messier activities, but you must ensure that it is safe. Is your cooker child-proof? Can you disconnect all electrical appliances not in safe use? We were dismayed to visit one group and find the children rolling pastry dangerously near an electric kettle boiling for the helpers' coffee.

3. Getting planning permission

Inquiries should be made at the Department of Town and Country Planning (address from your Town or County Hall). Many, though not all, halls have overall permission for a variety of community activities which covers playgroups. For a home-based group you *must* have planning permission. Be warned: the form for this is complicated; you may need the help of Planning Department officials. You may be asked to submit a street plan of your immediate area. If you have a mortgage make sure you are not contravening any of its conditions. (If you are registered as a charity, by the way, you are *not* running a business – see p. 123.)

Your neighbours have the right to object to your plans and if this happens you may have a legal battle on your hands. (A case at Gosport in 1970, where neighbours objected to a play-group in a private house, was successfully fought by the local Playgroup Association and the playgroup did open.) We think it best to approach neighbours individually, explaining the needs of the young children in your area. Try and arrange for inter-ested or antagonistic neighbours to visit a well-run home group; they may be pleasantly surprised by what they see.

4. Applying for registration

Under the Nursery and Child Minders Act (1948) and amend-ments contained in the Health Services and Public Health Act (1968), every playgroup must be registered with the local authority if it is to open more than two hours per day. This represents, in effect, official permission to operate a playgroup and is a legal obligation with which everyone must comply.

Having chosen your accommodation, either hall- or home-based, you should write to the Department of Social Services at your Town Hall, whereupon an official from that department will come to inspect your accommodation. He will want to check toilet facilities, the size of your space and the number of helpers; on these factors the number of children you are allowed will be decided. There is some variation up and down the country, but most authorities accept one lavatory to ten chil-dren, twenty-five square feet per child and one adult to eight children. The maximum number of children to one room recommended by the Ministry of Health is twenty-five.

The Fire Officer must also inspect your premises to check fire precautions; if an appointment with him is not made by the official from the Department of Social Services, contact him direct (address is in the telephone directory). He will want to see that your building has at least two exits which are freely acces-sible at all times. Any locks must be kept oiled and the keys hung where they are clearly visible, yet well out of a child's reach. A metal hook and eye is a simple locking device which fire officers prefer, as in an emergency the hook can be quickly knocked out of the eye and the door opened. Unless your heaters are safe for use with young children you will be asked to supply a fireguard conforming to British Standard Specification. You will be asked to instal a fire extinguisher and the Fire Officer will advise you on the size and type. This equipment can be bought outright – one of an average-size house costs £6–£7.

The number of children you will be allowed depends on whether only one room is considered as a suitable play area, or whether corridors, entrance hall, etc. are also taken into account. Outdoor play space is not included in these calculations. The Ministry gives local authorities guidelines which have been left flexible enough to take into account the layout of the premises, safety factors such as stairs, the proximity of lavatories and the training and personality of the supervisor. If you regularly use, say, a corridor adjoining your church hall, or the whole of the ground floor in a home group, then you have a good case for being allowed to take a greater number of children. However, we would strongly advise against too large a playgroup. If you have a very large public hall this advice may seem nonsensical, but it does protect the timid child and prevent playgroups becoming like battery baby farms!

As we said earlier, staffing ratios vary over the country, but are usually between eight and ten children to one adult, with a minimum of two adults in a playgroup at any one time. A single adult in a home playgroup will usually be allowed to take around five children, depending on the lay-out of the area to be used and the other factors already mentioned in connection with numbers of permitted children. There must be a second adult on call nearby, a neighbour or playgroup mother perhaps, in case of emergency.

5. Setting up your committee

As we have said, it is possible to run a playgroup as a 'one-man band', although anyone doing so runs the risks of isolation and exhaustion. Indeed to serve the best interests of the local community, it is advisable to set up a committee consisting of persons representing various sections of that community. Firstly, the head teacher from your local primary school is a must. Then,

he Health Visitor who serves the families most likely to use
our playgroup is essential. At least one parent, if possible one
vho has lived in the district for some time, plus yourself as
he person concerned with the day-to-day running of the playgroup, should form a good balance. If the accommodation you
re using already has a hall management committee, a repre-
entative from this should be on your committee. Since the
irst two at least are unlikely to have the spare time to help in
organizing and running the group, you will then also need other
people to share the work load. The committee should have an
ctive chairman, a competent secretary (to keep a brief account
of meetings and send out notices), and a treasurer experienced
n handling finances.

The Pre-School Playgroup Association's booklet 'The Business
iide of Playgroups' explains the legal status of playgroups,
describes in detail how to manage finances, gives a model con-
titution for the committee and says how to keep minutes of
meetings. All this may sound formidable and even unnecessary
n the initial stages. However, you are starting an organization
vhich you hope will continue for some years, so it is as well
o put it on a sound footing.

This valuable booklet also explains the benefits of registering
our group as a charity (not to be confused with registration
vith a local authority, discussed earlier). The advantages are
hat any income remaining after paying wages and other neces-
ary expenses is not liable for income tax and must be spent
o further the aims of the charity. In addition, you may as a
charity be eligible for help from other charities, say from a trust
und which exists to help 'needy children of the parish' – a
clause wide open to interpretation! If the accommodation it
ises pays rates, a charity can also claim a fifty per cent reduc-
ion. If your group works under the auspices of a church or any
other charitable body, you do not need to apply for separate
charitable status.

6. Raising funds and getting publicity

You will need to raise money before you start and, because the
supervisor will be coping with many other jobs, we think that
this chore should be someone else's responsibility. If you do not
already have a ready-made organization behind you, such as a
Young Wives Club or a Community Association, you may need
to gather a band of workers together right from the beginning
to help with publicity and fund-raising. Put up notices telling
of your plans to open in local shops, doctors waiting-rooms and
clinics. Ask if you can display a notice in local primary schools
or have duplicated handouts sent home by children with
younger brothers and sisters. When inquiries start to come in
from parents arrange a public meeting for them to explain the
aims of your playgroup and to ask for people to help. Try to
get your local newspaper to come – or at least to print an
announcement. If you feel apprehensive about arranging a
meeting yourself, invite your head teacher, a church minister or
a PPA area organizer to start the ball rolling. This is where it
helps to have a committee.

The Pre-School Playgroup Association has a very helpful pamphlet on fund-raising activities called 'But where does the money
come from?' A group which is registered as a charity may get a
grant from your local authority – the PPA pamphlet 'Local
authorities and playgroups' gives all the necessary information
– or from voluntary associations such as Toc H or the Rotary
Club. Bring-and-buy sales, coffee mornings, raffles (local shops
will often donate goods in return for free publicity), collecting
free gift stamps, dances, whist drives, bingo evenings – all these
can help. If you have a good contact with your school you may
be allowed to have a stall at their fête, say for 'nearly new'
children's clothes. Fund-raising efforts can involve interested
parents, making them feel it will be their playgroup. Point 8 on
p. 126 tells you how much money you need to start and how
to spend it.

7. Finding your helpers

For the day-to-day running of your playgroup, you will need two kinds of helper: one or two regular paid assistants, depending on the number of children, and mother-helpers, who usually come in for one day a week working on a rota system. A large, hall-based group may draw its helpers from local community organizations such as the Young Wives or from the initial public meeting. A small home-based group may be more informal, drawing in your helpers from among personal friends and neighbours whose children will be attending. You may feel that as you are charging mothers fees, you have no right to involve them in the running of the playgroup. However, by sharing the work load parents help to keep costs down and maintain social contact between neighbours. There will be many jobs for everyone, such as organizing a rota of mother-helpers, being responsible for changing the group's library books, looking after the maintenance of equipment; you can gradually draw in other parents for these jobs as you know them better.

Once you have chosen your regular helpers, go with them to visit two or more well-run playgroups and a nursery school or class if there is one nearby. Take time to discuss what you saw, notice the equipment, the layout of the room and the programme. It is as well to know before you start your own playgroup whether your ideas on running a playgroup are shared with your helpers or partners, and discussing the real situations you have observed will help clarify your attitudes. Do you and your helpers share the same attitudes on such basic principles as discipline, parent involvement and finance? If you differ very strongly on these fundamental issues, it would be easier to look for other helpers at this stage rather than when the group is already running. Try to choose helpers with warm, outgoing personalities who seem to be sympathetic to the needs of both children and parents. Do your best to ensure that all the people you hope to involve can work as a team. (See p. 142 ff. for extended discussion of working with helpers.)

8. Equipping the playgroup

It is possible to equip a playgroup for as little as £20, if you can rely on help from parents to improvise equipment. Look at the chapter on play, page 244, and read *Play With a Purpose for Under-Sevens* by Elizabeth Matterson (Penguin, 35p). Write to local factories and workshops, asking for any waste material – offcuts of wood, carpet samples, industrial cotton reels, and anything which can be used to provide good play experience.

It will, however, make your first term much easier if you can provide a broad range of activities and this is why we feel that £80 is a sensible sum to raise before starting a playgroup. The list on p. 127–8 shows how this should be spent; we have included only one expensive item, the climbing frame, because this is a difficult thing to improvise safely. (Note that all prices are approximate and will probably increase.)

Be sure to take out an *insurance policy* to cover yourself in case of accidents to children and staff and for theft or damage to your equipment. If a playgroup is run by a church, this will usually be covered by the general church insurance but make enquiries to safeguard yourself. If the church is merely your landlord, you should take out a separate insurance. This can be done through the Pre-School Playgroup Association at a very reasonable rate. You should also get in touch with the local Department of Social Security and your local tax officer for up-to-date information on questions of national insurance and income-tax contributions for playgroup personnel.

You will have to buy in small quantities to start with as funds will be short; but once your group is on a sound financial footing, it is much more economical to buy in bulk. Write away for at least three different equipment catalogues (addresses p. 343) in order to compare prices; ask firms if discount is allowed to members of the Pre-School Playgroup Association. Remember that as a general rule the sturdiest goods are the best buy. We have not suggested spending a large sum on books, as we anticipate that you will borrow from your library, either on a special playgroup ticket, or, if this right has not yet been negotiated with your Chief Librarian, then using one or two of your own or helpers' tickets.

Lastly, you will probably be given some toys but most will not be suitable for playgroup purposes. Accept everything with thanks, but only use equipment of a high standard; what you do with the rest depends on your relationship with the donor – you could use it for a raffle, or if it is too shabby, put it in your next jumble sale. You can be frank and say that what you have been given is not suitable for use in the playgroup so would you be allowed to sell it for playgroup funds.

How to spend your first £80

The prices given here are obviously approximate and likely to increase. We give them as a general indication of the sort of money you will need to spend in different areas.

General Expenses	£ p
Membership of the PPA	3·50
Insurance (see p. 126)	5·00
Sundries (cash book and register, postage, felt-tip pens, washing-up bowl, bucket, paper handkerchiefs)	2·00
First-aid kit (see p. 200)	1·50
	11·50

Basic Play Equipment	
Climbing frame	28·00
3 second-hand baby baths and stands (for water and sand)	2·20
½ cwt washed sand	·95
Clay	·64
	31·79

Domestic Play

1 small saucepan plus lid	1·30
1 frying pan	·70
1 kettle	1·60
Picnic set (cup, saucers and plates: 4 of each)	2·00
Dust-pan and brush	·80
Second-hand doll's pram plus non-toxic paint for refurbishing	5·00
	11·40

(All these should not be toys but should be bought from a hardware store, except the pram.)

Painting, Junk and Collage Work

Wood for 2 double-sided easels*	3·00
6 paint brushes (size 10)	·60
3 tins powder paint (red, blue, yellow)	3·80
2 rolls lining paper (from wallpaper shop)	·40
2 boxes fine art crayons	·50
Marvin glue	·36
6 glue brushes	·60
6 pairs round-ended scissors	·54
	11·70

Constructional Toys

1 large set of Lego	5·93
1 large set of wooden bricks	6·27
Pegboard 11″ × 11″ plus 100 pegs	1·12
	13·32
Total expenditure	£79·71

9. Fixing the fees

These should be discussed with the committee, though how you collect them and how much you charge will depend largely

* See *Play With a Purpose for Under-Sevens*, E. Matterson, Pelican, p. 116.

on the area your playgroup serves. Whether you charge on a daily, weekly, monthly or termly basis, we suggest you take fees in advance. This enables you to cover overheads if children are absent. In a low-income area, you may need to charge daily as some families will find it difficult to pay lump sums in advance.

To calculate your fees, add together all expenses – rent, wages, insurance, a fund for large equipment, a realistic sum (say 20p) for the daily needs of the group such as postage, first-aid-kit replacements, sellotape and so on. Divide this sum by the number of children you expect to have. If the answer gives a fee which is too high for the income level of the area, then you will have to hold a number of fund-raising activities each term.

Some groups ask for a £1 registration fee, to be refunded if the child leaves. This protects the group's income if a child goes without warning leaving an outstanding debt. Other groups charge a smaller registration fee, say 25p, which goes into a fund for large equipment. Some groups charge a half-fee for absent children or a token 5p if the child is away for a prolonged illness. Many groups allow the children of mother-helpers to come for a nominal fee, say 2½p – for if the child comes free, then the mother is considered to be working for 'reward', and the playgroup has to pay an Employees Liability Stamp. Others allow free places for needy children, perhaps on the recommendation of Health Visitors. Be warned, though, that allowing free places can cause contention among others. One group we know gives out small envelopes in which fees are handed in each week, so that only the person collecting them knows which envelope contains 2p and which 50p. Local authorities have the power to pay for children in need of playgroup experience: you should lobby your local councillors to press for such funds to be made available. The Acts which enable local authorities to do this are listed in the Appendix, p. 345. Handicapped children may have their fees paid by a voluntary organization, such as the Spina Bifida Association or National Association for Mental Health. We think it best that one of the regular helpers be respon-

sible for collecting fees. The supervisor is trying to build up her
relationship with the mothers and this can be hampered if she
has to press them for money. It is often worthwhile displaying
your accounts – parents may be surprised to see how much it
costs to run a good playgroup and may be more willing to help
with fund-raising. Here are the accounts of one church-spon-
sored group's finances, set out for an average day. This group
is registered for twenty-five children but has two free places.

Costs for an average day: hall-based group

Expenditure		Income	
rent	1·25	full fees: 20p × 20	4·00
supervisor's salary	1·00	absentees fees:	
2 helpers	1·50	10p × 3	30
equipment fund	·40		
apples	·15		
sundries	·15		
caretaker	·15		
insurance	·05		
	£4·65		£4·30

This group serves a large council estate and does not feel it can
raise its fees higher. This means that they might have a daily
deficit of 35p. Each term, therefore, they have to raise an additional £22·75 to make ends meet.

For comparison, here are the accounts of a typical home-
based group. Note that an allowance is made for rent: many
home-based groups do not do this, but it is more realistic to do
so. This group spent £2,000 on a playroom extension, so to
recoup some of this it allots £1 per morning rent. There are sixteen children in the group, which serves a middle-class residential area.

Costs for an average day: home-based group

Expenditure		*Income*	
rent	1·00	full fees: 14 × 30p × 20	4·20
2 co-supervisors	2·00	absentees fees:	
1 helper	·75	2 × 15p	·30
pianist	·15		
equipment fund	·35		
apples	·10		
sundries	·10		
insurance	·03		
	£4·48		£4·50

10. Opening day

Once you receive your official registration you are ready to open. Since it usually takes about two months from initial application, you will have had ample time to prepare for your first morning. Before starting the playgroup proper, make the first day a coffee morning when mothers and children can come in for an hour or so to get the feel of the place. This way neither children nor helpers need feel strained. It is best to start a hall-based group with a small group, say ten or twelve children, and build up the numbers slowly with as many helpers as possible.

This gentle start will give you time to take each child's particulars (see Settling in a new child, page 167). When doing this be sure to safeguard everyone's privacy by having the mother and helper sit away from the main part of the hall, so that they can talk without being overheard. Make it clear at this preliminary session that, when the playgroup opens, you will insist on all mothers staying with their children until they are settled in.

During all the weeks of preparation, you and your helpers should have learned each other's strengths and weaknesses and decided which task each will undertake. You will have discussed how your playgroup equipment is to be arranged: you will probably not have a great deal, so put most of it out for the children to look at. One group we know left some of their table toys wrapped, so the children had a 'Christmas Day' feeling as they helped to unwrap them.

Getting to know the children

It is essential to know each child and its parents as individuals and to be aware of their home background. Some supervisors find it useful to visit a home when the child's name is nearing the top of the waiting list; this is often a good way to make friends with the mother. Be very careful to avoid any hint of being a 'nosey parker.' You may not be invited over the door-step; on the other hand you may be pressed to stay and hear the mother's life story. Either way make your visit a short one!

If there are over twelve children attending your playgroup, it will be impossible for you to have a personal relationship with them all, to know all their individual needs and family backgrounds. To overcome this difficulty organize into smaller groups with each helper responsible for say, five or ten children, depending on the size of your playgroup. Each helper tries to become familiar with each child in her 'family group', to note his progress and to build up a personal relationship with him. At times of stress, say if he hurts himself or is off-colour, the same adult should look after him – being so young he will be confused if he is asked to make a close relationship with more than one or two adults in the playgroup. Usually the same helpers and children come on the same day each week: for instance, if Mrs Y. helps on Monday, Wednesday and Friday, then her group consists of children who come on those days, and Mrs X., who helps on Tuesday and Thursday will have in her group children who come then.

If your playgroup has a waiting list of thirty children, is it preferable to let all the children come once a week or fifteen twice a week? This is a difficult question. You may feel your-self under great pressure to accept certain children and worry that if you say there is no place for them you may never see them again. However, you must never exceed the number of children for whom you are registered: this is illegal, you could have your registration withdrawn, and in the event of an accident you would be severely blamed for having more children than stated on your registration form.

We do not recommend either that you accept a child for only one session a week. If a child is to adapt well to playgroup, he needs to have his first experience reinforced by a second visit, the second by the third and so on. A three-year-old may become confused if he is expected to hold onto the concept of a playgroup session for as long as a week – each attendance requires him to adjust anew to the group and to separation from his mother.

If you do decide to accept children once a week, guard against having more than one or two on this basis. A good playgroup generates a group feeling which is dependent on the regular interaction of the same children and adults. If you have too many children who are not familiar with playgroup patterns of behaviour, the whole group will suffer. What can you do to help those who are left outside? Tell your Director of Social Services and his committee, send in a list of names and addresses, with a brief note saying why you think each child needs to come to a playgroup. Attract as much publicity as you can by writing a letter to the local press, or an article in your parish magazine. Get the help of local doctors and social workers, and ask them to write to local councillors. Find out whether a new group can use your hall at different times or look for other premises in the area. Prepare helpers to become supervisors, especially by encouraging them to attend training courses. We know of many satisfactory groups who have splintered off from a parent group and who continue to support each other – exchanging table toys, holding joint fund-raising activities, sharing a waiting list and so on.

Some children need very little attention – most of their emotional needs are met at home and for them 'the play's the thing'; others need skilled handling and, unless they gravitate naturally towards another helper, it is probably best for them to be put in the supervisor's group – she is the person with the most training and experience and likely to be the most stable figure in the group.

You must try to have an accepting attitude towards all

children, both the angel-faced and the runny-nosed. It's easy to like the bright responsive child – but what of the one who is withdrawn, aggressive or overdemanding? You must be sensitive enough to know that these children need your help the most and you must try to learn to love them no matter how little you like their behaviour!

It's particularly important to avoid showing any signs of rejecting an unattractive child; children are very quick to notice facial expressions and interpret tones of voice. *Never* talk about a child in his presence, even when you are saying something positive; you may have said 'Sandra is settling well', but all Sandra understands is her name and she may be anxious, wondering what was said about her. Try not to label children and don't wholeheartedly accept other people's judgements on them. There may be a young tearabout on your waiting list, and neighbouring mothers may warn you that he will terrorize the group with his wild behaviour. Greet such a child with especial warmth; offer him some activity which will allow him to let off steam while you keep a watchful eye on him. Sometimes a whole family has a bad reputation and each successive child is labelled as a bad lot. Try to approach such children with an open mind, taking heed of other people's opinions but not necessarily acting on them.

If you have worked in a playgroup and finished the morning with a feeling of having been run off your feet, you may think it strange if we say that the adult's role in relation to children's activities is largely a passive one. Of course, you will be constantly offering help, pinning up fresh paper for the painting, helping to search for the right-shaped box for some junk modelling, asking and answering endless questions. But having provided a rich and stimulating environment, you should step back and allow the children to direct their own play. Sometimes you will be included by invitation, perhaps offered a cup of tea from the home corner or given some imaginary object 'bought at the shop'. It is a good rule only to enter into this sort of play if actually asked. The child's imaginary world is a very fragile one, easily shattered by a clumsy adult. Sometimes you will lead an activity – telling a story in the book corner, initiating some singing games. But this should only be for short periods – at this age it is more important to allow children to select their own activities, concentrating on what interests them. Does this sound like wasting time? Remember 'play is work' to the child, and this is how he learns best (see Part 4). Occasionally you may sit down near a neglected activity and begin to examine it. The chances are that some child will join you and start to play. We watched a supervisor get down on her hands and knees and begin to put together a road layout. In next to no time, two noisy boys had come to join her, and were soon engrossed in constructing a complicated road scheme. If she had said, 'Come and make up the roads,' they might have refused, but watching her start to work with it gave it an added value in their eyes.

You must also be careful to accept a child's creative efforts uncritically. When you are shown some blobs of colour, as a painting, or a strange collection of glued-together shapes, don't ask what it is. It is unlikely that the child will have reached the stage of starting out to make something; he is simply using the materials in an exploratory way. If you take time to watch your children working, you will be impressed by their concentration and by the way in which, having finished, they may show what they have made to a grown-up and promptly lose interest in it. It is adults who encourage him to want to keep it. As one experienced supervisor put it, 'To the children, the end product of their work is largely the waste product – it is the doing which is important.' When shown this 'waste product', praise it with a remark such as, 'You did work hard! Shall we put it on here to dry?' and leave it at that.

Many groups encourage children to take home paintings and junk models. If children ask for their work, let them have it; but be careful this doesn't develop into a situation where every child thinks he must take something home every day and so do mothers. Sometimes you must take a firm stand and resist pressure from parents and ill-informed helpers who want to ask the child to make something each session to take home. If a parent greets a child with, 'And what have you done for me today?' and the child has nothing to offer, he may feel that he has failed to live up to expectations. Yet he may have spent a busy morning building a make-believe train out of boxes with other children, experimenting with magnets in the science box, and listening to a story which has captured his imagination and enlarged his vocabulary. Supervisors should help mothers to understand that the most valuable part of a child's playgroup experience is often an inner growth which cannot be easily measured and still less taken home and pinned on the wall.

Getting to know the parents

By and large, people who work in playgroups are sensitive to the needs of children but less aware of the requirements of parents. The more you work with young children, the more you will realize that you can serve the child's interests best only if you consider parents and children together. In most situations involving mother and child one is very inclined to side with the child and stand in judgement over the mother. If you see a mother behaving badly towards her child – perhaps literally pushing him in the playgroup door and rushing off, or greeting him with a smack because he has dirtied his clothes – it is easy to feel pity for the child and anger for the mother. One has to remember, though, that a rejecting mother may have suffered rejection herself as a child, or she may be under considerable strain for one reason or another. She needs your help not your censure.

On the other hand, you will sometimes find yourself in the position of having to criticize a parent's conduct because it affects the organization of the playgroup. For instance, a mother may be repeatedly late collecting her child, even relying on your good will to bring him home. There may be a genuine reason for this, such as illness in the family; if there is not, you must refuse to tolerate this behaviour, pointing out that it isn't fair to you or your helpers. You may come across a mother who lavishes sweets on her child to eat in the playgroup or refuses to bring suitable footwear for outside play, although she could well afford to do so. In these circumstances, you must be prepared to act authoritatively, no matter how little you relish the role.

Once it is established that you expect the few rules in your playgroup to be kept, your energies can be freed to offer parents a supportive service in their difficult task. How best can you achieve this? Do you ever feel, if you have children, that you only exist by proxy, as wife to your husband and mother to your children? Many mothers have these resentful feelings *and* feel guilty about them. You can help by demonstrating that you see them as people in their own right and by showing your concern for their well-being. One way of doing this is to organize some sort of activity for them: a coffee club which is open during playgroup times and where mothers and helpers can mix and talk is usually very much appreciated. This is better held in a separate room if possible; we know of one group in a bleak church hall that uses the stage with the curtains drawn for a once-a-week mothers' club. The main value of having a time and place to meet is that mothers have a chance to talk over their common experiences. It's very reassuring to know that yours isn't the only child who still wets his bed at four-and-a-half or that other three-year-olds reacted to a new baby with exactly the same jealousy as your own. A mother can gain new insight into her relationship with her child in this way and be helped over a difficult period. As we argued in Part I, a playgroup can thus act as a valuable social centre for mothers, fostering a sense of neighbourliness and providing a kind of substitute extended family for isolated women.

Fathers, too, can benefit from talking together and being involved in the life of the playgroup. Try to arrange some evening meetings, perhaps with an outside speaker (see Chapter 9, Health education, p. 208). Remember that some fathers will never have a chance to see what goes on in a playgroup, so set up some of the equipment and have a small exhibition of paintings and other work, with well-mounted photographs of the children at play to illustrate certain aspects of the playgroup life. You may find one or two enthusiastic fathers prepared to help you with this. If such meetings are poorly attended, approach your local camera club to see if someone would come and take a ciné film of the playgroup. It's a rare parent who can resist seeing his child on a screen! Try to provide refreshments, making a small charge to swell playgroup funds. At one of the most successful meetings we attended, many of the mothers had cooked their own special dishes and as well as tea and coffee, a barrel of beer was provided. Whether it is advisable to organize outings or not depends a good deal on the area which you serve. You may know that your parents have a satisfying social life and that there is no need for the playgroup to add to it. On the other hand you may be in a district where mothers lead dull and monotonous lives and would be glad to contribute a weekly sum towards the occasional evening out.

Children quite often refuse to go home at the end of a playgroup session. Understandably, mothers can feel hurt and jealous at the child's apparent preference for you. Be quite firm with a child in this situation. Directing him to his mother by using such phrases as 'You must go with your mummy,' or 'I must go home to my own children now,' but add, 'I'll see you tomorrow.' – or whenever his next playgroup session is. The affection that a child has for you can act as a bridge between you and parents who are normally suspicious of anyone in a position of authority. One such mother was very distant with the playgroup supervisor, responding to all attempts at friendliness with 'No, miss' and 'Yes, miss' until one day she arrived in time to see her son give the supervisor a kiss and tell her, 'You're not a bad old b . . . . .'. The supervisor gave him a hug and sent him off to his mother, who after apologizing for 'the swear words', smiled for the first time as she said goodbye. It seemed that when she saw the supervisor accept her son, swearing and all, she could start to accept the supervisor.

Involving mother-helpers

Most supervisors like to encourage parents to play an active part in organizing their playgroup, serving on the committee or acting as fund-raisers. Some supervisors expect all mothers to help in running playgroup sessions on a rota basis, unless they have a special home commitment, such as caring for an invalid parent at home. Others only ask parents who have expressed interest to help. Some groups think it creates bad feeling to have paid helpers working with unpaid. Sometimes a supervisor feels doubtful about asking a mother to help, thinking that as she is accepting a fee, she should give a total service and not ask for unpaid help. Mothers may share this view: one was heard to say as she fled from her weeping three-year-old, 'I've paid my money, let them cope with his eternal crying!' We sympathize of course, but feel that more than a break from her child, such a mother needs help in understanding why he always cries and how to avoid it.

It isn't always easy to involve mother-helpers. Some supervisors are the type of people who tolerate children better than adults. Some supervisors, especially in small home-based groups, may feel embarrassed by the presence of adults. Others find mother-helpers notoriously unreliable, perhaps because of domestic crises or because they do not appreciate the importance of turning up when expected. Ideally, a group should have sufficient paid staff to function without mother-helpers – then it is easier to be patient with a mother who is more hindrance than help!

However, despite all these pitfalls it can be immensely valuable both to a mother and to the playgroup as a whole to involve mother-helpers. Give a new mother some guidance in what you expect of her – ask her to be responsible for watching over certain activities, explain the value of talking to the children rather than gossiping with other helpers, warn her of the need to stand back from the children's play rather than becoming over-involved. It is a great help to mother-helpers for the children to wear badges with their first names in big script and surnames smaller (see below). In fact it is useful for all visitors if everyone in a playgroup wears a name badge – supervisors, helpers and children. It is easier to make contact with a child and reinforce the feeling that he matters as an individual if you know his name. Mothers sometimes refer to all helpers by the universal

'teacher' or 'auntie' and of course children follow this lead –
try to encourage the use of names.

Peter
Simmonds

Figure 1

Some mother-helpers, because they are unsure of what is
expected of them, tend to cling to their own children and put
themselves in a teacher's role. We watched one mother nag her
child about recognizing numbers until he burst into tears, and
flung the blocks across the table, whereupon the mother, humili-
ated by this behaviour in front of the other helpers, slapped
him. It would have been much better to ask this mother to
supervise a specific activity, then she would have been too
busy to be so preoccupied with her own child. Helping in a
playgroup, a mother has the opportunity to watch experienced
people handle difficult children with skill and understanding.
Remember that it can be humiliating for her to see someone
else handle her child with more success than she can herself.
If you have the opportunity, explain that this is because adults
are usually more successful at managing children with whom
they are not closely involved.

It is normally beneficial for a child to see his mother involved;
her presence provides continuity between home and playgroup
and helps him build up a picture of his world as a coherent
whole and not unconnected fragments of experience. But
sometimes children do react badly, for exactly the same reasons
we mentioned when discussing the reaction of a child having
his mother as supervisor (p. 114). Warn mothers that this may
happen, perhaps describe your own child's reactions and give
her some guidance in meeting what she may feel to be a humiliating situation. None of us relish our own children behaving
badly in front of others. Suggest that she discusses with her

child the fact that she is coming to help at 'his' playgroup and how he must show her where to put things as she will not know. The pamphlet issued by the Pre-School Playgroup Association called 'You too can be a mother-helper' is very useful reading.

A mother can learn a great deal from working in a playgroup. She will be able to watch children playing with toys which are suited to their stage of development – well-made, often simple basic shapes that lend themselves to a variety of play purposes. She will see what fun children get from make-believe play, using props which she could easily provide – for example the home corner, with its pots and pans, cast off handbags, purses and dressing-up clothes. She will notice how absorbed children can be in experimenting with dough or playing with water – and realize that she could allow them to do this sometimes at home. The mother may learn basic principles for choosing toys – for instance that the younger the child, the bigger the equipment needed; that a good toy can be used for many purposes and that one well-made toy is better value than many poorly made ones. In the book corner, she may giggle over Gene Zions' *Harry the Dirty Dog* and share the children's delight in the richness of Brian Wildsmith's illustrations. According to the Plowden report, twenty-nine per cent of all homes have five books or less – so encourage mothers to borrow books from your own book corner, as well as from the local children's library.

Sometimes a mother with initial misgivings will discover that she has enjoyed helping in the playgroup. You may have opened her eyes to the very real pleasure to be experienced in working and playing with children. A busy housewife with her eye on the clock may not make the time to sit with her children to read a story or play picture dominoes. Freed from housework and working together with other adults, she may discover that she not only enjoys this contact with children but has a gift for working with them. To a person who has been a failure at school, whose working life was unrewarding and whose initial married bliss has largely evaporated into a dull routine, this feeling of being a success can come as a joyful surprise. These mother-helpers may in fact become your best assistants in the future.

Fathers have much to offer too. Pre-school children often see too little of their fathers and their lives are the poorer for it. There are many obvious ways in which fathers can help – toy-making and mending, becoming treasurer or taking some other office on the committee. We would certainly like to see more fathers involved in actual playgroups as everything that has been said about educating mothers in the choosing of toys and books and in the handling of children applies to fathers as well. Another point already mentioned is that little boys need a male figure with whom to identify, yet they spend a very large part of their lives surrounded by females. Have you noticed how quiet your four-year-old tearabout can become when a workman comes to mend something? A father supervising the woodwork bench or telling a story, possibly about his work, might have a good effect on the behaviour of your group. Try inviting in a friendly grandfather or a father on shiftwork, or a policeman or fireman in uniform. Or what about the local male head teacher – your playgroup may be a revelation to him!

Working as a team

Earlier in this chapter, we suggested that before you started, you and your helpers should discuss basic principles of playgroup practice to see whether you have a common viewpoint about the aims and organization of your playgroup, and that you should try to make certain that your personalities are compatible. If one of your regular helpers leaves, it is essential that you go through the same processes of discussion to ensure you choose someone who will fit in with your existing team. You will probably notice someone among your mother-helpers who would be valuable to the group as a regular helper. Unless you know them very well indeed, suggest that they come on a trial period of a term; then if they prove unsuitable, it is easier to tell them so. It also makes it easier for them to leave if they want to.

Be careful that you are not used as a therapeutic service by doctors or social workers. We have heard of several groups where people volunteered their services because a doctor thought that working with young children would 'take them out of themselves'. No matter how sorry you feel for them, you must remember that your first duty is to provide the ablest workers for your children. Again you may sometimes have unsuitable helpers 'wished' on you. Your group may, for example, be based on a church and your new minister's wife insists on coming to help. She may feel it is her duty to show the children how to make 'lovely calendars to give mummy for Christmas' or to gather everyone together at the end of the morning for lengthy prayers and a hymn. If this happens you must take a firm stand, remembering that if you allow yourself to be overruled, the children will suffer. As we have seen already in relation to parents, you will sometimes have to act authoritatively, to safeguard the life of the playgroup – by the same token you may need to stand firm on a decision and overrule helpers who disagree with you. Make sure you talk over any problem with your staff, but if after discussion you still cannot agree, you must be prepared to be assertive, no matter what status your helper holds outside the playgroup.

Much of what we have said about guiding, supporting and praising mother-helpers applies equally to regular helpers though you will expect a higher standard of work from them. Do all you can to encourage them to have a professional attitude towards their work, taking the definition of this word as following 'a calling which involves some sort of learning'. As soon as your group is on a sound financial basis it should pay for its workers to attend meetings, conferences and above all training courses; it should buy magazines and books to stimulate discussion and feed in new ideas. Unlike a school, which is composed of several classes, playgroups are usually units on their own and this is why it is so important for all of you to visit other groups, at least once a term. This also helps to combat any feeling of isolation. Make sure you have regular meetings to air problems, discuss the children's progress and propose new ideas. Some groups bring a picnic lunch once a month and stay on in the playgroup room with some equipment left out for their own children to use. Other groups meet in each other's houses in the evening. However you arrange them, don't underestimate the value of such meetings.

All work should be shared on an equal footing, supervisors and helpers taking a fair share of the menial jobs. It is a good idea to take it in turns on a weekly basis to be in charge of various activities. If they are no one's responsibility it is easy for, say, the dressing-up clothes to remain unmended, or the nature corner to consist day after day of a few fir cones and a wilting hyacinth bulb. Some jobs may remain the responsibility of one helper because of her special background; you may have someone with nursing experience for instance and think it sensible for her to be in charge of the first-aid box, or someone married to a physics master who is able to devise easy scientific experiments. You also need someone who can take charge if you are away; and it is good policy to have someone to take over if you have a visitor who is engaging your attention. This can be arranged quite smoothly if your helpers are all used to sharing the work load and know what to expect.

The hall committee

It is very important to build up a good relationship with your hall committee so that they understand what you are trying to do for the local community. Hall committees sometimes consist of older people who, having brought up their own children without the help of a playgroup, fail to see the necessity of them – they may even feel that you are offering young mothers a chance to opt out of their responsibilities (some of the arguments in Chapter 3 may help them change their minds); they may also be worried about the damage that young children might do to their hall, especially if it is new. Try to find other new halls which have had a playgroup running for some time and if possible take one of them to see it.

As we have already suggested, a member of the hall committee should sit on the playgroup committee and vice versa. In this way each gets an insight into the other's attitudes and there is more likelihood of problems being solved in a way satisfactory to both parties.

Hall committees often want to ban the use of sand and water. Reassure them about the protective measures you will take with floor coverings (see p. 262). Invite them into your own sitting-room and give them a demonstration of sand and water play, so they can see that if you protect the floor carefully your own carpet remains undamaged. If they allow water play but draw the line at sand which may scratch polished floors, give in on this point and make do with sawdust. When you have established a reputation of being good and careful tenants, you can discuss the possibility of using sand again.

In halls used by many different groups, conflicts do arise – and it is usually storage space which causes the most trouble. Playgroup equipment tends to be bulky and look untidy. Make a stand to get a large lock-up cupboard of your own, so that you can hide any unsightly equipment – you will be less likely to find that your home corner equipment has been sold in the Brownies' jumble sale! If your toys are misused by other groups using the hall, go in person to see the leader of the offending group rather than writing or telephoning; if you can take the misused piece of equipment with you, so much the better. Most adults are sympathetic to the needs of young children and confronted with you face-to-face will generally try to repair the damage and prevent a repetition of the incident.

We suggested earlier in this chapter that you have a written agreement with your landlord. Be sure to honour your obligations, pay your rent punctually, leave the premises clean. You could also send an annual or termly report on the state of your group, including a financial statement, so that you keep your hall committee in close touch with your affairs.

Caretakers

It is very important to take the trouble to win the cooperation of your caretaker. If this is a man, he may provide a much-needed male figure in the life of the playgroup; he may also prove helpful with broken toys, for instance, providing just the right size nut and bolt for a broken scooter. Some caretakers

resent playgroups using their premises fearing that extra work
will be caused. This is understandable. As housewives we can
sympathize with the caretaker who, having worked hard cleaning a floor, watches a procession of parents and children walk
over it and make it dirty again. One caretaker used to stand in
the porch, pointedly mopping up after each mother and child
had passed – hardly the way for this new group to establish a
friendly, welcoming atmosphere!

The most effective way of overcoming the resentment of
caretakers is usually to offer them extra money : they are often
on a very low income and an additional 75p per week can
make a great difference to their attitude. Caretakers are often
fussy about who uses their cleaning materials. Ask about this
and if necessary be prepared to use your own. Many a feud has
been started over a shared mop and bucket! Do your best to
keep caretakers informed about your plans; let them know
the dates on which you begin and end term, when half-term is,
when you hope to have a parents' evening and so on. Do this
directly – don't rely on the caretaker seeing the notice for
parents or on the memory of your church minister. The more
you show you respect them as responsible workers, the more
likely they are to show respect for you.

Links with the community at large

Primary schools

It is essential to have a good relationship with your local infant
or first school. Some head teachers and staff welcome and
support playgroups, seeing them as useful adjuncts to the school.
As we suggested earlier, try to have a local head teacher on
your committee. A school which has learnt to value its playgroup may allow it to run a stall to raise funds at the school
fête or jumble sale. As well as providing publicity, this is also
an open acknowledgement of the liaison which exists between
the school and playgroup. In Chapter 9 we discuss the value of
keeping records to pass on to your local school.

Some teachers may feel resentful of you, as amateurs,

impinging on the work of professionals. They may be suspicious of your motives, believing that you are making a good deal of money for very little work. They may have already received bad impressions from a poor-quality playgroup. It may be useful to explain your status to your school. One head teacher we knew said that she would be unable to recommend or support any groups in her area as they were all money-making businesses. In fact, the one on her doorstep was run by a committee of parents and other interested persons, and once she realized this, her whole attitude changed. Another way of overcoming an antagonistic attitude is to write to your head teacher inviting her to visit your playgroup and saying how much you would welcome her advice. If she comes, treat her like royalty, saying how much you hope these visits will become a regular occurrence. Listen humbly to all she has to say, even if you don't always agree!

Ask if you might be allowed to visit her school, mentioning that you would be especially glad to see the activities offered to five-year-olds. When you go, be sure to take a notebook and pencil to jot down any information which would be useful to your playgroup. Ask if you can take small groups of would-be school entrants in the term before they start school; try to meet their teacher-to-be, so that you can use her name when talking to the children about school; try to let them see their room and the school lavatories and cloakrooms. Discuss with the teachers the idea of passing on your children's records to the school.

If all these overtures fail, invite your local head teacher to be a speaker at one of your evening meetings. Most people are flattered by being asked to talk and most parents will come to hear a head teacher speak, especially on such a subject as 'What a child should know before he goes to school.' If you know she is a poor speaker, ask her to chair a meeting, inviting as your main speaker a member of the education committee or a senior education officer. If all your attempts to win her cooperation fail, don't despair; through observing the effect a good playgroup experience has on the children who enter her school, even the most uncooperative head teacher must acknowledge the value of your work – anyway, she will have to retire one day!

Secondary schools

You may be asked by your local secondary school to let last-year pupils come and help in your playgroup. We hope that you will be able to do this as these young adults can learn a lot from the experience of working with children, for exactly the same reasons as your mother-helpers: they will see skilled persons handling children in an environment designed for children's needs. Both girls and boys should come – boys become parents too.

This exercise will be of more value to both the playgroup and the school children if it is well prepared. We suggest you discuss the project with the teacher in charge. Ask that unless her students are making a one-off visit they should come regularly for half a term; too many changes of face may upset young children and the visitors will need at least six consecutive visits if they are to gain anything from the experience. Say what you expect from them and ask if you can come to talk to them about the basic principles of playgroup practice. The teenage group for example often want to *teach* young children, to show them how to paint a house or model a dog; you must explain why this is unwise – three- and four-year-olds are at a very different stage of development from school-age children; emphasize the importance of conversation at this stage.

Some of these young students will have an intuitive under-standing of young children's needs, others will be less mature. You may find that they themselves need to play, perhaps be-cause they were denied the opportunity at an earlier age. Some will want to show off their own skills, modelling exquisite roses out of clay or making paper boats for an admiring audience. If this happens too frequently, or if a student tries to overorganize your children, their play will suffer. Act authoritatively and direct them to some specific activity. We do not mean use them as dogsbodies to wash the coffee cups. Give them a notebook and pencil and ask them to describe examples of children's conversation, cooperative play, aggression or the various ways in which children use the water tray. This will help them to observe the children and provide a useful basis for discussion when they return to their school.

Youth clubs

A local youth club may like to 'adopt' your playgroup, especially if you are amicably sharing premises. The members may be prepared to organize a charity walk or sell raffle tickets to raise money for the playgroup. Try inviting them in – young people are often quick to realize the value of playgroups.

Old-age pensioners

Older people have an important role to play. You may have a friend who has retired but is still active enough to enjoy contact with young children and their mothers. Try inviting her along to your playgroup for a trial session and if you feel this has gone well, ask her if she would like to be a regular visitor. Young children can respond well to this age group, even though they may have had little contact with their own grandparents. The lap of a suitable 'grannie' can prove a refuge for a distressed child, who seems to find in an older person a satisfying sense of stability. Younger mothers, too, often respond to an older woman, valuing her maturity. Many older people are clever at using their hands and will make rag dolls or crochet a rug for the book corner. They may have a fund of nonsense rhymes and finger-plays that the younger helper lacks. And how they love to be needed and have their skills used!

Centres for the handicapped

It is worth contacting training centres for handicapped people (address from your local Medical Officer of Health) to see if they will make equipment at cost. Ask them to do a repetitive line, as it is uneconomic for instructors to supervise constantly changing work – they haven't the time to teach a variety of techniques to people with a limited work potential. One centre we know made screens which were used to portion off large halls most successfully.

Probably the most difficult of your relationships, and one that you may not have anticipated, will be those with professionally trained adults. You may be confident of your ability to work with young children, to get to know their parents, to be part of a team of helpers running the playgroup. But you may feel less sure of yourself when you come into contact with other members of your local community – health visitors, teachers and youth leaders, for example. Your dealings with these professional workers will be affected by questions of status and social background; not being formally trained for your work, you may lack the confidence to meet someone in an official position on something like an equal footing. Take Kay, for instance, a playgroup helper with great talents, an attractive girl with an assured manner, who confessed that she would not dare to approach the head teacher of her neighbouring school to discuss the difficulties of a child who was shortly to leave the playgroup and enter school. She said that she felt it would 'be a cheek' to make such an approach.

Playgroup workers often underestimate themselves in this way. In fact they frequently know more about individual children than anyone else except the parents, if only by virtue of having been in regular contact with the child in a relaxed situation. Do not be afraid of facing up to the responsibilities which such knowledge brings. By the very nature of the work you have undertaken, you are committed to making known the needs of the under-fives. To do this, you may have to cross swords with unenlightened officials or unsympathetic committees. If you are to influence people, you must present yourself as a concerned, informed person, ready to take into account other points of view, but never losing sight of the validity of your own goal.

Further reading

Starting a Playgroup, PPA publication
How To Form a Playgroup, BBC publication

8

Organization and Day-to-Day Problems

Organizing the programme

The atmosphere and programme of a playgroup is a direct reflection of the supervisor's own personality, especially if she has created it from scratch. If you are a cut-and-dried sort of person, you will probably have created a rather cut-and-dried programme; a more easy-going person is likely to run a more relaxed playgroup. You may know a playgroup run by an Art School graduate whose children turn out the most exciting and beautifully produced creations, but it makes one slightly sceptical sometimes just *because* they are so good. Somehow a three-year-old just couldn't do work like that on his own ...

One must therefore take care that the playgroup is run for the children and not merely to satisfy the needs of the supervisor. All the activities should spring from the needs of the children, not because it is 10.15 on the timetable, nor because the new helper is very good at sewing or you want to please and impress parents in some way.

How should the morning be organized so that the children get the maximum benefit?* There are basically two types of programme: the 'free' morning, and the three-part morning.

The free morning

We strongly advocate the free morning as being best suited to the needs of young children. All equipment is put out at the beginning of the morning and remains out until it is time to go

---

*Though we say morning, it may well be afternoon throughout, for those who meet at this time.

home. The children move freely among the various activities. They know they can spend as long as they like at any one place because nothing will be whisked away to make room for the next part of the timetable. All the activities arise spontaneously; for example, story-time can come at any part of the morning – a child may simply bring along a book and ask to be read to.

Contrary to popular belief, this freedom requires a far greater degree of skill on the part of the adults than does a more structured timetable. Supervisors and their helpers need to have a thorough understanding of what is meant by 'free play', not a free-for-all but freedom within certain limits so that a basically civilized atmosphere is maintained (see p. 221). They need to have enough invisible control to avoid chaos and to be able to feel when interest is flagging at a certain activity, or when tensions are rising over a piece of equipment; they need to know when a child is ready to be led on to something new, and when he needs to just stand and watch.

The children in such a playgroup should have been shown how to look after equipment as well as how to use it. They are aware that running wildly around in a confined space may disturb other children's work and even damage it. They know that after going to the lavatory they wash their hands without making a flood, even if they need help at first.

Sometimes, supervisors who favour a free morning are able to create such a busy workroom atmosphere that the adults feel almost unnecessary. The children are so engrossed in their activity and the equipment generates such valuable play that the helpers tend to stand back from any involvement. Watch this! It can develop into a speechless nomadic existence for children. Do remember here the importance of language. A child may not be ready to be extended further, practically, in an activity, but has he spoken about it with anyone? Has he had the chance to discuss with an adult and other interested children how he made it, its size, shape, colour, what it is for, or whatever else he wants to chat about? Once you have established an atmosphere of constructive 'business' where the children are happily occupied doing worthwhile activities, it will be much easier to find time to talk with the children, especially the non-talkers – the ones you never quite get around to drawing out because there is never enough uninterrupted time before more demanding children come along. So if the atmosphere is calm, stand back occasionally and look around to see who might gain from being talked with.

A supervisor in this kind of successful situation is like the centre of a maypole. Each child's invisible 'ribbon', his 'private line' to an adult, is attached to the central figure, the supervisor. If she has in her mind worked out a pattern for the ribbons to create – and the pattern can increase in complexity as she gains experience – the ribbons will intertwine and revolve in many directions, though the supervisor in the centre will still remain aware of the relationship of each ribbon to the others and to the central figure, herself. It is only when there is no preconceived pattern for the children's 'ribbons' to follow that they become impossibly tangled with each other and with the central figure.

Arrival of children

This is one of the most important times of the morning. The atmosphere you create for the children to enter into when they arrive sets the tone of the whole session. Once children have entered chaos they act chaotically, and it takes a great deal of skill and experience to recover a calm, purposeful atmosphere.

How can you avoid a bad beginning? Firstly, by not being in a rush yourself. If it is a dreadful panic for you and your helpers to get your own children and husbands off to school and work, and still catch the bus to playgroup on time, why not open fifteen minutes later? Whatever the timing, you should be able to have all the necessary equipment out by the time the main body of children arrive. Then they have something to do, and you are free to sort out any tensions before they escalate – you are just mixing up the last pot of paint when John and Philip start a fight about who can have a turn on the trike – your hands are covered in blue paint, if only you were not at the other end of the hall ... Meanwhile all this may be very disturbing to a new, timid child, who can only stand in a corner and be frightened.

Some playgroup premises happen to be en route to the local infant school so that mothers drop off their under-fives on the return journey, perhaps before your official opening time. Obviously you cannot expect young children to stand outside shivering in the cold. So there will often be a steady trickle of early-comers and their mothers to give you a helping hand. As it is likely to be the same children each morning, they will soon prove their worth as valuable assistants. In this way you avoid the problem of everyone arriving together and demanding attention simultaneously.

As the children arrive it is a good idea to have at least one helper by the door to smile and say 'hello'. This may sound silly, but we have seen children walk in, take off their coats and go to a toy without a word being spoken to them! The 'official receiver' can also tick off names on the register as the children come in – this saves time and tedium later on. The register should then be kept in a prominent position in case of fire (see p. 199). Another adult to help with coats and boots is useful too – she will encourage children to take off their own clothes, but is on hand to offer help where needed. (Do try and persuade mothers to put names on all clothing. A clothes peg to clip wellingtons into pairs is useful too.)

Most groups with a free programme open with a long period of free activity – usually lasting for about one-and-a-half hours. A basic list of the equipment for this might be: large wheeled toys, slides, climbing, balancing, swinging apparatus, paint, woodwork, clay or dough, water, sand, dressing up, home corner, constructional toys (e.g. bricks, Lego), road and train layouts.

Different children make use of this equipment in different ways. The old-stagers come bursting in, full of energy – they may have been cooped up in a flat since yesterday's session and are just raring to go! They go straight to the apparatus for large, physical activities, for climbing and swinging and balancing. Outdoor space is very useful here. Other children are eager to tell you all their news: the new baby, the red jelly for tea last night, the new wellingtons – an adult should be free to listen to all this. Another child may arrive full of anger after a fight with her brother and may want to bang about a lump of clay for ten minutes because she was not allowed to do that to her brother; another is upset because his mother has gone to hospital and so he goes straight to the easel and paints a picture about it to get it off his chest. Nearly all the children come in with something they are eager to play out, and you need to see the equipment is there to help them do this.

Because they have so much to express at the beginning, children don't usually need much stimulation from an adult at this time. Let them go to the toys alone, except of course a new or timid child, who may welcome an encouraging hand. Your main function is to listen and talk with the children hearing the news they bring with them, from and about home.

Some children always tend to go to the same piece of equipment every morning. You will have to use your judgement here about when to lead a child on to something different. Usually he will do this for himself when he has worked through all the delights and possibilities of his special interest. However, if your playgroup is in a large hall, make sure that all the children, especially the new and timid ones, have actually seen everything. We knew a little girl who only went on a slide for weeks until an understanding helper took her gently by the hand to see a new doll in the home corner. She was delighted and had a wonderful morning, playing with everything there. She had never dared to venture forth by herself – it would have involved crossing the hall diagonally, past the big boys on bikes and the banging at the woodwork table and so many strange children she had never seen before. But once she realized how nice the home corner was, she began to think there might be equally nice things in other parts of the big hall and so she gained confidence, little by little, to explore and to participate in all the activities provided. (The layout of your room and the 'breaking-up' of the large areas is very important in this kind of discovery also – see p. 227.)

Similarly, if someone brings an interesting object or a pet to show the children, make sure everyone has the opportunity of looking at it: if you are in a huge hall it might be worth saying, 'Look children, come and see what David has brought today.'

If you are introducing a new activity, have an adult nearby to sort out turn-taking and answer questions. The number of chairs at a table or the number of aprons is a good way of deciding how many children may have a turn first time round. Although children clamour to have a turn immediately, they will be more reasonable when asked to wait if they are confident that this new activity will be out again the next day, and indeed every day until all interest in it has waned. Interest does fall off, and if no one seems to be using a particular piece of equipment for a few days, put it away for a couple of weeks. It is amazing how the children will flock to it again when it reappears.

It is worthwhile having an adult in the Book Corner a good part of the time, so that the opportunity to hear a story is not lost to any child. Sometimes you will find that just by approaching this area of a room a small group of children will appear and settle themselves ready to hear a story. The Book Corner is a marvellous place to put a new mother-helper who does not yet know what to do and is afraid she will do the wrong thing. She can sit there comfortably and a few children will invariably gather around her so that she can lose herself in the intimacy of looking at books with an interested group. She can also see, perhaps for the first time, what good children's books are like, and how interested children can become in them.

A music table should also be provided. Some mornings there may be no music. On another day, a group playing at this table may encourage others to join with them, and when one of the adults goes across to the piano or begins to sing with the children, almost everyone is involved in playing or singing or dancing in a delightfully spontaneous way. This kind of successful group activity often pivots round one of the adults joining and subtly directing at just the right moment: too early, and it would not have come from the children's interest: too late and the interest would have gone.

Lunch

The mid-morning snack, which we shall refer to as 'lunch', is brought in on a tray, or better still, a trolley. The time varies but it usually comes after about one-and-a-half hours of free play or when the supervisor senses a lull in the intensity of play. Often it is just the break required to set the children off again on further activities.

In a free morning, the children take their lunch themselves when they are ready. This means that some check must be kept that one child has had her drink and another has not had three! But you will soon know who to watch in this respect. The children should sit down while they eat and drink together with an adult. This is a good opportunity to talk with the children – rhymes or songs often generate from the group feeling over lunch. In some playgroups, a table is set out as a 'Milk Bar' or 'Café'. The table is covered with a plastic tablecloth or mats which the children have helped to make, and a child hangs up a sign 'Open'. You may like to extend the shop idea and let the children take turns to be shopkeepers or waitresses serving the drinks.

Group times

Most children are very eager to join in at group times – whether for a story, music, game – and are full of anticipation that something exciting is going to happen. They know from past experience that group time is pleasant and interesting, and ends long before they feel fidgety and want to be off again, choosing an activity for themselves. They are ready to join in because there has been ample time to play freely since the morning began and now they feel like settling down in a more intimate group. The children who are ready to do this are learning to listen, because they *want* to listen.

Others, however, may not be ready to participate in group

activities and should not be obliged to do so. Watch out, for example, for children who are not yet mature enough to join in with a group, particularly younger children or those who have not been in the playgroup for very long and still need time to explore the activities. Many children at first play by themselves, then side by side with others, and finally in a group. This applies to group listening too. The best safeguard against having any square pegs in round holes is to leave out most of your basic equipment such as sand, water, paint, clay, large bricks, road layouts, and books so that any child who wants to can continue busily and quietly while those interested can join in a group activity. Other children may already be deeply engrossed in something else when you decide to have a group activity, such as a communal lunch – it is better if an adult quietly suggests to such a child that he takes his lunch when he has finished his work.

Take care also that a group does not become too large to be effective. Most children of playgroup age are not old enough to cope with sharing an adult among many other children. A child should not be further away from an adult's attention than he is likely to be in a large family. Six or eight children is the maximum. This is best achieved when group time is spontaneous; or you can organize a system of sub-groups within the playgroup with one helper in regular charge of each.

Group time should be really fresh and exciting each day. You can tell by the enthusiasm the children show in coming to join in with you. They will be very eager if they know you have something exciting in the box on your knee, or a new finger-play to tell them. It is only when group time becomes routine and dull that problems arise. The children get restless at having left an interesting activity to sit doing nothing for ten minutes while you keep saying 'sit down', 'sit still', 'keep quiet'.

Keep your time together short. 'Leave them begging for more' – the maxim of a successful comedian in Music Hall! Three to five minutes for younger children and not more than ten minutes for the older ones is a good guide. If you are showing something to the children, whether a book or a pineapple make sure they can all see. It helps to sit as near to the children's level as possible – on one of their small chairs if you have nursery-sized furniture. Changing the tone of your voice rather than the volume will help to sustain interest and ensure that everyone can hear as well as see.

Try to organize things so that helpers are involved in the group too, it makes for better relationships among you all, and implies that they recognize the importance of what you are doing. It is terribly difficult for even the most skilled supervisor to sustain attention when two or three adults are having a good old natter down the other end of the hall!

We would advise against having a news time in which children formally report their home news. It is an artificial situation which should not be necessary if a supervisor takes the numerous natural opportunities for conversation which arise during playgroup sessions. Some children always have lots to tell you, but they have probably told it already, earlier in the morning, and it tends to be the same children every day who hold forth – the quieter child is longing to speak but cannot bring himself to do so in front of the other children.

Going to the lavatory

Going to the lavatory can cause difficulties for a new child. Is it better to take all the children at a set time or let them go as the need arises?

A lot depends on how easy it is to get to the cloakrooms. Home-based playgroups have few problems here. In hall-based playgroups in a good modern building with cloakrooms adjoining the main hall, children ought to be able to go to the lavatory alone as at home though it may be necessary for a helper to go along the first few times to encourage handwashing and help fasten buttons. However, if the lavatories are across a dark corridor up the stairs, some of the younger or more timid children may need a helper to take them. This can lead to problems if one of your helpers seems to be spending most of her time and energy on the one task. The temptation for many supervisors is then to have a time when all the children walk to the lavatories together in a long line and queue up, waiting for their turn. Considering the physiological difference between us as individuals and the different amounts and times of fluid intake, we feel it is illogical to expect all children to want to go to the lavatory at the same time! And they are far more likely to play around and become troublesome in what is, after all, a potentially unhygienic situation, if they have to stand waiting, bored and restless in a queue, and then queue up again for handwashing.

We have seen a playgroup in a seedy downtown area which caters solely for disturbed children. The lavatories are down two flights of stone stairs and across a yard. But the supervisor is so convinced of the need for children to acquire a sense of responsibility that there is no set toilet-time. A helper takes those children who cannot go alone, but in time, many learn to tackle the journey themselves. As a final thought on this subject, consider whether happy, busy children visit the lavatory less than bored children.

Going-home time

This can be a tricky period – it is hard to strike a balance between giving yourselves enough time to put everything away calmly, and yet not having the children ready with their coats on and getting more and more restless twenty minutes before their mothers come to collect them. Ideally, enough equipment should be left out for a child to continue playing until his mother calls to collect him. Mothers then see their children actually at play and can enter into an easy situation to talk with the supervisor.

It is crucial that everything is put away in its right place ready for the next session; you may be late the next morning and so much time is saved if everyone knows just where to put their hand on what is needed. Have a plan of the storage cupboard pinned inside the cupboard so that new helpers know what goes where. The type of storage space will help you decide what should be put away first. The heavier and messier equipment is more likely to need adult help, so will probably be the first to go – for example, climbing frame, paint and clay. Equipment with lots of parts to check, like jigsaws, should be next so that there is enough time to hunt for missing pieces. Do encourage the children to put away only *completed* toys.

It is very worthwhile to take the time and trouble to show the children how to put things away. Although it is not essential that they help with every piece of equipment – some may be just too heavy or dangerous – the more they can do, the better. Try to follow the same routine every day so that soon the children know just what follows on from what. Eventually, an experienced supervisor can just say a word to a group of children and a chain of 'putting away' is set in motion with everyone knowing what they are supposed to be doing. Avoid clapping your hands and yelling 'Clear away now!' Ask the children quietly, group by group, to help clear up whatever equipment they have been using. If a child is in the middle of something interesting, ask him to clear up himself when he has finished.

Putting away is often a good time to praise a shy child – often the over-neat ones come into their own when they help tidy up. Or again, the big rising-fives can be encouraged to put their superior strength to good use when it comes to folding up the climbing frame! If you praise a child, however, do so quietly and individually so that if the next one drops his jigsaw all over the floor, he does not feel too bad about it. The children should not feel under pressure to be careful; it helps more if you can encourage them by praising a child for something skilful and helpful at his own level of development.

What happens when a child has put away his things and is waiting until his mother comes? If he does not know what to do he may become a nuisance and get in the way of those who are still clearing up. If you have a separate small room, you could have songs or finger-plays for the majority of the children while a few clear away. Do not have a story as it will be constantly interrupted as mothers arrive. Similarly with records, songs to join in with, or music to listen to – you have to be careful that the children are able to concentrate and that there are not too many distractions. A better idea is to let the children look at books. If you leave out a pile, they can choose one and sit down with their coats on until mothers arrive. Books are easy to put away when all the children have gone, and you can be sure that each child has had the opportunity to look at a book every morning. Have a helper at the door for a quick good-bye to each child – children like a sense of continuity of this kind.

The best leaving routine is for mothers to come in, see the children at play and help dress their own child. This gives you an opportunity of seeing the child with his mother. You will notice those who help too much, a gentle 'Susan, can you show Mummy how you can fasten your own coat now?' may help a mother to give her child a little more breathing space. You can praise the painting a child did that morning, or say how hard he worked at his jigsaw. This is a good opportunity to show mothers your values, to help them to understand what things please you, and that they please you because you feel they are good for the child.

Three-part morning

Some playgroups still model their morning session on the old-fashioned nursery-school timetable of free play, followed by a group time including lunch, followed by an organized activity when all the children sit down and are expected to do the same thing. We feel that this type of programme has many organizational difficulties and other disadvantages for both children and adults.

Nearly all playgroups start off with a long period of free activity. But what happens next? Somewhere around 10:30 a.m. you have to decide whether the children are to continue to play freely among the equipment provided for them, or to pack everything away to join a large group. Before you start putting everything back in the cupboards, think how much hard work and expense all this equipment has cost you. Is it sensible to use it for only an hour or so each day? Have the children had their fill of it yet? A compromise is to leave out the 'basics' and let them be really used.

Then, when you move on to a definite group time, the

actual period of transition can be quite a testing time. You will need to have a definite plan of campaign worked out with your helpers so as to ensure a smooth 'all change'. It is disastrous, for example, to have a vacuum – if the children are expected to sit still on their chairs for too long with nothing to do, there will be trouble. So at the first transition of free play to lunch, have lunch brought in all ready before you start clearing away from the free-play period. The children not involved in helping can go straight to a circle of chairs and take their drink, until eventually everyone is seated. Looking at books is the best way to keep the children busy as they finish their drinks at different times. Or, you may prefer to reverse this – the children choose a book when they join the group and then drinks are given out when all are seated. If lunch is included in the group time, whether it be rhymes or jingles or a story that is added, the children will certainly be asked to sit still for too long. Note that the pointers to a successful group time as discussed on p. 157 apply here too.

Organized activities

The next difficult transition is from lunch to an organized group activity. The children must be occupied while the equipment for the organized activity is being put out. If you have more than one room at the playgroup, you can take the group into a smaller room while some or all of the helpers are preparing the next activity. If there is only one room, you will have to keep the children's attention, while the helpers are getting out the equipment. Ask them to move quietly, talking as little as possible, and when they have finished, to come and join the group. This will emphasize the feeling of togetherness and imply that it is in the group that worthwhile things are happening. When everything is ready, the children can disperse for the third part of the programme.

There are a number of important points to watch out for in an organized activity. Remember that not all children may be up to the same level of competence in a certain activity, for example, one involving a manipulative skill. And once the children are all doing the same things, there is bound to be an element of competition, no matter how tactful adults are. Are you going to set the standard to suit the oldest, most skilled children? What about a new child who has only been to playgroup three mornings before and cannot use scissors properly yet? If you set your sights at his level and have the adults do the cutting out, the rising-fives are not going to find it very challenging.

The best solution is to leave out some of the more basic equipment from the first part of the morning, so that a less-skilled child has a chance to opt out without losing face. If he is allowed to play through the basic activities such as sand and water and painting at his own rate, he will eventually *want* to join in group activities.

Other children may start everything and finish nothing. Ask yourself whether such a child is really *ready* to join in with the others? Has he had his fill of the basic equipment and the large toys? He may have passed his fourth birthday, but for various reasons be only about two emotionally; so perhaps he still needs a two-year-old's push-and-pull toys, or the large bricks.

Some supervisors have said they find that an organized activity can give a fresh stimulus to a child who only plays with one thing, for example older boys who spend all their time in physical play. Other supervisors feel that some children will become a disruptive influence if left to their own devices and it is a help to encourage them to take an interest in one specific activity. We feel that you should first check that you are providing enough to capture the interests of *all* the children, especially those who have been at playgroup for perhaps two years and who may naturally enough be bored with exactly the same equipment coming out every day. Make sure that those old-stagers have enough equipment to develop their play as they themselves develop intellectually (see p. 313).

What organized activity you decide to do is entirely up to you and varies from day to day. You may hit on something which proves so popular that the children keep asking for it again and again. Fine. Why not try putting something like this out at a small table for, say, four children to do during the first free-play period? It may then become part of routine activities. Other days, a well-planned activity will misfire completely. Was it too advanced? Were you expecting too much manual dexterity from the children, particularly the younger ones? Or was it too easy – did they finish and become bored? Was all the equipment needed ready at hand?

If you are planning something round a specific event such as Christmas or Easter don't start too early (see highdays and holidays, p. 190). The children gain satisfaction from doing rather than keeping, so avoid folding up your Christmas frieze at the end of the session waiting for it to be added to, yet *again*, the next day. If children are going to take home something they have made, let them do so, whenever possible, *the day they make it*. It will lose its excitement if it is kept at playgroup until the day you break up for Easter!

Occasionally you may find that you are praising a child's efforts and encouraging him only to discover that when he takes his work home his mother makes rude noises about 'that bit of rubbish' or 'a tortoise doesn't look like that'. In this case you should try to help the mother understand what her child is capable of doing at his particular stage of development, and encourage her to praise her child's effort rather than his results. This may involve inviting her to see the other children's work – she can then compare what her child has done with others of his age. You could also keep a few paintings that show some development – this is a valuable starting-point from which to explain other areas of children's development.

The main difficulties in organized activities often come towards the end of the period when the children are completing their work at different times. How can you keep the quicker children occupied while the slower ones finish off? You don't want to gear everything to the quicker ones, or else some children will rarely have the satisfaction of completing. Finishing off the next day is not satisfactory either, children usually lose interest if faced with the same thing the next morning. The best solution is to leave out some basic equipment so that any child

who has finished can quietly get down and find something else
to do.

Changing from a three-part morning to a free morning

After reading this chapter, we hope that some of you who have
had a three-part morning will want to try changing over to a
free morning. If you decide to do this, it is essential to discuss
your ideas with your helpers first. Ask them round for coffee
one evening rather than trying to explain with twenty children
milling around during the morning.

Your helpers may be resistant to a change. In many play
groups an organized activity makes helpers feel they are being
useful. If you are unsure of yourself and your skills in relation
to children, it is very comforting and rewarding to help them
make something which shows concrete results. It requires a
much more subtle understanding of children's needs to feel
equally rewarded after having only talked about the softness
and stretchiness of clay while they banged and pulled it around
for the first time and never even thought about making anything. It is up to you as supervisor to explain that you are not
assessing a helper's worth by the quality of Indian hats everyone goes home wearing, but by the quiet sensitive manner they
develop with the children; how they know just when to join in,
the precise moment to lead on in an activity, and, just as
important, when to keep out of children's play. (You should
also explain your new ideas and the importance of 'play' to
parents who would prefer more structured programmes.)

So make sure your helpers understand fully what you are
aiming at. Give them every opportunity to ask questions and
discuss their worries with you and each other. Arrange for
them to visit another playgroup where the methods you are
suggesting are already working well. Then still don't rush
things. Have *another* discussion evening to report back on these
visits. How can these methods be adapted to our group? How
will particularly difficult children react to the change? How can
we be prepared for certain behaviour problems which may

increase with a new routine? When should we explain to the mother-helpers – a coffee morning perhaps?

You then need to decide on the practical steps of your changeover. The basic rule here is 'go slow'. If you don't hurry the change too much it can be quite painless, with everyone, adults and children alike, managing to keep pace. First of all, keep more or less to the original three-part programme, but gradually extend the first free-play time. Then leave out an increasing amount of general equipment during the latter part of the morning, until eventually so much is still out that only one table has a set activity on it. By this time you will be trying out your music and story activities at different times as the opportunity arises. You can also try different ways of having lunch. Don't be discouraged if you have one or two difficulties. You can learn a great deal from thinking them through later – why did it go wrong? How can I avoid that happening next time? Do my helpers understand what went wrong? Do they now understand how to put things right? If you have kept the changeover period gradual and consistent, things should be ticking over nicely in about four weeks though this is a very approximate time and depends a lot on how frequently your playgroup is in session.

You may eventually decide, even though the change was smooth and painless, that you and your staff prefer the old way. Well and good. But if you are going to revert to your original programme, follow the changeover procedure in reverse, slow but sure again being the basic rule. If you change things too suddenly, some of the children may become very worried and confused – and so indeed may your helpers. You may also find a compromise somewhere along the line between the two kinds of programme which you feel suits your particular playgroup very well.

Settling in a new child

Most children settle into playgroup quite happily, especially if the group is well established. Even so, starting playgroup is usually the first big separation from mother. If it goes smoothly a child is more likely to feel secure about future big steps such as starting school, going to stay away from home or generally meeting new people. So, since this may represent his first encounter with the 'outside world' it is important that this 'world' be warm and welcoming.

It is also important that mother is welcome there too; that she approves and is approved of. If she simply disappears after bundling her bewildered child into the arms of a strange lady who says 'Mummy's going shopping,' this will look like desertion. In all good playgroups, mothers are asked and *expected* to stay until their child is well and truly settled. When they come along to enter their child's name for the playgroup explain why you like mothers to remain with their children initially, then they will have a chance to organize themselves to be present at their child's first few sessions. Supervisors can also gain much information about new children by seeing them with their mother. They can assess the quality of the mother–child relationship and thus predict how the child may respond to playgroup. The mother will also be able to see for herself what kind of toys he has to play with, what activities he most enjoys, how he gets on with other children and whether he is the only child in the world who sucks his thumb when listening to a story. Supervisors should try to find time to give an occasional word of explanation and encouragement to a new mother – what is going on may look almost as strange to her as it does to her child. Another thing you can do is to organize a coffee morning towards the end of the holidays for all the children and mothers starting playgroup in the next new term. During this morning some of the equipment is put out for the children to play with and the mothers are able to ask questions and discuss details about their own child with playgroup staff; children also have an opportunity of meeting some of their future playmates. You may notice addresses which are near each other to point out for a time when the children will be ready to come along to playgroup with a friend's mother. Meanwhile, perhaps a lonely mother will strike up a friendship with a new-found neighbour and the children can play together at home. So you will be helping the child and his family *outside* the playgroup as well as inside.

If when term begins you find there are a lot of new children due to start, it is best to stagger the days these children come along so that there are not too many new ones all together. Ask new children to be brought along for a short session only for the first few times; half-an-hour may be quite enough for some children who find the stimulation of so many new toys and so many strange children and adults very tiring. These short sessions are usually best mid-morning when you are not engrossed with welcoming the other children, or in the hurly burly of clearing away. There is more time to talk and explain during the middle part of the morning. A new child may enjoy having lunch with the other children as a sort of 'weaning activity' away from home. Eating is, after all – unlike so many other things at a playgroup – something he is familiar with and *knows* he enjoys!

When the newcomers arrive, offer the mother a chair in a special place which is to be hers during the settling-in period. The child may immediately fix himself on her knee and refuse to move. All well and good: reassure her that this often happens and that he will join in with the others in good time. Point out an obviously happy and confident child who behaved in a similar way on first coming to playgroup. When she is secure in knowing that many children cling at first, she will not be so busily pushing him away to join the others – something which only lengthens the natural settling-in process.

Many children will soon take off on their own to join or watch an activity, but do ask the mother to wait in her special chair, no matter how engrossed her child appears because – if he decides to trot back for a cuddle or to tell her about what he has been doing he must know just where to find her. He is then much more likely to rejoin the group he has been playing with. Gradually, the return trips to mother will become less frequent until eventually she really does feel superfluous. Now is a good time for her to go.

At first she may just go into the kitchen for a cup of coffee.

But she must tell her child where she will be. Some playgroups have even encouraged mothers to bring their ironing so that they can do it in the kitchen at this time! Then you and the mother may feel the child is quite ready to cope without his mother there at all. If so she will just bid him a quick, cheery goodbye and off she goes. Providing he has not been pushed but allowed to settle at his own rate, there should be no trouble at all. However, take the precaution of keeping a special eye on a new child the first few times he is left just in case anything unexpected happens to upset him.

So much for the majority of children. But there are a few under-fives who take longer and need more help to bridge the gap between home and playgroup. It is more important than ever, with such children, that their mother stays and feels she is doing something worthwhile in staying. (Perhaps some knitting or mending she brings along would help to reinforce this feeling even though you have explained to her how important it is for her child.) If a child seems to be taking an unusually long time before he shows signs of wanting to join in, try bringing an activity *to him*. Often his mother will tell you that 'he loves doing jigsaws' or 'he's very good at crayoning'. Let the mother and child do this activity together in a playgroup situation. You can bring up a table to help them have a corner of their own and a place for the newcomer to shelter behind. It is a big step forward for this type of child to be doing *something* in the playgroup even though it is still with his mother. The next stage is for a helper to join in, perhaps just with interested comments at first, and later actually participating in the activity.

Try to arrange for one specific helper to be assigned to settling in a child. It is much easier for him to relate to the same person each day than to a new face. This is where family groups are so valuable (see p. 132). After a couple of sessions of playing with the child, your helper will be able to say 'Should we do it like we did yesterday, Sheila?' or 'Shall we build a bigger tower today, Peter?' This kind of continuity can be very comforting for a child whose whole world seems to be rapidly changing all around him. Once he has learned to trust and enjoy the helper's company, he may well go with her to join (or more likely at first, just to watch) another group of children. If he has been told that his mother is staying on her special chair until he gets back, he will be much readier to move.

The mother of a child like this may have to 'go in the kitchen' or 'go to post a letter' many more times than other mothers. A series of short absences, gradually getting longer will ease the process as gently as possible. But she should always tell her child that she is going and where she is going, having first made sure that the helper in charge of her offspring knows she is about to leave and is ready to be with the child. The day will no doubt come when this child just does not want to go home before all the other children. Then you can all stand back and feel very proud of your achievement.

We have already mentioned holding a special session just for new children and their mothers before term begins. As well as this, it is extremely helpful if mother and child can pop in two or three times for about ten minutes before the child starts attending regularly, to see a normal session. This helps a new child to get the feel of where he is going; some children have had little or no opportunity to mix with or see other children. The strange sight of playgroup needs time to settle in their minds. These sessions also help a mother to understand what is done and not done in playgroup, so that she feels less likely to drop a brick when talking with you.

When a mother brings along her child on these visits, it is a good idea to discuss with her the proposed starting day in relation to events at home. If, for example, a new baby is on the way, try to arrange things so that the playgroup beginner is well and truly settled before the baby arrives. It would be harmful for him to feel he is being pushed out to playgroup so that his mother can stay home and cuddle the new baby. Again, has the mother got a clear run in front of her, so that she is able to stay to every session until the settling-in period is well and truly over? She may be going into hospital in which case, again, the child must be settled *before* she goes. As a general rule, if a mother cannot stay an odd morning, then it is best if the child does not stay either. This may sound rather harsh, but by letting the child remain without her, and then finding he is upset, you may undo a lot of hard work which may take months to make up.

The next Monday

Often when a child has settled in well and is happy for his mother to leave we tend to focus our attention elsewhere. Of course, you cannot continue to give a child all the individual help he has had during the settling-in period. However, the week-end break, or perhaps a few days of absence because of illness, may mean that a child feels insecure again on the first day back. If this happens, it is best to start your usual settling-in process again. At the first signs of the child clinging to his mother, suggest that she stays. Reassure her that things will move much more quickly this time and her child will very soon be at his independent stage again. Remember that if he has been away because of illness, he may not yet be feeling entirely fit and this may also account for his clinging to his mother.

Tiredness

For most children, starting playgroup is a very exciting time. They are plunged into a new world full of new toys and new children and much more hustle and bustle than they have been used to at home. Consequently, many children become extremely tired after a full morning, especially until they are used to the new routine. They may then be very cross and difficult to manage at home in the afternoons.

A child may be also extra hungry when he gets home – another source of crossness. Perhaps he now has breakfast earlier than he used to, so that he can be out in time for playgroup; or he may not have time to finish his breakfast. Again, some children at home are constantly nibbling snacks which keep them more or less full. At playgroup they will not be doing this – they will be far too busy to think about nibbling all the time – so they may be very hungry by dinner time and mothers might arrange for meals to be ready a little earlier than before.

You might also suggest that the child would probably enjoy some extra cuddling during this period. It is a reassurance for him that his mother still loves him even though he is a big boy at playgroup now. Some mothers find that settling down together for 'Watch with Mother' is a very pleasant way to unwind after a morning's hard work and play. A child may even revert to a short nap after dinner although he had previously given this up. Alternatively, a mother may bring forward bedtime half-an-hour or so, especially if she has to wake up her child in the morning to be out in time for playgroup.

Using the lavatory

Do not forget to ask a mother what word her child uses when he needs to go to the lavatory. One supervisor who had failed to discuss this topic with a mother was perplexed for a long time by the new little boy who kept asking to 'drop bombs'! Can the child go to the lavatory unaided? It is usually best to let his mother take him along the first couple of times so that he learns from her first where it is, how to pull the chain, etc.

Some children have strange rituals regarding their toilet routine. Also it may be an area of tension for the child emotionally if mother has been rather strict about toilet-training (see pp. 49 and 53) so it is as well to ask all about it. Make sure he is not worrying about knowing the way, or that there is a dark corridor to go along, or that the lavatory seat is too high (portable steps help here). This kind of worry can make all the difference to a young child settling down well at playgroup.

Occasionally, a child who can normally cope with things himself may be wearing a particular garment which may cause him some bother; new stiff buttonholes perhaps, or tights. Ask a mother to let you know on the days her child is wearing such clothes so you can offer help when needed.

The best age to start playgroup

It is impossible to give hard and fast rules about this as it all depends on the stage of development the child has reached when mother brings him along. However, as a general rule, it is better not to take children into playgroups before they are three. Some local authorities will allow two-year-olds to attend, but we believe that most two-year-olds are not ready for regular three-hour separations from their mothers (see p. 59).

If, as sometimes happens, the Health Visitor or doctor suggests you accept a child and mother in great need, then let them come together for short periods. This way, the mother is getting a break from the problems at home, and the child is being weaned gradually so that when he is three, he will more than likely go to playgroup quite happily, and then mother will have her well-deserved break. Meanwhile perhaps the mother in her chats with you may gain some good ideas on ways to occupy her child at home so that he is not so difficult to manage there.

Essential information

It is very important for all concerned that supervisor and mother understand each other from the beginning. If you have had your explaining talk when the mother came to put her child's name down, then most things will have been cleared up naturally. This is a time to get your essential information from the mother and also to give her a wider knowledge of the playgroup. She needs to know what you mean when you say you prefer children to come 'suitably dressed', and why you do not encourage children to eat a bag of toffees for their lunch. If she has seen going-home time on a wet day, she will understand why you like the children to bring a clothes-peg to clip their wellingtons together.

The initial talk with mothers usually takes place when she comes to see if you have a vacancy. Remember, this is your first point of contact with a new parent, and if you are really convinced of the importance for both her and her child of their future involvement in your playgroup, then this first meeting may prove all-important. This is the first bridge between playgroup and home. You may be one of the few people she has come across who has ever shown any interest in her or her child. In such cases it is probably quite easy to make her feel at home once she is over her initial shyness. On the other hand, just *because* she is so unused to people caring about her and her problems, or perhaps because of a deeply ingrained attitude towards authority and education generally, she may appear suspicious of your friendliness and even aggressive towards you. So you may well have to exercise great tact and diplomacy in explaining your aims and attitudes, so that she is assured that any questions you ask stem from a genuine concern and not from wanting to pry.

Application forms

This is the simplest and most effective way of reminding mothers of what was discussed at your first meeting. A printed or duplicated sheet of this kind gives your playgroup the professional image which will ensure that parents maintain a healthy attitude to your aims and values. It should not, on the other hand, be intimidating in tone, so the wording is most important. Too many 'children are expected to ...' and 'parents must ...' are not a good idea. Different areas will respond to a different approach. The following example might act as a guide.

Highlands Pre-school Playgroup

6 Green Street, Anytown   Tel. 1234

Supervisor : Mrs Joan Smith

The playgroup is a self-supporting local venture. We are, however, a member of the Pre-School Playgroups Association and registered by the local council. The group is run in a church hall and garden, and is designed to provide three- to five-year-olds with a wide range of educational activities. There is no attempt at formal instruction, as we believe this is best started at primary school. We recognize the importance of play and hope to provide every opportunity for children to learn through play in a happy and relaxed atmosphere with companions of similar age.

Times of sessions:
9.15–12.00 on Monday, Wednesday, and Friday during school terms

The playgroup session will include:
free play, which includes painting, clay, and many forms of creative activities, sand and water play, bricks and constructional toys, puzzles and matching games, imaginative and family play, and a book corner. The session also includes music, rhymes, and stories. Weather permitting, there will be outside play.

Lunch
consisting of milk and a quarter apple is served at approximately 10.30.

Fees
are 25p per session, payable by the week in advance.* (There is normally no refund for absence of up to two weeks. Refunds may be claimed for sessions missed in the third and subsequent weeks.)

Clothing
Please send children to playgroup wearing practical play clothes, and bring wellingtons for the garden. Please mark clearly all outdoor clothes, particularly wellingtons; a clothes-peg is useful to clip wellingtons together.

Parents and the playgroup
Children thrive best when parents are actively interested in their education. Therefore, we encourage parents to take an active part in the running of the playgroup. Mothers are invited to offer an occasional morning each term to be with the children. Offers from fathers to mend toys are always welcome. Parents are always wel-

---

* In many areas it may be impossible to expect parents to pay a week in advance' although this does help to reduce your clerical work. The payment of fees is dependent upon how family income arrives, i.e. weekly pay-packet or monthly cheque. The application form needs to be adjusted accordingly.

1. A mother helps settle in her child

2. Making things

3. Making music

4. Painting

5. Enjoying a story in a family group

6. Learning to communicate

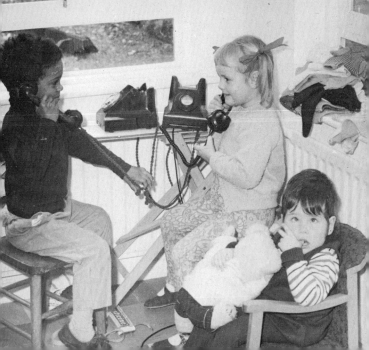

7. Learning to care for animals

8. Carpentry

9. A tea-party with a guinea pig

10. A teenager becoming familiar with the world of children

11. Balancing on a line of bricks

12. Logs and trees make a natural climbing frame

13. Happy to see each other and lots to talk about at the end of the morning

come to come to playgroup and discuss their children with the staff. Regular open mornings and evenings are held when we rely on parents joining us to make these a success.

Tear off here

APPLICATION FORM

Name of child: Date of birth:
Home address: Telephone no.:
Family doctor:
  tel. no.:

Mother's place of work during playgroup hours:
            tel. no.:
Father's place of work during playgroup hours:
            tel. no.:
Immunizations:
Has your child been immunized against tetanus?
Allergies, e.g. to plasters:
      milk:
Any physical abnormalities, e.g. fits:
      speech defects:

It is also useful to find out the following information to help you talk with the children, especially during their settling-in period: names and ages of brothers and sisters; other people living in his home, e.g. granny; special word or phrase for going to the lavatory. PPA has produced an illustrated leaflet for new mothers.

Different attitudes of mothers

How the mother feels is obviously of great importance at this early stage. Remembering how closely interrelated the child is with his mother, it is clear that we cannot settle in one without the other. No matter how happy a child's life is at playgroup, if he goes home and senses that his mother worries about what he is doing there, he will be thrown into conflict. Occasionally, for example, you may come across a mother who asks why the children are not learning to read and write, or why they are allowed to get their hands so messy at the clay table. These are perfectly natural inquiries. Most mothers will be satisfied by a careful explanation of children's play needs and by observing the child's satisfaction. If not, we feel it is a very risky situation for the child to continue coming to playgroup. Usually it is the mother who decides to take the child away, and if you feel you cannot influence her any more, you will have to harden your heart and say goodbye to that child. As a consolation, his place can be easily filled by another child whose parents appreciate all you are trying to achieve. Fortunately, this situation crops up very rarely.

The average mother, however, probably feels enthusiastic but nervous when first bringing her child to playgroup. She should have visited your group two or three times already and had her initial discussions with you, so it is certainly not a completely strange world she and her child are entering. However, she may still feel her child's reactions will 'tell tales' about her skills as a mother. If he does not say 'Please' and 'Thank you', what will you think of her? If he does not join in immediately, will he be thought withdrawn? If he cannot write his name with the crayons, will he be considered dull? No matter how good a mother she is, there is bound to be a certain amount of apprehension on her part and she will need reassuring on all counts.

Deep inside she may be full of sadness at this parting. If, like many mothers, she devotes most of her time and energies to her children, she is bound to feel a sense of loss. For this reason she may cling to her child longer than he needs, even to the point of inhibiting his settling in. An experienced supervisor will realize that this mother would probably be helped by becoming a mother-helper; a discussion with her on this possibility may help to dissolve some of her fears.

Most mothers are sensible enough to realize it is unwise to show their child that they are upset and so will put on a brave face, and when the time comes, bid their child a cheery 'goodbye' and leave straight away. But if you feel that the poor woman is going to worry herself sick until lunchtime in case her child is upset, why not offer to telephone her mid-morning just for a few reassuring words? If a telephone is not available (as is often the case) you could suggest that she comes to the side window in an hour's time for a pre-arranged signal which says everything is fine. It will make so much difference to her first few hours away from her child, and will be a very positive influence in her attitude towards you and your playgroup.

Sometimes, when the youngest child in a family begins playgroup, the mother is so familiar with the whole ritual – she has been through it perhaps two or three times before – that she may tend to be a little too breezy about the whole thing. She may need reminding that, although she is experienced in all this, her youngest child is not. It is still *his* very first day and he may need just as much time to settle as his elder brothers and sisters did; indeed, his pattern of settling in may be quite different from theirs.

Dumping children is something of which supervisors occasionally complain. A few mothers do use the playgroup as a 'dumping ground' for their children and take no interest in what they do there. This kind of mother presents problems; but if those running the playgroups are themselves convinced of the importance of the mother's wellbeing then that is half the battle. Any woman wants a break from her child – don't we all? It is terribly difficult to be a good mother twenty-four hours a day, three hundred and sixty-five days a year. The very reason that she is so fed up with her child at home may be that she's unable to keep him interested and happy. Perhaps she secretly longs to know ways to occupy him so that she does not always feel guilty at being inadequate. If in the course of conversation with her you can admit how your own children weary and drive you to distraction, she may warm towards you. Offer praise for any small thing her child can do. Make sure that she does not look upon the playgroup as a school – for many people the day they left school was probably the happiest day of their life! Let her see that parents are welcome in the playgroup; if she can make friends with other mothers, she may be more willing to become involved.

Home visiting is an idea worth trying with an uncooperative mother. A friendly chat about her child might persuade her that if you genuinely care about him, you just might care about *her* too. But do be most careful not to give the impression of prying into her private life. It is best not to call unless you have previously suggested a time to her. No one likes to be caught unawares and it certainly would not do much good for this particular relationship. If, however, in spite of all your efforts it is impossible to make headway you may have to be content to concentrate on helping the child.

Further reading

'Settling a child into a playgroup', Sutton and Thorne, PPA publication.

Discipline

In this section, we will be writing firstly about discipline, meaning the general order which should exist in a good playgroup and secondly, how you should treat an unruly child.

Every group, whether consisting of children or adults, needs to have rules. Some playgroup workers, told that children should have 'free play', interpret this as meaning that the children should be allowed to do as they please and are slow to enforce any sort of discipline. This is doing the children a grave disservice. Every child in a playgroup needs guidelines, rules, to tell him what he can or cannot do. Without these, he will take the law into his own hands and this will result in group chaos. We suggest that you have as few rules as possible, but that those you do decide to have are enforced by all the adults involved.

What rules do you have and why? Some are designed for a child's own safety. For instance, he mustn't go beyond a certain point which gives access to an outside door; or, he must not be allowed on a stage, because there are some props from a drama club's production stored there which he might pull over on himself. Wherever possible make out-of-bound places inaccessible to children, otherwise you will all waste a lot of energy checking that no child is where he shouldn't be. A row of chairs or a piece of garden netting on plastic coated hooks, across a corridor or across the steps to the stage, will create a psychological barrier as well as a minor physical one. Such a barrier may be a challenge to some children, however, and then something child-proof must be erected. If your stage is an Aladdin's Cave of forbidden delights, take three or four children up at a time, satisfy their curiosity by showing them around and then be quite adamant that they may not go up without you, but that you will take them again tomorrow. If the playgroup is providing them with a rich variety of play, the stage area, once their curiosity has been satisfied, will seem much less compelling. Some supervisors in house groups decide not to use the sitting-room as a play area; rather than wasting time and energy repeatedly shooing children out, put a latch on the door above the children's reach.

Other rules are designed to protect property. Obviously children cannot be allowed to hit windows with hammers, or submerge the dressing-up hats in the water tray. Unless a child is very disturbed, it is unlikely he will want to do either of these, especially if he is being provided with a wide variety of things to play with. If he can pummel a big lump of dough, bang large nails into wood and, above all, act out his hostility in the home corner, he will be much less likely to act aggressively towards other children.

It is essential that the discipline given is consistent. What may be considered exploratory play by one member of the staff may be intolerable to another. For instance, a new child, just starting to settle, may pour water into the dry sand tray. Do you stop him or allow him to find out for himself how much water needs to be added to dry sand before it is wet enough to hold its form? If someone puts the brush from the red pot into the blue pot to discover what happens when you paint with two brushes in one hand, do you stop him or not? These sorts of things need to be talked over at regular staff meetings so that a child isn't confused by being allowed to do something one day, and scolded for exactly the same thing on the next. It seems to us that once a child is settled, he should be allowed to play in an exploratory way as long as he is not damaging property or being over-wasteful of material. Regretfully we must sometimes limit play. For instance, children often want to carry sand into the home corner for make-believe meals, and although one sympathizes with this most supervisors would consider it too messy and wasteful of sand. If you feel this way, don't expect the child to accept your decision arbitrarily, explain why sand must be conserved. Children are more reasonable than we think. At the same time make sure that there are plenty of materials for make-believe play in the home corner – haricot beans, conkers, dough (see p. 267).

Disruptive children

Discipline is also very much concerned with how children behave towards each other. If a child is hurting another child, or being wantonly destructive, it is useful to crouch down so that your faces are level, holding his hands and making sure he looks at you, telling him firmly, 'You mustn't do that,' and insist that he stops – you may need to remove him from 'the scene of the crime'. Then, still holding him by the hand, try to interest him in some other activity. Usually the most disruptive child responds to this treatment if it is repeated by the same adult each time; if he does not, and you feel that his behaviour is beyond the bounds of normality, it may be that you should consult your Health Visitor, who may suggest that the child needs treatment at the Child and Family Guidance Clinic.

The behaviour of an individual child must not be allowed to disrupt the life of the group. If, for instance, a group of children are listening to an adult telling a story or singing a song, the child who doesn't want to join in should play in such a way that he doesn't disrupt them. A child who persists in battering his tricycle into the back of someone's chair should be told firmly that he can't do that, removed from his trike and taken into another room or to a far part of the hall. Explain that you know he doesn't want to listen, but the others do, and that you have something that you think he will want to do. You then produce a special toy, say, a musical box, or look at a book with him or perhaps suggest you both sit down and play with the clay.

Do you think this is rewarding a child for his naughtiness? Would you have preferred to sit him in a 'quiet chair' doing nothing for several minutes? But isn't this a negative form of discipline? A disruptive child is usually asking for attention, and whilst most of the group is happily occupied, this is a chance to give him some individual attention, and thus improve your relationship with him. One writer has said that to deny an aggressive child attention is like denying medicine to a child with a cough. Try to see yourself as creating a therapeutic community, not a repressive one.

Let us consider the word 'naughty'. A child's behaviour is dictated by his needs, and the more we try to answer his needs the less 'naughty' he will be. For instance, a child needs to explore the properties of water. If a legitimate opportunity to do this is denied him, he may stamp through puddles in his new sandals or bail out the lavatory with his shoes. Most adults would call this behaviour 'naughty'; the child, if he could express himself in these terms, would say he was answering his need to understand the nature of water.

Similarly a child needs to be noticed, to be given individual attention within the group. If you tip all the beads out of their container, an adult will at least notice you enough to scold you. In a good playgroup, adults will be giving the children individual attention without the child needing to ask for it. This is more likely to happen if each adult is responsible for a small group of children, with whom she can build up a relationship, (see p. 132). In fact 'relationship' is the key word to remember when discussing discipline. A child wants to please an adult he knows and likes, and prefers not to attract their displeasure. Conversely, he will be little affected if some adult with whom he is not personally involved is cross. It is the same with adults; we value the good opinion of our friends, but in the main disregard the comments of strangers.

It can be very hurtful for a child to be placed outside a loved person's approval. If a child does behave badly, and you show your displeasure, this must be for a short period only. Try to think and act positively; replace 'You mustn't do that', with 'You can't do that because ... but come and try this'. Always make your point clearly and firmly but briefly and then lead the child on to something else.

A four-year-old, Debra, greeted a new helper by thumbing her nose and poking out her tongue. The helper ignored this behaviour, but said, as if to herself, 'My next job is to mix the paints and I shall need a helper.' Within seconds, this child was at her elbow, and was allowing the supervisor to put on a protective apron, and most cooperatively stayed to mix the paint and polycell. A series of such incidents over the next few days built up a relationship between the child and adult, and the rude behaviour disappeared. When Debra began the same face-making at the next new helper, a look and a head shake from the first helper were enough to let her know that this was unacceptable and she stopped at once.

Sometimes you get a gang of older children, often boys, who play in such a way that the rest of the groups' activities are spoilt. If at all possible, get such children into an outside play space; play which is quite unacceptable inside will pass unnoticed outside. We watched two five-year-old boys pivoting a plank on a box, and then, with one boy each end, they ran around until, with a great clatter, it fell off. It was in a small hall and the other children were terrified of coming into range of this orbiting plank, so the supervisor had to stop the game. The boys weren't being naughty, they were exercising a good deal of skill. But it was noisy and too dangerous for indoors. Once outside, they could play the same game to their hearts content without upsetting any other children. If you have no outside play space, draw a chalk line across a big space in which you provide the sort of equipment children may use for vigorous play, and keep all other activities in the rest of the hall. Whenever possible take an energetic group out to a park.

Troublesomeness from a group of older children may also come from boredom. If they came to playgroup at three, and are being offered the same sort of activities eighteen months later, then of course they are bored, and the only way they can relieve their boredom is by making a nuisance of themselves.

Sometimes the personalities of two children will clash. The best thing here is to ensure that they play in different parts of the hall; and if you have family groups, that they 'belong' to different adults. Also try to predict where trouble will arise and plan your programme and the layout of equipment in such a way as to avoid it. For instance, you may be used to having one big circle for a group time, and find that it is then that children hit or pinch each other. Try having smaller groups, no more than eight or ten. This means that the children are closer, both physically and mentally, to a controlling adult, and because organizing the group is a much quicker affair, they are less likely to be sitting with nothing to do except play or fight with each other.

Sometimes a favourite toy will cause fights and the adult has to act in a disciplinary way, ensuring that each child has a fair share of it. We know of one group that had a huge engine donated to it, which started so many rows that the helpers banned it from the playgroup – until other equally attractive wheeled toys were bought. Three-year-olds find it very difficult to accept turn-taking; most four-year-olds won't fight over a toy if they know they can have a share of it later. A kitchen-timer can be useful here, children seem to accept the impersonal decision of the ringing bell without argument (we find it invaluable for enforcing bedtimes at home).

Should you ever smack a naughty child? We think not. A child who is lashing out in a temper tantrum should be picked up and held firmly, removed to the side of the room, and contained until he is quieter. Your facial expression is important, remember that the other children and helpers are watching you to see how you deal with an upsetting incident. It requires a good deal of control to remain calm if your own leg has been bitten or kicked, but if you can, both the aggressive child and those who are watching will be greatly helped.

Biting can cause particular distress amongst helpers and children, perhaps because it seems such a primitive act that we ourselves feel threatened by it. Never, never bite back – some people do! If it is right for the adult to do it, why was it wrong for the child? Probably the best way to deal with this situation is to have one adult soothe the frightened child who was bitten, and another to take the biting child who also may be frightened by the intensity of his feelings. Hold him, talk to him, and thereafter make certain that some concerned helper keeps an eye on him. Ask yourself why he needs to regress to such an infantile level. Is he under too much pressure at home, for instance, by parents who expect too high a standard of behaviour? Is there tension because of the arrival of a new baby? Is the child confused because of the break-up of a marriage? Without being too 'nosey' try to find out the child's home background so that you can anticipate problems and give him extra attention.

To sum up

1. Have as few rules as possible, but ensure that all adults concerned know them and enforce them.
2. Remember that the more you answer the play needs of your children, the more acceptable their behaviour will be.
3. The better the relationships within the group, the easier discipline becomes.
4. If the general atmosphere of the group is calm and orderly then so will be the children's behaviour.

How noisy is noisy?

Whenever a group of people – adults or children – are gathered together for any kind of social activity, there is bound to be some noise. We live in an increasingly noisy world – whirring machines in the kitchen, constant radio and television, road and aircraft traffic. There comes a point when both adults and children suffer from living in too noisy an atmosphere – adults may complain of a headache, a child may become timid or withdrawn, refusing to go back to a noisy group. We are well advised therefore to encourage children to speak and act quietly, and cut down on unnecessary uproar.

Some adults equate noise with naughtiness, a left-over from Victorian times when children were 'to be seen and not heard'.

Perhaps as a swing away from this, other people now equate noise with enjoyment; a supervisor will say with pride when giving directions on how to find her playgroup; 'Don't worry, when you are *that* close you will soon hear us!' If it is suggested that a group is noisy, the supervisor may say, 'Noise never worries me,' as if this was a testament to the strength of her nerves, and proof of her dedication to the principle that for children to enjoy themselves they must be noisy.

Other supervisors blame the conditions under which they work for their high noise level, either the ceiling is too high or too low. However, we once visited a group with a time lag of a term between the first and second visit. On the first visit, the noise was unbearable; as one little girl put it 'you can't do any thinking at playgroup'. On the second there was a different supervisor, many more activities had been introduced and the noise level had been greatly reduced. So it would be silly to blame the high level of noise entirely on the hall conditions, other factors have to be considered. How can we help children to play happily, actively, busily, satisfyingly and thus not noisily ?

First of all there are some practical steps you can take to reduce noise. Some activities, such as woodwork, inevitably cause a row; you cannot hammer softly. Indeed it is very satisfying to make a big bang as hammer and nails make contact. If possible, therefore have your woodwork, under supervision, away from the main play area. There might be a cloakroom, or cubby hole where this can be put. Whenever possible put it outside. If you have only one room, put it in a corner and possibly restrict its use to one part of the programme. Carpets are a good way of muffling noise, so try to collect some for different activities. A collapsing tower of bricks can make a thunderous noise, but is dampened if they fall on a carpet. Obviously the larger the carpet the more noise will be reduced, but remember they are heavy to put away.

Outdoor shoes can be deafening on wooden boards. The ideal combination is sandals and wellingtons. Wellingtons for going outside on damp days, and sandals because they are quiet on wooden floors (slippers sometimes slide). Suggest this sort of footwear on your first meeting with the mother, and on your admission form (see p. 175). Mothers may not know that summer sandals often last longer if the toe is removed, when they make ideal indoor shoes. Make sure they are wide enough over the top.

Figure 2

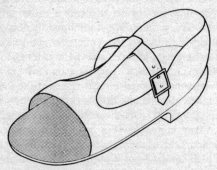

shaded part cut out, far enough back to
give foot sufficient width

People often fail to oil playgroup equipment, and put up with a squeaking trike or pram wheel. Make a point of going round once a month oiling all wheels and joints – not too lavishly, and wipe off any surplus. Children love to help with this.

Cover the ends of seesaws with rubber carpet underlay and tack pieces on to the ends of trucks. This also helps to protect woodwork, and is especially helpful in a home playgroup where there is less room for manoeuvring and paint work can get damaged. If your tables and chairs are moved about by the children a good deal, tip the legs with felt or rubber.

Apart from these practical steps how can we help children to play reasonably quietly? Children who have been living without outside play areas sometimes react to the large space of a hall and the company of other children with over-boisterous play, shouting and shrieking. Some supervisors may permit them to do this to compensate for their cramped living conditions, but is it really a service to allow them to 'go mad'? Certainly they need to be introduced to the joys of rumbustious physical play, and as much as possible in the fresh air. If your playgroup has nowhere to play outside make sure to visit a recreation ground.

Sometimes you get a child from a home where everybody shouts instead of speaking. Sometimes a child shouts out of devilment, as a way of attracting attention to himself. It's no use crushing him for this – he may respond to one person getting to know him, probably the most skilled adult would be best. Be firm with him and show him that some noises you will not tolerate. Encourage him to play with basic materials, which have a soothing effect (especially wet clay, which he can use in an aggressive way) or with noisy playthings – the woodwork tools, the drums, a game of football, where the noise he makes is legitimate. Other children from flats who are used to a quiet atmosphere find the noise of a group frightening. They have been trained not to disturb the neighbours and will need a variety of play experiences, together with the building up of a warm relationship with an adult, before they can allow themselves to make a really loud noise. They can be encouraged to make a loud noise, in a *controlled* way, at group times – making giant steps in music and movement, or loud claps and jumps to synchronize with the 'pop' of ' "Pop" – goes the weasel', and many other rhymes and finger plays.

If your group as a whole is too noisy ask yourself whether you are offering enough activities? Bored children become noisy. When did you last introduce a new activity? Write down everything you give your children to do, and compare it with Chapter 10.

The voices of the playgroup staff are important. Children copy the pitch of an adult's voice; if you whisper to a child, the chances are he will whisper back. A playgroup supervisor who is often having to raise her voice as an instrument of discipline, and make herself heard across a hall with 'Stop that ...', 'Don't do that ...', 'You mustn't do ...', is herself contributing to noise in no small order. If this is a situation you recognize, then look at your group and see how it can be improved. How are you using your helpers? Is each one supervising a small group in some activity? Having helpers in different parts of the playgroup means that there is always some adult regulating the noise level in that area, so there is no need for an adult to bellow across to control some child. You may notice that when your supervisor withdraws from the group to talk to a visitor the level of noise rises. This is because, although she may be physically present, her influence is withdrawn, and in some subtle way the children sense this and react accordingly.

A book can only give guidelines for each playgroup supervisor to answer the question of noise. Busy children in a group will produce a busy noise, boisterous play will produce a more robust sound. If you have an opportunity, ask the Infant Adviser of your local education department if she can recommend a good nursery school or class you can visit, or ask the local area organizer of the Pre-School Playgroup Association if she knows a good playgroup to visit. Then you can compare your own group with others of acceptable noise levels. If after such a visit you think your playgroup is too noisy, start a campaign to train both the adults and children in your group to be quieter; praise them when they close doors softly and handle equipment with care.

High days, holidays and religion

Make sure that your celebrations are geared to the needs of the children, not the adults, in the playgroup. Under-fives are still at the stage of finding out, at their own rate, the possibilities of all the activities you provide. Only later, when they are mature enough to work in groups and also skilled enough with the materials, should creative work in groups be embarked upon. Complicated friezes, wall pictures, and many other types of formalized handicrafts belong to the Infant Schools and beyond. If you enjoy making this kind of thing, why not do it at home and bring it along to show the children? They will be delighted.

Christmas

There is usually enough pre-Christmas hysteria outside the playgroup and the children will welcome the stability of the usual routine continuing at playgroup. However, because Christmas is so special, you may feel, despite the advice at the beginning of this section, that it would be nice for a very small group of rising-fives – perhaps three or four children – to make a wall decoration or some paper chains. Throughout this activity keep checking who is getting most out of it and who is doing most work. If you have begun with some pre-conceived idea of what to make, it is inevitable that one of two things will happen. Either you will over-direct the children, forcing them to make what you want, or else you will be tempted to make most of it yourself. Either way, the children will gain little from the whole project. Decide on something to make which can be completed in one, or at the most two, sessions, and resist the temptation to begin too early. The children are concerned with immediate results and will be very disappointed if their work is put away for a month until Christmas.

You may like the children to take home a present for their parents at Christmas. If so, make it something very simple, which can be completed in one session, preferably on the last day of term. A suitable present might be a very simple card or calendar, or a bulb the child has planted and looked after himself (see p. 329).

Many parents spend a great deal of money on toys for their children at Christmas. And often, because they have nowhere to look for guidance on the choice of toys, their hard-earned money and good intentions are wasted. Supervisors can help a great deal here.

We strongly advise against all forms of Christmas concerts and plays performed by the children. The amount of rehearsing, the great deal of extra work for the staff, and the strains and anxieties for the children are just not worth it. We heard of one playgroup child having nightmares because he could not remember his lines in the Nativity play. There is also a danger of an unpleasant element of competitiveness creeping in among mothers. Instead of the playgroup being a uniting force in the community, tension is created between 'Joseph's' mother and the mother of a mere 'angel'! As far as the children are concerned, they merely understand that Joseph follows 'Mary' (who is really Jane), who carries a doll and then stands still while 'the others' come with stuffed toys and pile them by the doll's cot!

If you must have some kind of show, hire a Punch and Judy man or a conjuror who is used to under-fives. Invite mothers to come along and watch with their children on their knee ready to protect any child who is frightened. Similarly, if you have arranged for a playgroup father or the caretaker to be Father Christmas at the party, be on the lookout for the child who may be terrified by this strange figure, who, like puppets, does not fit into any familiar category of experience. Prepare the children for Father Christmas's visit by talking about him beforehand. Describe his appearance and emphasize what a good, kind man he is. Let the children know what he will do when he visits the playgroup.

Christmas parties will involve staff in a great deal of extra work, which barely equals what the children gain from two solid hours of eating carbohydrates. However, in some areas, a Christmas party can be the turning point in the upward struggle for a playgroup to become accepted as a real and important part of the community. If you feel pressure for a party from mothers, particularly from those who previously have shown little interest in the playgroup, arrange a meeting at the end of November. Ask for volunteers to form a committee to organize the party. It makes for better liaison if the supervisor is included on this committee. Refrain from using the word 'committee' though, if you feel it will frighten people away. Mothers who have been diffident about becoming involved in the playgroup may welcome an opportunity to join in doing something simple and familiar such as making jellies. After Christmas you will be able to build on the new goodwill created by the party.

Easter

All that we have said regarding Christmas festivities applies again here. If you feel it is really worthwhile for the children to make something to take home, keep it very simple and make it as near to Easter-time as possible.

Birthdays

Again, birthday celebrations should be short and simple. Keep a list of birthdays so that you know whose birthday is coming up next. A birthday is very exciting for the birthday child but not for the other children. Under-fives are not mature enough to share some one else's celebration. We remember one of our own children who was born in April, coming home from playgroup in November and crying because 'all the children sang "Happy Birthday" to Mark and I want it to be my birthday *now*.' If you have family grouping and only the birthday child's 'family' sings to him, there is less chance of other children being jealous and the birthday child gains just as much. The mid-morning lunch time is often a good moment to sing 'Happy Birthday' and to give the appropriate number of claps.

Outings

You may like to establish your own regular annual playgroup outing for parents and children. A coach trip to the seaside or a pantomime, for instance, will create a tremendous amount of goodwill towards the playgroup and give overworked mothers a relaxing day out. The section on Visits, p. 290, gives suggestions and guidelines for organizing your trip.

Religion

Religion is an intensely personal matter whatever your beliefs, and because of this, some supervisors get rather carried away by their own feelings on the subject. The aim of this section is to take a balanced look at religious education in playgroups.

First of all make sure that you are not imposing your views dogmatically as if your religion is the only one or the best. Respect the views of minority groups – an increasing number of playgroups are becoming multi-racial.

If you feel, because of your own beliefs, that in some way you must introduce formal religious practices into your play-group, it is only courteous to discuss the matter first with your helpers and the children's parents. For a large playgroup the subject will have to be brought up at a parents' evening. In a home playgroup you can probably discuss the matter less formally with parents individually. It will make for poor home–playgroup relations, as well as serious conflicts in the child's mind, if the playgroup gives him ideas which differ from those he hears at home.

Avoid having a specific time for religion in your playgroup, or using a special tone of voice or facial expression. If you do any of these things, the implication is that religion is some-thing special and separate from ordinary life. Far better to help a child to adjust to and understand his environment so that he sees religious practice as a normal element in the real world.

Your choice of stories should be dictated by the usual rules (see p. 307). If you want to tell the Christmas story, give it in a very simple version; never tell the Easter story in a play-group, and if you are in a church hall resist the temptation to use evidence which may be left around of various religious festivals. For example, you may arrive at playgroup one morn-ing to find the palms left from Palm Sunday. It is better to put such things away before the children arrive rather than risk creating confusion in the children's minds by telling stories beyond their understanding. Similar care needs to be taken with the pictures you show to the children. Many adults find it difficult to change the images presented to them in their early years and still see Bible characters looking like chocolate-box figures, unrelated to anything else in their experience. Above all, let the children enjoy what they do with you and it will have a greater impact. It is useless trying to use stories to impart abstract moral principles to children of this age group

- they are too young for abstract ideas and interpret things much more literally.

If your own convictions make it imperative for you to pray with the children remember that the whole idea of prayer is far too complex for under-fives. But there are a few prayers and hymns which can be made meaningful for this age group. Parroting the same few lines each day before drinking milk is hardly conducive to faith.

It is often best to make up your own prayers to suit the occasions. For example, if a child has brought his pet tortoise to playgroup, you might like to say, 'Thank you God, for giving us small animals and please help us to look after them.' Change the subject of your prayer each day to avoid any stereotyped rituals developing. Young children cannot be expected to close their eyes when being asked to pray: it is a meaningless gesture, unrelated in the child's mind with anything except going to sleep. We have seen far too many playgroups where 'Hands together! Eyes closed!' only serves as a means of getting the children's attention – not necessarily anything to do with religious feelings. There can be something frighteningly unpleasant to a small child about adults sitting in judgement with their eyes open, checking that all the children have theirs closed.

No matter how deep and sincere your own religious views, you *must* think them through very carefully and examine your motives for wanting to introduce them into playgroup life. Because of their openness to new ideas, it is tempting to try to pour adult standards of behaviour and moral concepts into children. Question your right to impose your views on the children, for they will try hard to grasp everything told them by adults they admire.

Churches

If your playgroup is run in a church hall you may feel a responsibility to the children to have some specific religious education in the playgroup. Many church hall committees show an admirable awareness of the needs of the under-fives when they open their doors and offer practical help and support to playgroups.

But there are still many people who are shocked at church buildings being used for secular activities and may even see the playgroup as a means of recruitment to the church. If you feel pressure is being put on you by such people, you must try to help them to see the playgroup as a service to the community, and any rewards for this (if rewards are needed) are to be gained from the involvement of any church members in the running of the playgroup. A playgroup where fathers help make and mend equipment, the youth club digs out a sand-pit, and the mothers work with the children must surely provide opportunities for practising the values of true Christianity for those who have chosen that faith. But this is very different from imposing it on young children who have no choice in the matter.

But whatever you do and whatever your religious convictions, the fact remains that children grow up gradually forming their own judgements about right and wrong, gained from their own experiences of the way people react to the children themselves and to each other. We can only learn to love others by being loved ourselves. It takes far more than religious preaching to help a rejected child grow up warm and tolerant of other human beings. Gentleness and affection on the part of adults in a happy playgroup, where children are learning to share, give and take, and forego some of their self-centred activities for the common good, probably have a much greater influence on the child's moral development than a strong diet of prayers taught by rote or stories which concern abstract ideas.

9
Health and Welfare

General health and hygiene

Washing and lavatory facilities

These may not be ideal, despite the stringencies of Ministry regulations. Some playgroups are fortunate in having a conscientious caretaker who regularly disinfects lavatories and cleans washbasins. However, many more find it necessary to clean the lavatories before the morning session begins. Existing hand-washing facilities may have to be supplemented with bowls of clean warm water placed at child height. If you provide individual hand-towels, make sure they are changed frequently. Paper towels are more hygienic as they can be thrown away after use, so preventing cross-infections. The children must learn from the start to wash their hands after going to the lavatory; all the helpers will probably have to be extremely vigilant to make sure they do. Explain to the children the reasons for this ruling and long-term habits of hygiene are more likely to be established. The task is easier when there is no set toilet-time and children are free to go to the lavatory individually when the need arises, as they do at home. Some playgroups insist on handwashing before the mid-morning snack. Unless a child's hands are particularly dirty, we feel that this is unnecessary and, for the majority, time-wasting regimentation.

Heating and ventilation

This often presents serious problems in old, draughty halls which are often difficult to maintain at the statutory temperature of 58°F. A cold child is not a happy child and if there are persistent problems in heating premises adequately, ensure that all the mothers understand and send children suitably clothed. In some areas, it may be necessary to keep a box of passed-down sweaters and cardigans for children whose parents are unable to provide enough warm clothing. This is particularly important in playgroups where children play outside regularly. Helpers should wear warm clothing too. Sometimes, far from being inadequately heated, halls may swelter under a sub-tropical fug! This can be just as unhealthy as a cold, draughty one. It is easy to forget to open windows during the busy morning session and a gradual build-up of heat occurs. The straightforward solution is to make window-opening the responsibility of one particular adult, say half an hour after playgroup starts.

Wet clothes

Some playgroups provide drying facilities for wet hats and coats, but the vast majority have to make do with putting clothes on hangers to help a little surplus moisture dry off. Children should not spend all morning in wet shoes and socks; mothers should be asked to supply indoor shoes. If the group is in an area where this request will cause embarrassment, a few spare pairs of slippers or sandals will have to be provided. A look-out must then be kept for children with foot infections such as a verruca.

Chest X-rays

All regular playgroup staff should have regular chest X-rays as part of the satisfactory health record which they must supply. This may be a source of irritation to some staff, but like other health regulations they are only intended to protect the children – it is surely reasonable that adults in daily contact with small children should be known to be free from TB. (All teachers in State schools have to be X-rayed.) Difficulties do however arise in those areas where Health Departments insist that even mothers who help perhaps only once a term on a rota basis should also be X-rayed. It seems to us unrealistic and unnecessary to enforce such a regulation; we do not ask our next-door neighbour to be X-rayed before leaving our child at her house for an odd morning. In areas where Mobile Mass X-ray Units are being closed down, a mother may have to travel miles, perhaps dragging a toddler along, to her nearest X-ray Unit – and all so that she is legally able to help in a playgroup for approximately three hours! More enlightened authorities are waiving this regulation for mother-helpers; if your area insists on going by the book, badger the department concerned (with the backing of your PPA area organizer and branch) to reconsider the rule in a more realistic light.

Accidents and emergencies

Fire prevention

including regulations and drill for the playgroup, should be understood by the supervisor and all her helpers. The Fire Officer who initially inspects your premises will advise on the best means of prevention and drill for your accommodation (see p. 121). Make sure all adults know where the fire extinguishers are and how to use them; a plan showing their whereabouts should be pinned up inside a storage cupboard. Fire drill should be practised at least once a term – more often if there are different helpers on different days. A bell or alarm must be kept specifically for this purpose. The children must learn to go outside immediately through the recommended door and to wait together outside to be counted. The supervisor should take with her the register to make sure everyone is outside, but pause for nothing else. Someone must have responsibility for checking that no child is left in the lavatories or any other room.

Accident prevention

requires commonsense and an awareness that children in their first five years are highly vulnerable. We strongly recommend buying 'Accident Prevention and First Aid in Playgroups' published by the PPA. This small, useful pamphlet should be hung up inside your cupboard so that it can be referred to immediately, should an emergency arise. Calm, sensitive and adequate supervision is the best way of keeping a playgroup accident free. The layout of equipment should be planned with the children's safety in mind: certain activities such as woodwork, or cutting, will need an adult constantly on the look-out for potential trouble. Broken toys, trailing electric wires, unsuitable heating equipment and glass containers should all be locked away – a high place is merely a challenge. Do not allow the children to play games involving banging doors: many a nasty trapped finger has resulted. Coat-pegs and table-corners at child height are also at eye height, so watch for tussles near these. Delegate to someone the responsibility for regular checks on climbing equipment. Train the children to give a wide berth, in front and behind, to swings. Check that the outdoor space contains no poisonous berries. The local Health Department can supply posters to display where mothers can see them.

First aid

should be a familiar routine in every playgroup and at least one person on the staff should attend a First Aid Course. The British Red Cross Society, 9 Grosvenor Crescent, London SW1 or The St John's Ambulance Association, 1 Grosvenor Crescent, London SW1 each provide courses; their headquarters should be able to suggest suitable courses in most areas. If the helpers change each day, it may be necessary for more than one person to attend the course.

Every playgroup needs a First Aid Box, always kept in the same place, which must be easily accessible and known to all the adults. Someone must be responsible for regularly checking and replenishing the contents. A large biscuit tin with a well-fitting lid, or an airtight food-container is suitable. Providing your own contents is often cheaper and more useful than buying a ready-made kit. Keep one specially for your playgroup if you share the premises with other organizations.

First aid box – suggested contents

1 pair sharp scissors
1 pair tweezers
  cotton wool (several small packets are more hygienic than
    one large)
  paper tissues (ditto)
12 sterilized swabs for cleaning wounds
1 bottle of Savlon detergent cleanser to be used diluted for
    washing wounds (for those who are not happy with just
    running water)
  safety pins, assorted sizes
1 tube of antiseptic cream to soothe small burns, stings,
    grazes
1 packet of adhesive plaster plain dressings to be cut to size
    for small cuts and grazes
  sterilized Vaseline net dressings, individually wrapped, 5 at
    2″ × 2″, 5 at 3″ × 3″
2 eye bandages
  conforming roller bandages: 2 of each width – 1″, 2″ and
    3″; a 2″ crepe bandage for sprains
2 triangular bandages (head scarves can be used instead), for
    slings, holding dressings in place, binding broken bones
1 packet bicarbonate of soda for stings or burns
1 packet salt
  teaspoon
  a tin of small sweets, one of which, combined with a cuddle,
    is often sufficient to soothe minor bumps and grazes
  notebook and pencil with which to keep a record of injuries
    and illnesses

The telephone number of the nearest doctor and hospital
should be prominently displayed by the first-aid box.
  As we said above, provide yourself and your helpers with a
copy of 'Accident Prevention and First Aid in Playgroups'
from which many points in this section are taken – you
will find in there treatments to cover most contingencies.
Be sure someone present can cope with the most frequent: sand

in the eyes, trapped fingers, stings, burns and scalds, foreign bodies in nose or ear, head injuries, fractures and sprains, nose-bleeds, poisoning, puncture wounds, deep cuts and splinters.

Emergencies

of a minor kind may not be unusual – such as a sick child who would be better at home. Don't worry if you cannot tell what exactly is wrong: you are not expected to make a diagnosis. It is sufficient to be aware that a child is not his normal self and to channel help his way. For a young child no medicine in the world does as much good as the comfort and reassurance of 'my mummy'. Whoever telephones or fetches the mother must approach her calmly and offer as much reassurance as possible. A mother with no home telephone may ask that the doctor be contacted for her. Some supervisors manage to make an arrangement with a GP near the playgroup for him to come in an emergency.

Occasionally a real emergency may arise and a child has to be rushed to hospital. If the supervisor and helpers have a pre-arranged plan for what to do on such occasions, there is more chance that someone will be free to cope with the intense fear (as well as physical discomfort) that the child may experience. It is, of course, vital to contact the child's mother immediately. Not only will her arrival reassure the child, but her consent (or that of the father or guardian) will be necessary before blood transfusions or stitches, etc., may be given. If neither parent nor guardian is obtainable, a message should be left for the mother stating which hospital the child has been taken to and asking her to go there. Supervisors working on their own in a home-based playgroup should know where their nearest help is: which neighbours are likely to be in during the mornings the playgroup is in session and which of them, if any, has a telephone. If the child is taken to hospital by private car some-one at playgroup should phone the Casualty Department to warn them that he is on his way. If an ambulance is sent for the driver will contact the hospital. One person whom the child knows should accompany him and take a note on which are the following:

1. Child's full name, address and telephone number.
2. Name, address and telephone number of place of work of mother or father.
3. Name of child's family doctor.
4. Whether or not the child has had tetanus injection.

Do try not to simply turn the child over to the hospital staff. No matter how kind and considerate they are, the only face familiar to the child will be that of the playgroup staff member with him. Her task is not completed even when a parent arrives: the mother will probably need someone to comfort her and to answer her questions on how the accident happened. The hospital doctor too will need essential information which the mother may be too upset to provide. See *New Safety and First Aid* by Ward Gardner (Pan Original, 30p) for further reading.

Infectious diseases

Infectious diseases can spread very quickly among groups of small children and it is therefore essential that commonsense habits of hygiene are established and maintained in your playgroup. All mothers should be encouraged to have their children inoculated and vaccinated, though this cannot be enforced. A child should not be excluded on account of this, provided he has an otherwise satisfactory health record; it is, however, essential to know if he has had an anti-tetanus injection in case of accident. Mothers should always be told when a playgroup child has an infectious disease; they can then keep their own child away from playgroup if they wish or at least be on the look-out for symptoms. All pregnant mothers and women who suspect they may be pregnant should contact their GP immediately if there is a case of German measles at playgroup.

Most mothers have their own instinctive way of knowing when their child is not well or 'sickening for something'. A supervisor familiar with her playgroup children will also sense

Common infectious diseases of childhood

Disease	Usual incubation period (days)	Interval between onset and appearance of rash (days)	Period of exclusion from playgroup	
			Patients	Contact, i.e. the other members of the family or household living together as a family
Measles	10–15	3–4	10 days after the appearance of the rash if child appears well	Children under 5 should be excluded for 14 days from the date of appearance of the rash in the last case in the household. Any contact suffering from a cough or red eyes should be immediately excluded. A child who is known with certainty to have had the disease need not be excluded.
German measles	14–21	0–2	7 days from the appearance of the rash	None
Chicken pox	11–12	0–2	14 days from the date of appearance of the rash	7 days

Disease	Usual incubation period (days)	Interval between onset and appearance of rash (days)	Period of exclusion from playgroup	
			Patients	Contact, i.e. the other members of the family or household living together as a family
Whooping cough	7–10	—	28 days from the beginning of the characteristic cough	Children under 7 should be excluded for 21 days from the date of onset of the disease in the last case in the house. A child who is known with certainty to have had the disease need not be excluded.
Mumps	12–28	—	7 days from the subsidence of all swelling	None
Scarlet fever	2–5	—	14 days or until nose and throat swabs taken by doctor are negative	7 days

(Based on list issued by Ministries of Education and Health, June 1956.)

something amiss when a normally happy child cries a lot, or a sociable child is unusually solitary and inactive. She may even be able to pick out a potentially sick child when she greets all the children as they arrive at playgroup. A sick child should be wrapped in a clean, warm blanket and either cradled in a sympathetic lap or laid on a bed either in an ante-room or away from the other children in a warm, well-ventilated place, until his mother arrives. *Never* leave him on his own.

Skin diseases

are usually highly infectious, especially impetigo and scabies. Children suffering from either must be excluded from playgroup until cured. The Health Visitor's advice should be asked about letting children with eczema on their hands play in sand and water – unfortunately this kind of play, while emotionally valuable for such children, may increase their discomfort.

Coughs and colds

will be almost constant in the winter months. A box of paper tissues is essential. Train the children to put used tissues in a large paper bag fixed by a clothes-peg or bull-dog clip on the side of a table. Encourage children to bring handkerchiefs to playgroup and to use them effectively for sneezing into. Many children will need to learn how to blow their noses properly!

The Health Visitor

The role of the Health Visitor in relation to playgroups differs in different parts of the country. In some areas playgroups are just one part of her many responsibilities; in others, one particular Health Visitor who has attended a special course is responsible for playgroups alone. This second system enables her to build up a fund of knowledge to help supervisors. The frequency of her visits depends upon her assessment of how much help you require; it is, of course, extremely valuable for a playgroup to have a good relationship with its Health Visitor. We recommend asking her to join the playgroup committee; if she has been in touch with families in the area for a number of years, she will know many of their problems and their strong points. It may be she who initially recommends the first 'customers' when opening a playgroup. To her a supervisor can direct her concern about a child's progress or a mother's anxieties. She should be able to advise you on where to obtain literature and charts to display around the playgroup entrance for mothers to look at.

Health education

So many of our attitudes and patterns of health are laid down in the early years that it seems worthwhile to consider health education with the pre-school child. Mothers of young children may receive only small and spasmodic amounts of help once their child stops his regular check-ups at the Welfare Clinic. It is probably only when her child is really ill and needs the doctor that a mother receives any direct information on his physical development. Yet all mothers (ourselves included and, we are told, mothers who are doctors too!) tend to worry about minor physical problems. With opportunities to see our own children alongside others of a similar age and background, we can begin to appreciate the wide variety of human behaviour that is considered to be within the bounds of normality. Allowing mothers to watch and work in a playgroup provides them with excellent opportunities for such reassurance.

A mother may be unduly worried that her child is small for his age or that he has a slight lisp. Even though she hesitates to go to the doctor for fear he thinks she is fussing, she may continue to worry and seek confirmation from the playgroup staff that her child is normal.

Supervisors who suspect that a child is suffering from some minor handicap also worry about the best way to handle this problem. Whatever you do, you should take a cautious approach and avoid causing a mother undue alarm. It is more than likely that she is aware of the problem herself; she may even find it a relief to find someone to discuss her fears with. As always, this type of situation is much easier for all concerned if there is a good relationship between mother and supervisor. Indeed when a mother has spent time in the playgroup and observed her child with his contemporaries, this may provide the confirmation of her fears that leads her to make the initial approaches to the supervisor for advice. If a mother does become very distraught or aggressive, try to put yourself in her shoes. What if her nightmares are confirmed and she does have a handicapped child? One could not predict one's own emotions under such circumstances.

The supervisor's role is *not* to diagnose a condition; to realize this is of vital importance in discussion with the mother. The aim should be to alert her and to channel specialist help in her direction. Any doubts about whether or not a child is abnormal should be put to the Health Visitor. The earlier a problem is dealt with, the greater is the chance of successful treatment. This is particularly important with minor speech defects. Unfortunately, the majority of authorities do not give speech therapy until children begin school and by this time once-trivial defects can develop into serious ones. Encourage the local Medical Officer of Health to see the need for early treatment. He will probably plead a shortage of cash – but do not be put off!

Talks for parents

Some mothers have only the vaguest ideas as to the Health Visitor's function, not realizing that she is trained to help with a wide variety of problems in the home. Why not ask her to give a talk one evening to parents on a health subject? The local GP or school dentist might also be willing. Topics for once-weekly evening talks could include suitable clothing (particularly footwear), nutrition for young children, dental care, road safety, home nursing of sick children, ways to occupy an ill child at home and children in hospital. This last is a particularly helpful topic – mothers often need advice in preparing their children for hospitalization. The National Association for the Welfare of Children in Hospital (NAWCH), 74 Denison House, Vauxhall Bridge Road, London SW1 will provide material for discussion. On the need for play facilities for children in hospital see *Play and the Sick Child* by Eva Noble (Faber, £1.12½). There are many short films which can be shown to stimulate discussion. Some playgroups provide speakers during a coffee morning in a room adjacent to the playgroup. In this case supervisors must ensure that the speaker understands that mothers may need to bring their under-threes and that he may need to adapt his approach accordingly.

Nutrition

This is a subject which should be raised with a mother when she enters the child's name for the playgroup. The mother may, for example, say that her child doesn't drink milk at home. Rather than just accepting this, the supervisor should explain how important it is for young children to drink milk and that it is worth trying the child on it at playgroup, because, as with so many things, children will copy what others do. Most playgroups provide a plain digestive biscuit with the morning milk, always finishing with a slice of apple or carrots. If children bring their own snacks, an element of competition can creep in and what the children bring tends to escalate from a simple biscuit to whole packets of toffees or crisps – ruinous to teeth, and providing only sugary or starch additions to the children's diet. If a mother fears her child will be hungry because of food fads or food refusal, explain that constant sugary snacks will only take the edge off his natural appetite and reinforce unhealthy eating habits. Many mothers with this problem find that once a child starts playgroup, he returns home after a busy morning with a good healthy appetite for his midday meal which the sensible playgroup snack has not affected.

There is a lot of scope in the playgroup itself for discussing the nutritional value of different foods. It can be linked, for instance, with nature study when the children are shown a vegetable or fruit. *Milk*, at 35p in the Macdonald 'Starters' Series, is another useful standby. The readiness of children to grasp the basic ideas behind nutrition should not be underestimated. We remember Stephanie, a three-year-old, announcing 'I've finished my protein part, can I have dessert now?' Another three-year-old went through a phase of asking his mother at every meal, 'Which is the goodest for me on my plate?'

Welfare milk is available free for every child at your playgroup – ⅓pt daily for each child. Playgroups in England/Wales should apply to Department of Health and Social Security, Alexander Fleming House, Elephant and Castle, London SE1. Playgroups in Scotland should write to Scottish Home & Health Department, 12–14 Carlton Terrace, Edinburgh, EH7 5DG. Application form FW20 is sent to applicants. The playgroup chooses its own milkman and pays him initially. The cost is then refunded quarterly upon the return of the completed form (W.F./D.N. 16). Forms for further refunds are sent with the quarterly payment. (Refunds often take several weeks.) No reimbursement is given for children marked absent on the registers, so it is a good idea to allow for two to four absences in your order, depending on the size of your playgroup, and divide the milk between those present.

Dental care

is a subject of considerable importance since there is a great deal of dental decay among young children in this country. The playgroup is a good place to try preventive work. Discuss with the children what we eat and why; this can be supplemented with pictures of animals which have strong teeth and the food they eat. A very attractive frieze on this topic is produced by the Oral Hygiene Service, Hesketh House, Portman Square, London W1A 1DY, at approximately 25p. A useful book to look at with children is 'Teeth' in the Macdonald 'Starters' series. Encourage children to use a toothbrush correctly, telling them why this is important. Explain why we eat an apple or carrot after biscuits. Going to the dentist is frightening and a visit to the playgroup and its parents from a dentist experienced with young children may do a great deal of good.

Road safety

This is a topic of some controversy since there is disagreement on how much under-fives, with their limited understanding, can really grasp about the subject. We do not consider the Tufty stories (published by the Royal Society for the Prevention of Accidents) particularly effective in the message they aim to put across. However, the fact remains that road accidents are a curse of our society and we cannot begin too early to alert children to the dangers. A recent piece of research in Sweden* showed that for a variety of reasons, including immature eyesight and hearing, children up to as late as ten years of age are unable to cope safely with the complexities of busy traffic. After testing a variety of methods, it was found that the most effective way of teaching road safety to children combined indoor and outdoor training, especially when this was supported by parental instruction and example. We suggest therefore an initial session for parents to hear a speaker and discuss ways of helping children, backed up by constant reminders in playgroup about care in crossing the road. Use opportunities which develop around play with road layouts to discuss road safety. Try to find a policeman or 'lollipop lady' who can speak effectively to pre-school children.

But remembering that the Swedish research showed that indoor learning by itself achieved little, we recommend taking the children out into the street two at a time and crossing at the zebra with them, explaining and discussing all the time. The Green Cross Code chanted parrot-fashion is more or less meaningless to under-fives – so choose a *single* point from the code, talk about it, then go on to the street with a couple of children to practise it.

Keeping records

When a child spends two years of his short life in a playgroup, the supervisor and her regular helpers come to know him very well – his strengths and weaknesses, the areas in which he is most advanced and those in which he may need help. They should also know much about his home background and the quality of relationships within his family, particularly that between the child and his mother. In other words, they will

* Sandels, 'Young Children in Traffic', *British Journal of Educational Psychology*, Vol. 40, part 2, June 1970

have a clear, all-round picture of the child in his everyday environment. It seems to us a great loss if the most important parts of this picture are not passed on to the head of the child's infant school, if he or she is willing to accept your observations. Where there are already good relations between the school and playgroup this should be straightforward: heads or reception class teachers who have accepted the quality of your work are likely to appreciate the value of the information being passed on to them.

We are sympathetically aware that sometimes, even with the best will in the world, a supervisor cannot influence her local infant school head to regard the playgroup positively. In a case where, despite all efforts, links cannot be established with a school, the Local Authority Playgroup Advisor should be asked to intercede.

We suggest that you ask the head what would be the most useful information to record from her point of view. There is no point in your writing page after page if all she wants is to know if the child can put his coat on! An ideal arrangement is for all supervisors of playgroups who feed into a particular infants school to meet together with the head to discuss the type of information she would like to receive. This again helps towards standardizing these records. Within a group of several playgroups there is probably someone who can get record sheets duplicated free of charge. If anyone can type, this is greatly appreciated: a pile of hand-written comments can try the patience of a saint!

The observations you make should be as brief as possible. Not only is there a greater likelihood that they will be read, they are also more likely to remain as *observations* rather than *interpretations*. It can be very dangerous, but nonetheless tempting, for lay people to dabble in pseudo-psychological classification – a danger which, quite rightly, often puts people off receiving records. There is also the criticism of giving a dog a bad name: it would be very unfair to send a child to school with the damning label of 'unmanageable' or 'over-aggressive'. In any case, such terms can be quite subjective; children may be very difficult with one adult yet respond well to another.

We suggest, therefore, that regular staff meetings should be held towards the end of each term to discuss the children who are leaving for the infants school. A group discussion among all the adults who have been in contact with a child since he started playgroup is likely to provide the most balanced picture of his development. It is not necessary to go to great lengths to give a full record of a child's normal development. It is far more valuable to note down any abnormalities so that professional help may be alerted all the sooner. There should be space at the end of the form for any other relevant information – anything which may have influenced his behaviour, such as hospitalization, a new baby in the family, the absence of the mother in hospital, father's absences, moving house, taking a long time to settle in or frequently being absent from playgroup.

The design of the form is determined by the need to keep it as factual as possible. The example we give* overleaf shows the type of heading it is valuable to include. They are not all relevant for all playgroups, and some will have additions to make. Nor is it necessary to fill in every line unless there is something unusual to record.

This form may seem rather daunting in the amount of details it includes but you will find it very helpful to look back on. (Tutors might find it a useful exercise to give to students.)

*The authors wish to thank Science Research Associates Limited on whose pre-primary profile the above record is based.

Greenways Playgroup,
16, Smith Street,
Notown.

Name of supervisor   Tel. no.
Date
Name of child
Address   } *This information*
Date of birth   } *will have been*
Home telephone number (if any)   } *gathered when*
Name, address and tel. no. of mother's employer *the child enters*
                        father's employer } *playgroup*
Immunization details
Number in family
Place in family
Any known physical abnormalities,
   e.g. allergies
        hearing or sight defects
        asthma
Any major illnesses which led to hospitalization.
   How long was he in hospital, approx.?

	Years	Months
He has been at this playgroup for	☐	☐
another playgroup for	☐	☐
(name and address)		

	Rarely	Often
Puts on and takes off own coat	☐	☐
shoes	☐	☐
Drinks without spilling from cup	☐	☐
from a straw	☐	☐

	Not yet	Needs help a lot	Needs help a little	Needs no help
Can wash and dry own hands	☐	☐	☐	☐
Goes to toilet by himself	☐	☐	☐	☐

	Not yet	Just beginning	Well	Very well
Builds with bricks	☐	☐	☐	☐
Enjoys fitting things together, e.g. puzzles, construction sets	☐	☐	☐	☐
Enjoys conversation with adults	☐	☐	☐	☐
children	☐	☐	☐	☐
Do others understand what is said?	☐	☐	☐	☐

	Not yet	Just beginning	Well	Very well
Knows colours	☐	☐	☐	☐
Says rhymes, sings songs	☐	☐	☐	☐
Enjoys – listening to stories	☐	☐	☐	☐
looking at books	☐	☐	☐	☐
discussing pictures	☐	☐	☐	☐
Uses – paint	☐	☐	☐	☐
scissors	☐	☐	☐	☐
pencils and crayons	☐	☐	☐	☐
dough and clay	☐	☐	☐	☐
glues	☐	☐	☐	☐

	Not yet	Not clearly	Clearly	Very clearly
Tells what he wants or needs	☐	☐	☐	☐

	Usually	Seldom
Takes turns with other children	☐	☐
Fights or cries when doesn't get his own way	☐	☐

Prefers to play alone	☐
with a few children	☐
with many children	☐
with children who are younger	☐
same age	☐
older	☐

Makes friends easily	Yes ☐	No ☐
Responds to advances of other children	Yes ☐	No ☐
Is often frightened	Yes ☐	No ☐
Apprehensive of strange adults	Yes ☐	No ☐
Seems to have had a lot of accidents	Yes ☐	No ☐
Wets his pants during the day	Yes ☐	No ☐

His best friend who is coming to Infants School with him is:

Any other relevant information:

Part 4
Playing and Learning

10

The Purpose of Play

What is play?

An important part of your work in playgroups is to convince
firstly mothers and then other less committed adults of the value
of play. Why are opportunities to play so important to the
development of young children?

Firstly, let us try to imagine the human infant as part of the
greater animal kingdom. When Charles Darwin first tried to
convince people that their near relatives included not only
Aunt Edna but also the orang-utang, people were naturally
more that a little ruffled at the idea! But there were compensa-
tions. Adult human beings, it emerged, had by far the most
developed brains of any animal and our adult behaviour is
different too; we are able to gain (and lose) from past experience
to build up cumulative knowledge of the world in a way that
animals lower down the ladder cannot.

Man varies in another important way too from other mam-
mals: his youth is much longer. The young human child therefore needs protection for far longer than any other mammal. A
young foal, a few moments after birth, will shake itself, stand
up alone and walk, even if it is wobbly at first. Compare this
to the human infant who will be approximately fifteen months
old before he takes his first few tentative steps.

The longer an animal has to develop into adulthood, the
longer the time it has in which to learn. We call our long slow
period of development childhood. How can childhood be put to
the best use so that a human infant matures into a thinking,
civilized adult? It has been demonstrated that animals which
learn more also apparently play more. Simpler living things

such as fishes and insects do not play, the young behave and appear as the adult, their mature behaviour is based on the instincts they were born with, not on the acquisition of patterns of behaviour which reflect a steady build-up of experiences. Play is in fact a vital part of the learning process for young children.

Susan Isaacs calls play 'Nature's means of individual education. Play is indeed the child's work, and the means whereby he grows and develops.' It may be a new idea to some adults to think of children *working* when they are *playing*. In fact, the word has unfortunate associations in its use – we tend to say, 'Oh, go away and play' when we really mean 'For heaven's sake, just go and do *anything* and let me finish what I have to do.' In other words, the adult in this type of situation is not really caring about 'play' at all. The pressures of everyday life make it difficult for mothers at home to see clearly and objectively that children need to explore every aspect of their environment, their own physical capabilities, and all the people with whom they come into contact. For the under-fives, play is not the jam but the bread of existence! If you closely and unobtrusively observe the play of a young child, you can see the surprising intensity with which he becomes involved in it. He is completely absorbed – thinking, doing, learning.

In Part I we discussed the factors which may hamper the development of a modern town-dwelling child. Fewer and fewer children are now able to play with the real stuff of their environment in its natural setting. Because they are often so far away from the countryside, it is increasingly difficult for a young child to study the natural world intensely and in detail. Nor is he able to climb and physically experiment with danger to gain confidence in and awareness of his own body's capabilities. If he is isolated from his own age group and from a variety of caring adults, how can he practise the social skills which he will need as an adult to live happily with other people? If so many of these valuable practical experiences are taken away from him, it follows that he must somehow be helped to replace them if he is to develop as fully as he is able. The playgroup supervisor must constantly bear in mind that the play environment she creates in her playgroup should go some way towards compensating for frustrations imposed on young children by urbanization.

Broadly speaking, a child needs four types of play; physical play, creative play, imaginative play and manipulative play. We describe each of these and the best equipment for them later in this chapter. Before doing so, there is one difficult question to be dealt with – so-called 'free play'. Lately, there has been a lot of controversy about the subject of free play – some opponents favour, for example, a more structured approach for certain children. In the absence of any decisive research we continue to advocate free play provided it is accompanied by a thorough understanding of child development.

There is a great deal of argument about precisely what this term free play means. The basic principles behind it are clear enough; as Susan Isaacs expresses it: 'Children need freedom and choice if they are to grow up responsible and independent beings. They learn to exercise responsibility by having it, just as they learn to walk by trying to walk, to swim by swimming, to dance by dancing. They can't learn to be controlled and responsible by mere teaching in words, nor by the power of our wishes – but only by their own efforts, corrected by their own experience.'

What exactly do we mean by free play? Paradoxically, it may be easier to begin by discussing what it does *not* mean. It certainly does not mean a free-for-all, with children allowed to run wild all around. Complete freedom of this type – with all the noise and bedlam that it produces – terrifies a child, and a frightened child cannot learn. For this reason adults in a playgroup have an important responsibility to protect timid children from the uncontrolled rages and rantings of other children. A child also needs to be protected from his own emotions – it is extremely comforting for him to feel that an adult is capable of controlling him as an individual and all that is going on in the group as a whole. Ideally, this control is an invisible one, 'felt' rather than 'seen', but the children and any sensitive observer will be aware of its presence.

Providing they are for the common good and not for the

supervisor's convenience, a minimum number of rules is necessary in a playgroup. For example, the children must know they are not allowed to throw sand, knock down someone else's tower or kick another child. These rules must be stated and insisted upon at the very beginning, until each child knows the limits to which he may go. When children have no framework within which to function, their play degenerates into chaos. It has no purpose. All the adult can then do is to step in, too late, with a list of 'don'ts' which result in the children having no freedom at all. It takes time, patience, and effort to establish the right kind of framework, but if you are consistent, the rules will become accepted by the children and the playgroup will run much more smoothly as a result.

With so much control from the adults, where does the freedom of 'free play' come in? The freedom is the freedom of choice within the framework you have set up. The breadth of freedom depends upon the play equipment provided and the practical problems of interrelationships within a group of people. It is the subtle interweaving of these two factors which makes for effective free play. A child is not free to play with water if the supervisor does not provide water play; that is something she has imposed. But more than this, a child must accept that he cannot play with the water you have provided if there are enough children playing there already and he can see there is no more room. He must control his immediate desire to play with water and wait for a place to become free – this is a self-imposed discipline, the best kind of early training for the social disciplines which will be demanded of him when he is mature.

Free play, then, means freedom for the child to choose his own activity and follow it as he wishes, providing he keeps within the limits set by the adults or the situation. If a child is to accept these limits, it is essential that he sees them as reasonable ones. We do not ask a three-year-old child to sit still for twenty-five minutes, nor do we expect a timid child to climb to the top of a tree.

The role of the adult

A child develops intellectually each time he plays; the degree of development depends on the quality of equipment provided and whether there is an adult to show an interest in discussing any discoveries he has made or wishes to make. What does this mean in practical terms? How should a supervisor and her helpers behave in the practical running of a playgroup session?

Firstly, the adult needs to see herself as a 'provider' rather than a 'doer'. She provides the place, time and equipment, and the major part of her physical activities take place before the children arrive. Once she has provided for their needs she should step back and take a seemingly passive role. We say 'seemingly' because although she is not physically active in playing with the children she is constantly though unobtrusively watching for any new needs that may develop.

A large play area cannot be visually absorbed by one person alone, so your room should be divided up into areas of responsibility – one adult responsible for all the children and activities in each. The supervisor then has the overall responsibility for all the areas and the people in them, skilfully balancing things so that a coherent and harmonious whole is created. This may sound more like a plan of battle than a way to work with young children but you cannot expect children to accept and understand the limits of what they are allowed to do if adult roles have not first been worked out – it is only when a real framework of roles has been established that the adults and children feel part of a well-run group. As an adult stands and watches she can enlarge her own understanding of children's behaviour and needs. She will come to realize the intensity with which children play. She will understand how wrong it is to shatter the world a child has created for himself with an adult's breezy 'What are you making Johnny?' She will see the importance of only entering the home corner on invitation and that even poking her head inside 'to see everything is all right' is enough to break the magic of an intensely personal world inside. She will become aware of the need to speak quietly and individually to a child – how can a child be expected to con-

centrate and become involved in the job in hand when he
constantly interrupted.

There are, of course, times when an adult must intrude. A
fight over whose turn it is to go on the trike or who may put
on the only available apron and be the next to paint, needs wise
handling to stop the situation escalating. But if you remember
that part of your role is to predict tensions you can take steps
to avoid them arising. For example, you will sense the moment
to subtly distract a child who is about to claim something out of
turn.

It is very important that a supervisor should discuss all these
points with her helpers and explain the nature of their role.
New helpers in particular often feel they must prove their
worth – and see this in terms of making things with the children. The supervisor should cut across any feelings they have
of not being seen to do enough and help them to understand the
more difficult task of being an unobtrusive but involved figure
in the background, always ready to extend a child intellectually
or renew flagging interest in an activity. This means helping a
child to find out and do things for himself, not doing them for
him or expecting him to do things to an adult standard.

Adults working in playgroups should also be aware of children's need for good language development (see p. 290). How
can an adult remain unobtrusive yet help a child to learn to
communicate verbally? In many ways, this is one of the most
difficult things to do in a playgroup. Keep a child's play needs
to the forefront. Is he playing well and thoroughly absorbed?
Good, then leave well alone. Has he reached a point in his play
when an adult's remarks might draw together and form into a
coherent whole the impressions and ideas he has gained from
his play? Now is the time to enter quietly, discuss and question
and extend his interest and ideas further. The older children
in particular are beginning to understand cause and effect. They
need to be questioned 'why?' Never confuse this with telling
a child what to do next; there is a world of difference between
the two approaches. The skill of talking to children should be
thoroughly discussed in staff meetings and ways of improving
the helpers' techniques suggested. Try to arrange visits to other

playgroups where adults have mastered this. Contact the Nursery/Infant Advisor at your Education Authority, or a Playgroup Course Tutor for names and addresses of suitable playgroups for visits and follow up with a staff discussion.

Lastly, each child's work must be accepted on its own merits. We remember one very skilled supervisor praising a delightful painting by an unusually artistic four-year-old. The next moment she was praising with equal enthusiasm the messy daubs of a four-year-old who had just begun playgroup and had done very little painting. Each child was praised not for the results of his labours, but for his individual effort.

Children who don't join in

Occasionally you may have a child who seems to wander around aimlessly, not joining any group or activity. How should you deal with such children?

Some children may be overwhelmed by the richness of the environment they have suddenly been thrust into, the numbers of people, or, in less effective playgroups, the general noise. Surely such a child should be allowed time to absorb his new situation gradually? Although he is perhaps physically immobile, he is still learning and gaining a great deal from what he sees and hears. He also needs to feel that you care about *him*, not about what he is playing with. He certainly does not need a succession of overbearing, grinning ladies dashing up to him and saying 'Let's go and do a painting' or 'Let's go and play with clay'. Indeed you should involve him indirectly by arousing his interest and letting him drift into the orbit of an activity by himself. We have seen one experienced supervisor walk slowly past a very quiet little boy, sit in the book corner and begin to read aloud 'to herself', with the attractive pictures in the book turned towards the child. Very gradually he inched towards her, ending up a couple of feet behind, looking over her shoulder at the book. The supervisor did not break off from her reading but went on as if oblivious of his presence. Naturally enough, two or three children of more outgoing disposition joined them and, for the first time, this little boy experienced the satisfaction of participating in a group. A very gentle 'Should we look at this book now, David?' encouraged him to stay for another story. This kind of situation was repeated daily by the same adult until eventually the child was fully integrated into the playgroup. Family groups (see p. 132) are valuable with these children; they allow one helper to be responsible for the child and a steady relationship to be built up quietly and unobstrusively.

Further reading

Play With a Purpose for Under-Sevens, E. Matterson, Penguin, 35p; *Playgroup Activities*, B. Crowe, PPA, 25p; *The Playgroup Book*, M. Winn and M. Porcher, Fontana, 35p

Indoor play

Firstly, give careful consideration to the layout of your room. Children do not take kindly to radical changes (nor do helpers) so make sure you think it through at the outset. The layout is also closely connected with the general atmosphere you are trying to provide. Does the room look warm and beckoning to a newcomer? Can a child see lots of exciting and interesting activities which encourage him to join in? Is there a calm but busy 'children's workshop' atmosphere to set the tone for all you do?

If you are one of the very few in a purpose-built playgroup, then the task is relatively simple. Home playgroups, too, are at an advantage in that there is no need to use artificial means to create a homely atmosphere. The vast majority of playgroup workers, however, battle along in cold, dingy church halls.

Break up large areas into small bays or recesses each with an activity giving a feeling of privacy and security. Covered clothes-horses, screens, cupboards, the piano, even a line of chairs can all be used at right angles to the wall to help create these separate areas. Separate quiet activities from noisier ones, and then group together quiet activities such as the book corner and the manipulative toys. Put activities needing constant supervision, such as woodwork and cutting out, near each other so that one adult can keep an eye on both.

Traffic lanes must be kept clear so that a child does not have to walk too near a precariously balanced tower of bricks and knock it over with a doll's pram. Cycles and scooters must not be allowed to interfere with the quieter activities. You could limit these toys to outdoors or to a corridor or room adjacent to the main play area. If none of these is possible make absolutely sure that the children understand why they may only ride their bikes in certain areas. If they can play with this kind of toy at home, you may consider banning them completely indoors. Try to provide all the activities which the average home cannot.

Plants and flowers (real, not plastic) brought by both children and the staff help to make the place look more homely, and so of course do pictures on the walls displayed at children's eye-level. If you have to clear everything away at the end of each session use Philip and Tacey's 'Plastitak' – this is a putty-like substance, a small lump of which will attach a picture or painting to a wall and not mark paintwork. It can be peeled off at clearing-up time. A long sheet of corrugated paper can have pictures stuck on to it and be quickly attached by the corners to a wall and then rolled away again at the end of the session. Better still try and persuade your hall committee that a few well-placed children's paintings would add a touch of gaiety to otherwise depressing premises.

Above all, try to imagine what the room looks like from a child's eye-level. Does it appear as a haphazard jumble of strange equipment, or does each activity present itself clearly and look attractive and inviting? Is there an obvious route across to the activity in the far corner, or would a timid child not attempt to get there? Overleaf is a basic guide to the layout of equipment in the average hall.

Choice of equipment

As we saw above, there are four main types of play for which equipment should cater: physical play, creative play, imagina-

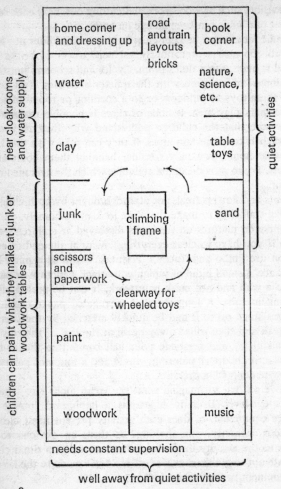

Figure 3

tive play, manipulative play. Your playgroup should provide a balance of equipment for all these types of play. You should also take into account the special needs of certain groups of children. For example, under-fives living in tower-blocks have a very great need to run free and every attempt should be made to provide outdoor play space and equipment. Children from culturally deprived homes may need extra intellectual stimulation. This does not mean the formal teaching of reading, but rather providing pre-reading experiences in a more structured way. A child from a particularly strict and rigid home may need to be helped towards the emotional release which good creative play can provide.

Given these needs, there are certain activities which must be provided in all playgroups. There are what we call basic equipment: water play, sand play, paint, clay, large apparatus for physical play including push-and-pull toys, bricks, road or train layout, home corner and dressing up, book corner, story-telling, music table, nature table, junk play, woodwork, constructional toys, three or four examples of matching and sorting equipment, jigsaws.

A new playgroup should aim at having as much as possible of the above equipment (although you would be well advised not to put everything out simultaneously until things are well established – see Equipping the playgroup p. 126). As finances and storage space develop you will naturally add futher things. When doing this always bear in mind the main categories of play. Beware of adding too much of one kind of toy – a well-balanced collection is the ideal.

Care of equipment

Supervisors must be continually concerned about the care of playgroup equipment. Most do this automatically because they know how much time and money it has cost to provide. But there are other reasons, too. The care with which you handle and maintain equipment sets a standard which the children will imitate. If you gently insist that no puzzle is put away till complete or that a piece of Lego found under the piano cannot be put in the dressing-up box just because that is nearest to hand, then gradually the children will do the same. Learning to take care of equipment gives children responsibility for it and learning responsibility is an important part of what a child gains from playgroup.

Broken toys should be removed immediately – they may be dangerous, but even if not, they discourage children from looking after them. The supervisor needs to have a set plan for the mending of toys. Some playgroups organize a fathers evening once a term when, armed with a variety of carpentry tools, sellotape and paint, a mammoth attack is launched. You may prefer to make some arrangement with the local youth club or pensioners club. Don't fail to ask the help of mothers when the dressing-up clothes and the doll's bedding need a wash and iron. A certain amount of clearing out and cleaning may be done during a playgroup session with the help of the children – clearing out a cupboard or washing down the painting easel can be great fun.

There is a world of difference between the amount of handling a toy will stand in a home where just one or two children use it, and when it is constantly used every day by a large group. Some equipment should be reinforced before it is brought to playgroup: screws may need tightening, cardboard box corners strengthened inside and out with sticky tape, book jackets covered with transparent plastic. Good storage arrangements also help, particularly with smaller toys. If each toy has its own container and is clearly labelled, there is less chance of odd bits and pieces being put in the wrong place.

Storage

Available storage space will tend to dictate the amount and size of equipment you buy; all the available space must therefore be put to the best possible use. Most hall playgroups have to clear away every scrap of equipment at the end of each session, so much time and energy go into 'packing up'.

The best way to store small equipment is on shelving placed at children's height. The shelves should be narrow from front to back so that toys do not get stuck behind each other. The children can learn to choose their equipment from the shelf and put it away when they have finished with it. More often, a large cupboard which can be locked and has some of its shelving at child height has to be used as a compromise. Work out the best arrangement for storing your particular set of equipment and pin up a plan for helpers to follow and for days when you are not at playgroup.

Toy chests, large strong cardboard cartons and hampers, fitted with castors whenever possible, are useful storage equipment and can also be used for playing during the playgroup session. Avoid having them too big or they are impossible to move when full. They can be fitted under the hall stage and make stacking simpler. When filling them, make sure that all small equipment is packed away in its own container, otherwise a collection of odds and ends will accumulate at the bottom. You can make a smooth-running trolley to fit under the stage in a church hall (or other narrow space) – see below.

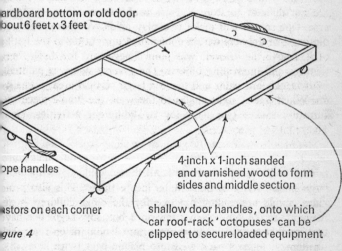

cardboard bottom or old door
about 6 feet x 3 feet

rope handles

castors on each corner

4-inch x 1-inch sanded
and varnished wood to form
sides and middle section

shallow door handles, onto which
car roof-rack 'octopuses' can be
clipped to secure loaded equipment

Figure 4

This storage trolley was designed by local art students and fits neatly under the stage of a village hall. Why not contact the art school in your area to see whether they might launch a project for students to design something suited to the needs of your particular playgroup?

One enlightened hall committee provided a continuous row of storage chests down the two long walls of the hall. The lids of the chests had gay cushions on to provide adult seating.

Some toy manufacturers such as E.S.A. (see p. 343), are now producing excellent though expensive storage equipment for playgroups. These are usually lightweight, being basically wire baskets of various sizes on castors. One can sometimes buy ex-supermarket baskets and display racks at auctions. Second-hand tea-trolleys are useful for wheeling equipment in and out of the main play area and can be used in the home corner when the playgroup is in session.

Junk shops occasionally produce useful pieces of furniture such as chests of drawers. It is also worth contacting your local Education Department School Supplies Officer. He may be able to get you, for a nominal price, second-hand school furniture which can be cut down to small children's size. Screens are not difficult to store and are useful to divide up a large area. One screen will make two play areas. We have seen an old chest of drawers with a door nailed upright on to the back of it. Above the drawers was pinned peg-board for displaying pictures and interesting objects. The reverse side was painted with blackboard paint and made a large vertical area to chalk on. When put at right angles to the wall, the whole piece of furniture makes two bays for two different activities. (See Figure 5.)

Shoe shops will usually give away shoe boxes. Coffee tins and any tin with a smooth rolled edge make good small containers, so do plastic seed trays. All these should be labelled in large simple script to help adults locate things. This also provides simple pre-reading practice for the older children – to realize that the symbols written on a box say 'Lego' because that is what goes inside is an important landmark on the road to literacy. Jigsaws pack well into plastic bags (with holes in) tied up with a pipe-cleaner. Mark each piece of a puzzle on the back with the same number to help place an old piece someone finds.

Very few playgroup supervisors are satisfied with their storage facilities. Indeed, most are extremely hampered in their work

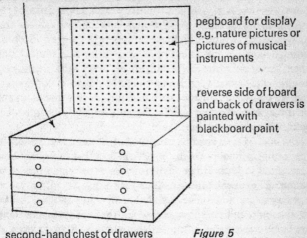

chest top, covered with fablon or painted
and used for nature table, musical instruments etc.

pegboard for display
e.g. nature pictures or
pictures of musical
instruments

reverse side of board
and back of drawers is
painted with
blackboard paint

second-hand chest of drawers   *Figure 5*

by very bad conditions in which they are expected to drag
heavy, awkward-shaped pieces of equipment in and out twice
a day. Unsympathetic hall committees should be pressed continuously to provide storage facilities. It is worth pointing out
to such committees that it is usually only playgroups who will
rent a hall regularly during the mornings.

Outdoor play

Outdoor play space is an enormous asset. You may only have a
small ugly area of tarmac, but it is still worth using. Outside
space offers so much more than fresh air and exercise, although
the importance of the latter should never be underestimated –
an increasing number of children are brought from home to
playgroup by car, never enjoying the exhilaration of a run on
frosty mornings or shuffling through piles of leaves along the
pavement. Even a single oak tree overlooking the asphalt square
can be used to point out the changing seasons. In more developed outdoor areas, all that nature offers out of doors can be

used as equipment – sheltered spots under trees become houses or hidey-holes; acorns, pebbles or leaves can be used for playing shops.

A much wider range of behaviour is acceptable outside than in. Behaviour which can make a supervisor angry indoors – running, leaping and shouting – can make her smile fondly when she sees it outside. And yet, we have seen many playgroups where good outdoor space is not put to maximum use. 'Oh, we go outside for the last half hour,' or 'It's much too cold for the little ones today,' are comments regularly heard. Let us look at these two attitudes more closely. Firstly, a set time to go outside. We feel very strongly that the children should be free to play outdoors when they wish, and that there should be a free flow in both directions throughout the whole playgroup session. The over-exuberant four-year-olds who often worry supervisors are much more amiable if they are allowed to have a good romp and climb outside when they arrive in the morning. Some supervisors complain that there is then a perpetual fastening and unfastening of coats. It may be necessary to have one helper to put on coats, but the more children go in and out, the better they will get at doing it themselves. They can also learn to help each other. If the novelty of this freedom means that children are endlessly in and out, do not be worried. They will soon grow accustomed to the idea, and will begin to stay longer in one place. You will have to train them to shut outside doors quietly to avoid a continual slamming and extra heat loss. In warmer months the outer door should be hooked back so that indoors and outdoors become one. French windows are ideal for this purpose and help supervision enormously.

(Another reason why it is essential that playgroup supervisors should be in at the very beginning of the planning of any community centre, youth club, or building that may eventually be used for a playgroup. They can then point out the needs for french windows, toilets nearby, suitable storage facilities, and so forth.)

Supposing it is too cold outside? Make sure you are not really meaning it is too cold for adults! Obviously children must not be allowed to get cold and uncomfortable. Mothers, as we have said elsewhere, should be encouraged to send their children to playgroup with warm, sensible clothing and wellingtons for wet weather. If the children are adequately clad, there is no reason why they should not play outdoors. A cold child can always come inside again, and most children will generate enough heat to keep themselves warm. Avoid using the seasons as a guide. With the vagaries of the English climate they are no sure guide to the temperatures – it can be warmer in March than August. In fact, there are very few days throughout the whole year when children are unable to play outdoors at least part of the morning as long as the supervisor is convinced of the importance of this type of play.

Equipment and layout

The opportunity to play outdoors is so important that supervisors should try to use whatever space they have, no matter how unsuitable it seems at first. A delightful book, full of photographs and ideas used in playgrounds around the world, but which could be adapted for playgroup use is *Planning for Play* by Lady Allen of Hurtwood, published by Thames and Hudson, £2.10 – rather expensive, but well worth ordering from the library. Organizing an army of fathers on a Saturday morning to clear broken glass and tin cans, worked wonders at one downtown playgroup. The mothers made coffee and the results showed, as well as a new play area, a great deal of pride and goodwill among the playgroup parents. If your only available area has no fence around it and funds do not immediately run to this, use a line of chairs as a boundary. We have even seen a piece of string mark off a boundary, but the supervisor was extremely skilled and fully confident in her ability for 'remote control'. Barbed wire is dangerous and should be screened with a line of chairs until it can be removed. If you have grass, put in a mound to add variety. Shrubs and trees provide shade for sunny days, as well as secret places and natural climbing apparatus. Put an outdoor climbing frame next to a tall tree – the two together form a rich complex piece of apparatus for climbing, hiding, crawling, and swinging. Good cheap sandpits can be made with second-hand bricks forming the side walls to prevent the sand spreading. A cover will be necessary to keep out cats. You may be lucky enough to salvage a chopped-down tree with its main limbs still intact. This can be laid down outside to provide all manner of games. The local Parks Department may help you with this. Further suggestions for suitable equipment for physical play are given on p. 238.

On really fine days, given enough space, take most of your equipment outdoors: woodwork is far less noisy there, and the spills from water play matter much less. Some children may notice that the paints look different colours from when they are inside the dingy hall.

If you have absolutely no outdoor play area, then have regular nature walks, visits to parks, zoos, recreation grounds and public playgrounds (see p. 290 Visits).

Physical play

Urban society has robbed the child of his natural environment. Why do so many of our city fathers consider busy main roads are sufficient substitute for trees to climb, mud and water to splash in, or even enough space in which to run and jump and allow a child to learn the strengths and limits of his physical powers? One of the most pathetic sights of our times is to see the collections of gleaming, unused trikes and pedal cars, stacked in the entrance halls of tower-blocks. There is just nowhere for children to use these birthday presents, given by well-intentioned adults.

Safety

Children will often attempt and indeed need to attempt, the most daring and seemingly dangerous feats. How should you react to this? As a general rule they will not attempt anything they do not feel capable of. It is only when an adult suggests to them 'Can you go any higher Mary?' or 'Why not try that upside down, Peter?' that they are pushed into situations for which they may not be yet ready. In fact one may also be reinforcing a timidity which the experience should be helping to conquer. No matter how dangerous or precarious a position a child has adopted, never let them see that you are scared. Your fears will quickly be transmitted to him and that is when accidents happen. It is also essential there are no group pressures as to what must be achieved in physical activities. A child needs to develop at his own rate in acquiring physical skills just as he does in other aspects of his development. If you want to praise a child praise him quietly and individually so that no one else is tempted to copy merely to gain approval.

Given that we allow children all the freedom they require to experiment and practise physical skills there are nevertheless certain precautions that must be taken.

1. Check all your large equipment regularly for safety, particularly any kept outside, e.g. climbing frame, ropes and ladders, trucks etc. Beware of screws working loose and splintered wood. Anything potentially dangerous must be removed immediately and not put back until mended. Buy equipment only from reputable manufacturers so that if any part goes radically wrong and you do not consider it to be caused by fair wear and tear you will have some redress.

2. Footwear. Ideally, children should be able to play barefoot, particularly outdoors in the summertime. However, splintering floors, poor heating and other factors often make this impractical. Rubber-soled shoes are a second best, but not wellington boots. Some leather and composition soles can be slippery when wet. Socks or tights without shoes are dangerous because slippery.

3. Clothing. Nasty accidents occasionally happen when belts, braces or anorak-hood cords hook on to a projection. Little girls sometimes catch their feet in a dress hem – tucking dresses in pants helps here. Watch out for safety-pins, badges and 'jewellery'.

Choice of equipment

Provide a good balance of all types of equipment, bearing in mind any special needs of the children in your care. For example, children from flats need a wealth of material to stimulate physical play and lots of space to carry it out in. All children need equipment for climbing, balancing, swinging, crawling, pulling and pushing.

Equipment for physical play may be the most expensive you have to buy and possibly be the source of your most expensive mistakes. There is a great deal of equipment on the market, much of it apparently similar in purpose. Contact as many other playgroups as you can to look at their choices. Learn by their mistakes and save yourself a lot of money and annoyance. Send away to toy manufacturers for their catalogues (see p. 343 for list) – these are free, and once you are on a manufacturer's mailing list, you will be sent new editions as they come out.

Three main factors will influence your choice of equipment: available play space, storage facilities, finances. Bear these in mind when you visit other playgroups. One climbing frame, for example, though large and versatile may prove impossible to stack away in the ramshackle hut your equipment has to be kept in. If space and money are at a premium, look for flexibility – can a piece of equipment double up to make something else?

Here is a list of suggestions for equipment for indoor and outdoor physical play –

CLIMBING FRAME – an essential for all playgroups and usually the most expensive item. Must be collapsible to allow storage.*

(i) Dome-type frame (see Figure 6) usually metal and because they need pegging in the ground mainly suitable for outdoor use. Not much room for many children at one time. A tyre can be hung from the centre or a plank to form a slide, inclined on one outer side.

(ii) Ladder-type frame (see Figure 7) – wood or metal and consists of three basic ladders, fitted together to form a square

* *Which?* August 1970, published a useful illustrated report on climbing frames. However, it should be noted that evidence was collected after watching 7–8-year-olds at play.

archway. They are simple to erect and lend themselves to the addition of various slides and extra wooden rope ladders, planks, tyres and ropes.

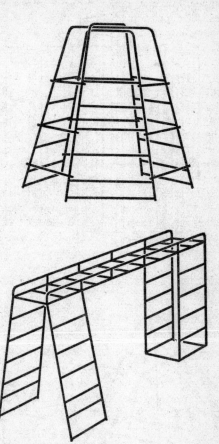

Figure 6

Figure 7

(iii) Cube-shape frame (see Figure 8) – usually wooden and collapsible for indoor use. The shape lends itself to imaginative play – a house, going to the moon etc. Many models have a platform with a small hinged door. This door can be a finger-trap so some playgroups remove it. Additional extras are usually available, e.g. slide.

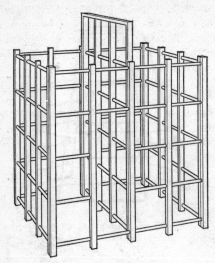

Figure 8

(iv) Planks and trestles (see Figure 9) – very flexible, lends itself to a variety of additions, e.g. slides, ropes.

Figure 9

VARIPLAY TRIANGLE SET (Figure 10) A stimulus to group play. Expensive, but offers a wide variety of combinations of the various pieces and each piece can be bought separately. Use it as fully as possible – some playgroups tend to set it up in the same position each day, which is a great waste of its play possibilities. Needs a lot of space for manoeuvring so only recommended for large halls or outdoor play areas. Sold by Goodwood Toys and Arnolds, addresses on p. 343.

STEP UNIT AND HIDEY HOLES (see Figure 11) – easily made by carpenter fathers etc. Expensive if ready-made (Goodwood), but very versatile. Storage may be a problem, although small equipment may be stored inside them.

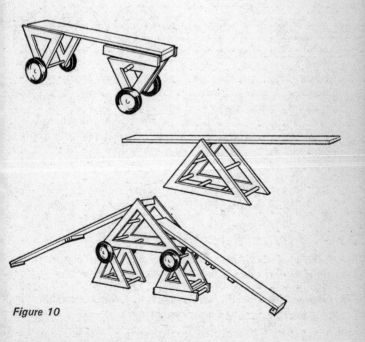

Figure 10

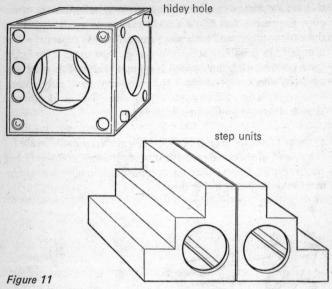

hidey hole

step units

Figure 11

ROPES – synthetic-fibre ones are best. Put in large knots for footholds. Attach to girders in the roof, climbing frame, door lintels (of unused doors). Also rope ladders.

TRAMPOLINE – stand on a piece of carpet to prevent sliding. Needs constant supervision but a marvellous way of using up surplus energy.

PLAY TUNNEL – great fun for crawling through, but some children may be frightened of being trapped inside. Establish from the beginning that no one is allowed on top of it or it will collapse very easily. (See pp. 245–6, Figure 12.)

SLIDES – perhaps *too* popular with supervisors. They are costly and have only one use. Regular safety checks necessary.

SWINGS – positioning very important, never have other children running past. As a 'one-only' toy they may cause turn-taking problems. A swing frame is much more useful if you ring the changes and hang from it rope ladders, trapeze, ropes, tyres etc. Regular safety checks necessary.

SCRAMBLING NET – may be hung from swing frame. A delightful activity, often overlooked.

SEESAW, SWING BOAT – beginnings of group play for younger children. Not much exercise, but children enjoy the regular rhythm. The E.S.A. 'Rock-a-cart' is a rocking boat, seesaw and cart combined. Made in tubular steel, cost approximately £10.

EQUIPMENT FOR BALANCING – line of bricks for balancing, narrow planks supported on bricks or chairs, stepping-stones (sawn-off rings of trees).

BALLS – large and small to stimulate different kinds of play and practice in throwing, kicking and catching. Never buy hard balls – young children's aim is too haphazard. 'Gamester' balls made of perforated plastic are good for indoor use. Arnolds make these in two sizes – $2\frac{1}{2}$ inch and $5\frac{1}{4}$ inch diameter (address, p. 343).

BEAN BAGS – easier than balls for children to catch and often more suitable for indoor use. Simply made from scraps of strong material and filled with rice.

SKITTLES – good for older children. Plastic ones (bottles from washing-up liquid rubbed with steel wool and painted) are quieter than wood.

RUBBER QUOITS

WHEELED TOYS – trikes, pedal car, scooter, wheelbarrows, trucks. These provide lots of scope for muscular development and coordination but may cause turn-taking problems. Make sure they are not the only activities you provide for physical play, and ask yourself whether if the children play with them at home they need them at playgroup.

GO-KART – choose ones with a steering apparatus for greater safety.

PLAY-WHEEL – tyre with hardwood centre on castors – highly recommended. (See pp. 246–7, Figure 13.)

PUSH-AND-PULL TOYS – most children have outgrown these by three, but some may still need to go through the phase at play-group.

Improvising equipment

The equipment listed above is obviously expensive if all bought new. How can you improvise? Firstly, keep your eyes open for second-hand materials and cast-offs. Junk shops are a valuable source of furniture made of strong seasoned wood – old deal tables, for example, make planks of perfect size and strength for many activities. Watch out for woodworm, sand-paper thoroughly if necessary, remove nails, hooks, etc. Cut down noise by tacking pieces of rubber carpet underlay to offending edges. (Underlay can also be used as an anti-slip device, and to protect paintwork and furniture.) One rarely finds the right kind of large equipment at jumble sales. There are usually too many trikes and little else.

Here is a list of things to look out for:

Stout wooden boxes – get a variety of shapes and sizes, ones with rope handles are particularly useful; they may need sand-papering.

Beer crates, plastic milk crates.

Strong steady chairs.

Ladders – various lengths. Taller ones may be used horizontally as monkey bars, supported on strong boxes, chairs or tables. This type of apparatus costs little and can be arranged many ways by the children – they can paint it from time to time. Add small items such as a flag, hooter, blanket and you have a car, or tank, or ship, etc. Once the playgroup is financially stable, a real climbing frame should be provided.

Tyres – many garages give these away free in various sizes. Perfect for swinging on, suspended from a rope, or stacking, balancing, rolling etc. A tyre cut through longitudinally makes a good moat.

Floorboards – balancing, sliding activities.

Bricks – stepping stones for balancing and to support planks.

Barrels.

Logs – horizontal for crawling, balancing; slices for stepping stones.

Telegraph poles – some G.P.O.'s sell these off at a nominal fee. Well sanded and sawn up they have numerous uses for balancing, stacking, stepping stones etc.

Stilts – make home-made ones from treacle tins pierced at the top with string threaded through to loop over feet.

Cardboard cartons – collect from the local supermarket and use for storage. Children can paint them, stack them, wear them and hide in them. When they are broken throw them away and get some more!

Play tunnel – simply and cheaply made with wire and cheap cotton material for crawling and hiding in (see Figure 12.)

Materials: 25 yds strong galvanized fencing wire about ⅜" if possible (approx. 75p); a large piece of material, such as an old bedspread, canvas is ideal if you can afford it; strips of strong cotton or canvas 6 ins wide; solder; flex – use with solder for a strong join.

Make the wire into ten coils, each approximately 24 ins in diameter. Solder each end to form a circle. Fold material in half and sew up side to form a tube slightly larger in diameter than the coils. Stitch coils to inside of tube. Oversew each end of tube to end of coil. To make tunnel stronger, bind the coils with 6-inch strips and stitch to inside of tunnel.

Slide – if you have a grassy mound outdoors a strip of linoleum firmly pegged down to the turf down one side makes a safe, simple slide.

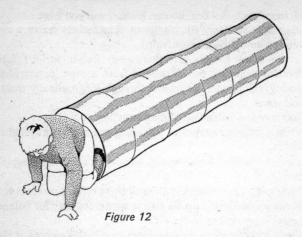

Figure 12

Playwheel (Figure 13) – you will need: 1 tyre (any size from the local garage), 2 pieces of wood, 4 nuts and bolts, 4 castors, 2 handles.

Cut two circular pieces of half-inch plywood, large enough to fit over the rim of the tyre used. Drill four holes through the wood close up to the tyre rim. Insert four bolts through the holes – see Figure 1.

Tighten the nuts on the bolts to clamp the tyre between the plywood discs – Figure 2.

For extra strength screw two cross joints to the underside of the playwheel. Attach four castors to the ends of the cross joints – Figure 3.

Add handles on the top – Figure 4.

Paint the tyre with tyre paint.

Enlist the help of local people. Fathers may be willing to have a Saturday morning club, or to give up a couple of evenings a term to mend old and make new equipment. Will your caretaker help? Pensioners Clubs very much enjoy a link with young children. Investigate the occupational therapy at nearby centres for physically or mentally handicapped adults. Is there

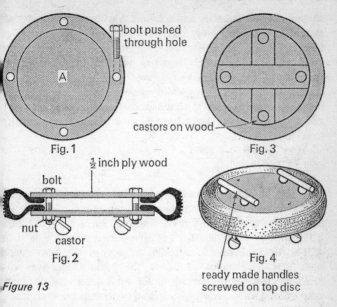

Figure 13

Fig. 1 — bolt pushed through hole · A

Fig. 2 — bolt · nut · castor · ½ inch ply wood

Fig. 3 — castors on wood

Fig. 4 — ready made handles screwed on top disc

a prison or mental hospital in your area? Woodwork departments of secondary schools may welcome the opportunity of providing their boys with a 'social service' aspect to their work. Such boys may be very interested to come and watch their work being used in playgroup – an apprenticeship for fatherhood? Contact local factories and shops and make appointments to see managers and directors. Factory waste products may be valuable in a playgroup: perspex offcuts for junk modelling, wood offcuts for woodwork, large industrial cotton reels for building and modelling, carpet samples for flooring in the home and book corners.

Creative play

How can a child who has never handled a wide variety of natural materials gain concrete understanding of relative sizes, shapes, weights, capacity and colours? A wide range of materials should be provided every day in playgroups – all manner of objects familiar to adults are fresh and new to a playgroup child and provide endless hours of valuable experimentation, particularly the messier varieties of play which are seldom acceptable at home. Young children need lots of time to experiment and come to terms with the properties of creative materials and they will never again have such a leisurely opportunity to do it.

Aprons

You should always provide protective clothing for messy play and insist that children wear it. If a new child feels threatened by being asked to put on a strange garment, give him a little time to see that other children accept it as a rule – he will soon come round to it. Plastic aprons are best. Avoid ones that have tapes to tie at the back. Under-fives can rarely do this for themselves or for each other and the tapes snap off and knot irritatingly. Velcro fastenings are best. E.S.A. and Philip and Tacey make aprons with velcro at approximately 30p each. Snap fasteners are the next best type – Galts make a simple one with a front-fastening, again at about 30p. For some strange reason manufacturers rarely put hooks on their aprons for hanging them up, so you will have to do this yourself. You can also make your own aprons perhaps with the help of some mothers. Figure 14 opposite gives a good basic shape. The apron is cut from PVC or plastic. It is fastened in front with press studs or velcro. For playing with water, stitch nylon sponge round the hem to stop water running on feet and floor. Children can also wear plastic cuffs, although these are not essential if sleeves are well rolled up.

A man's shirt, or plastic mac can be worn back to front. Shorten the sleeves and put elastic round the cuffs and neck. Tie with broad tape at the back of the neck. In some areas mothers can be asked to provide aprons marked with the child's name to keep at playgroup. The number of aprons

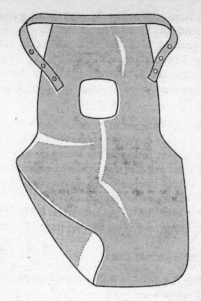

Figure 14

provided at an activity is a good way of regulating the number of children who can play there at any one time. If you are consistent in this, the children will soon learn to hand on their aprons to someone who is waiting for a turn.

FLOOR COVERING If the floor surface is precious it will have to be covered. A large sheet of heavy-duty polythene is best. Failing that, old plastic tablecloths or thick newspapers are adequate.

Painting

Children love painting and become very absorbed in it. A child should always be left to enjoy paint and develop skills at his own pace until one day his apparent haphazard splodges of colour may suggest something to him – 'I have painted a train'.

It is a stage later still before he says 'I am going to paint a train,' confidently picks up a brush and does so. An interesting and well-illustrated book on this subject is *Pre-school and Infant Art* by Kenneth Jameson, Studio Vista, £2·50. This book will help you explain to mothers the stages that children pass through as they learn to paint – they are given here in outline.

1. Joy in colour
    indeterminate splashes of paint,
    colouring whole page one colour – all blue or all red (some children stay at this stage for a long time),
    vertical lines painstakingly painted with tremendous concentration and then coloured all over and 'spoilt'.
2. Emergence of recognizable shapes
    enormous head with legs and arms, no body; the head is very important and often fills the page,
    pin men,
    recognizable human forms.

You can keep a good example of each stage to pin up and discuss with parents.

Equipment

Easels are better than horizontal surfaces which may cause smudged pictures and stained sleeves. Get double-sided easels if possible as painting is very popular. One can also get three- and four-sided easels – these are very expensive to buy (about £17 from E.S.A. and Goodwood) but can be copied. They also save storage and floorspace. Some easels have a blackboard on one side for chalking.

If you can't afford easels – though you should aim at getting some as soon as finances allow – you can cover trestles with washable cloth or polythene and lean them against a wall. Clip on three or four sheets of paper, depending on the length of the table. Put the paint on boxes or small tables between each child. Alternatively, let the children paint on the covered floor or directly onto plastic-topped tables.

BRUSHES The younger the child, the larger the brush. Size 10 or 12 are best for playgroup use. Round- or square-ended are equally suitable. Arnolds, Galts or E.S.A. supply brushes in a range of prices. Buy good ones, they will last longer, especially if thoroughly washed at the end of each session. Store bristles upwards to prevent splaying.

PAINT Powder paint is the most economical. Margros 5 lb tins work out the cheapest at £1·07 each, if you can arrange to bulk buy with another playgroup. Some local education authorities will arrange this for playgroups. Red, blue, yellow and black are essential – you can add other colours as your finances allow. Mix the paint quite thick so that it will not drip and the children can enjoy the feel of it. A little cold water paste or flour mixed in will make it go further and also thicken it. Some playgroups prefer to buy ready-mixed paint. Margros sell this in plastic containers, 20 fl.ozs costs 38p.

CONTAINERS Mixing paint fresh each morning is time-consuming and unnecessary. A week's supply of each colour stored in plastic detergent bottles saves work. Pour a morning's supply into smaller containers each session. Glass jars are dangerous and yogurt pots tip up easily. One can buy non-spill plastic pots which have the added advantage of taking only one brush each. This helps children learn to keep colours clean and separate. A simple non-spill pot can be made by cutting the middle third from a plastic detergent bottle and inverting the top section into the bottom third (after first removing the nozzle). See p. 252.

PAPER Sheets should be large (try 18 ins. × 20 ins). Sugar paper can be bought in bulk. Butcher's paper, lining paper, unprinted ends of newspaper rolls from the offices of your local newspaper, computer print-outs from factories and offices are all useful sources. New children who tend to go through paper at a rapid rate can be given ordinary newspapers but try to avoid sheets with photographs on – the children may think they are expected to colour these. Ring the changes by provid-

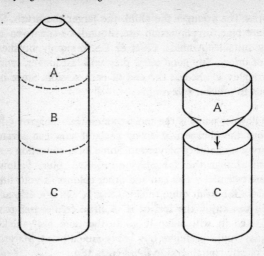

Figure 15 **Non-spill paint pot**

ing different colours – not always white. Change the shape too – squares, circles, triangles.

CLOTHES LINE AND PEGS Something of this nature is necessary to peg paintings up to dry. Remember, however, that for a child the pleasure and purpose are 'doing'. He may well forget all about his picture by dinner-time and not be at all concerned about taking it home. This is quite normal and mothers who have had this point explained to them will usually accept it, even if Mrs Jones's child (who may well be a year older) is taking *his* painting home.

Variations of painting

From time to time you may sense interest in painting is flagging. Some of the older children, and those who have done a lot of painting, will enjoy variations on the brush and paper technique.

COLOUR MIXING If you provide only primary colours – red, blue and yellow – some children may discover how to make new colours out of them. Add black and white paint later and a fuller and more exciting range can be experimented with. A new colour often stimulates new interest in painting for children who have not done any for a while.

FINGER PAINTING Very popular. Clothing needs to be well protected. The paint must be very thick, about the consistency of porridge – adding cold water paste is the cheapest way to achieve this. Plastic-topped tables are delightful to finger-paint on directly, without paper. They provide a large smooth surface which can be easily wiped clean. Otherwise newspaper and the more absorbent types of paper can be used as the paint, being so thick, does not soak in as would ordinary paint.

FOOT-PAINTING Great fun in a well-established playgroup; chaotic in one that is not!

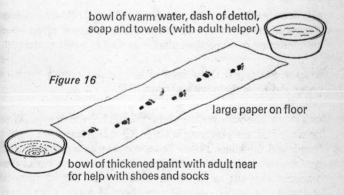

bowl of warm water, dash of dettol, soap and towels (with adult helper)

Figure 16

large paper on floor

bowl of thickened paint with adult near for help with shoes and socks

COMB-PAINTING Mix the paint as for finger-painting and cover all the surfaces to be painted. Use real combs or stiff cardboard ones to make patterns.

POTATO PAINTING Thickened paint again for this, soaked into squares of sponge placed in tin lids. Cut a large potato in half and cut out a simple shape on the inside flat surface. Press the potato surface onto the sponge and stamp the pattern onto a large sheet of paper or plastic table-top. The flattened end of a carrot or cotton reel with a wiggle of string stuck on with Marvin can also be used.

WAX PAINTING Use a piece of candle or a wax crayon to draw an 'invisible' picture or pattern on a large piece of paper. Mix a pot of very thin paint and wash it over all the paper. The children will be delighted by the gradual emergence of the 'magic' picture. Don't forget to discuss with them why this happens.

DECORATING New equipment for the home corner, or even cardboard cartons can be painted by the children. This helps them to be involved in caring for the new equipment as well as providing an opportunity to practise their skills.

SHADOW PAINTING Make blots of different coloured paints. Then fold the paper in half. The resulting 'marbled' effect gives an interesting concept of symmetry as well as a nice pattern.

STRAW PAINTING Drop small dabs of paint onto a piece of paper and blow them with a straw.

CRAYONS The younger the child, the thicker the crayon. Wax ones are best for playgroups. Galts' 'Chubbi-stumps' are a good length and thickness. Plastic boxes for storage are quieter than tins. Provide large sheets of paper. Children can use both sides. You can also cut up wallpaper with heavily ridged patterns and stick the pieces onto a larger sheet of paper. Cover with kitchen paper and rub over with crayon. A print of the picture underneath will appear. Other rubbings can be taken from pieces of bark, coins, floorboards and woven plastic matting.

COLOURED PENCILS These are fine as an occasional substitute

or addition to crayons. They are not in themselves very satisfying to young children, and can cause much frustration if the points keep snapping. So provide pencils with soft leads. Fibre-tip pens come in bright colours and are pleasing to use. Train the children to replace the caps to stop the pens drying up. Under-fives are not ready to colour in outline drawings or trace and should not be asked to do so at playgroup.

CHALKS The commercially produced blackboards and easels are generally too small and rickety for regular use. Hardboard painted with blackboard paint provides a cheap blackboard. Some painting easels have one of their surfaces as a blackboard and children enjoy standing up to chalk on a large surface.

Water-play

How often do we ask children not to splash in puddles? How many times does a young child ask to help with the washing-up or wash his doll's clothes? As adults we appreciate the delights of a warm bath to soothe away the cares of the day; water has a therapeutic value for all of us. Most children don't have the opportunity to play naturally in streams and rivers, puddles and ponds : water-play at playgroup can help redress this and costs virtually nothing. As well as having lots of fun with water, children need to become aware that it obeys its own laws and to discover for themselves what these laws are. They need to practise pouring and measuring. Water is delightfully soothing and makes few demands on a child. Confused, unhappy children, bed-wetters and those who have had problems in their toilet-training will gain much from the therapy of long periods in which to concentrate and relax with water-play.

If you are worried about the mess, give careful consideration to where you put the water. A washroom with a tiled floor is ideal providing all the children know it is there. If it is in the main room, which is easier for unobtrusive supervision, try to arrange for it to be set apart, perhaps in a far corner so that spills can be more easily confined and other children are less likely to interrupt what is often a quiet, contemplative activity.

CONTAINER If you can afford them, use containers commercially produced by educational suppliers. They are usually on castors and have a plug for emptying. Put the plug in upside down so that the children cannot pull it out. If you have to improvise, make sure your containers are rust-proof with a large surface area and a depth of water of about eight inches. A deep container is less messy as the water will not splash out so easily. Old-fashioned galvanized baths are suitable. Baby baths are rather small so if you have to use them provide two: one for the younger children and one for the older. The kitchen sink can be used as long as it is not next to the cooker. Children love running the water from the taps through their fingers. Provide a strong, safe non-slippery surface to raise them to a suitable level to reach the sink and check that the hot water supply is not set at a dangerous temperature. Always use warm water, but add cold water first, so that there is no possibility of scalding. You may like to add a few drops of TCP.

FLOOR COVERING – large ground sheets, plastic tablecloths, anything water-proof in fact. Polythene is slippery when wet. The children's feet will remain dry if you tuck their shoes under the floor covering.

PLASTIC BUCKET AND SMALL CLOTHS should be kept nearby. Let the children realize that it is not a great tragedy if some water goes on the floor, but that you do expect them to be responsible for their own mess, so that they mop it up and then carry on playing.

SMALL EQUIPMENT Keep all small equipment easily accessible in a large plastic bucket, either under the water container or on a covered chair by the side. Provide as wide a variety as possible, avoiding anything which rusts or is made of glass. Because it is the water itself which attracts the children initially, avoid having so many objects that the water cannot be seen. Vary what you provide each day. Make sure there is a balance of objects which will float and sink as well as room for the water to flow.

Small containers of different capacity – yogurt cups, jugs, teapot, plastic beakers. Try not to have only random containers. A graded set of measuring jugs from an educational supplier is useful for older children. Galts make aluminium jugs, varying in size from a centimeter measure to a meter measure. You can improvise a set of these from plastic detergent bottles cut to varying heights. If the time seems ripe, talk to the children about 'How many little jugs fill the big jug?', 'Can you fill the jug half full?' This will help them to incidentally acquire concepts and language of number and ideas about capacity.

Polythene funnels – a large one and a small one. Rubber tubing, two different bores and lengths – although if they're longer than two feet you're asking for trouble! These are useful for making syphons and other experiments.

Plastic detergent bottles and squash bottles.

Plastic lemons to make thin jets – but beware – the children are bound to squirt these at each other!

Plastic foot pump, the sort used for air beds – if you are confident you can control the excitement.

Sponges, pebbles, corks, stones, cotton reels for threading to make a row of barges etc.

Feathers – the children will discover they do not sink. Discuss why.

A variety of containers with holes in (a hot skewer or knitting needle easily pierces holes in yogurt pots and plastic bottles).

Plastic colander, sieve, tea-strainer.

Variations on water-play

1. Bubble-blowing – add washing-up liquid and bubble pipes or twist an 'O' shape on the end of a pipe cleaner – one per child. Blowing bubbles with the hands is very satisfying.
2. Colour the water with food colouring or powder paint.
3. Wash the doll's clothes.
4. Wash some of your equipment.
5. Bath the doll – this can be very helpful for a child coping with an adjustment to a new baby at home.

One of the best yet often forgotten ways of stimulating fresh interest is by *talking* with a child who is playing with the water. There may be a case for letting younger children play uninterrupted but often it is the adult's questioning at just the right moment which can crystallize vague thoughts in a child's mind. Older children who have had time to explore water at their own rate, will enjoy discussing why the big plastic fish floats and the tiny pebbles sink. Why does the syphon only work when you hold the funnel lower than a certain point? Simple experiments in water-play are suggested on p. 339.

Sand

A summer afternoon on a crowded beach. Look around at the many people building sand castles! Not only a range of children of all ages, but fathers and mothers too, grandads down to toddlers all preoccupied with the basic material around them. But summer holidays do not last for ever and few of us have enough opportunity to play and experiment with sand as much as we would like. Indeed, there are many children who have never been to the sea.

Playgroups can go some way towards helping here by providing both wet and dry sand – the properties of each differ sufficiently to make two worthwhile activities. Children will concentrate for long periods on playing with sand. Sand stimulates lots of discussion about size and shapes and capacity, so a helper standing near can develop both language and early experience of number. The younger children and those new to playgroup will experiment digging, pouring and patting the sand with their hands. Older children will develop their play imaginatively and make tunnels, moats and forts using the small equipment listed on p. 261. On p. 266 we point out how dry sand can help an over-fastidious child towards 'messy' play because he can so easily brush it off and feel clean again.

BUYING SAND Always buy washed sand to avoid clothes and hands being stained yellow. This can be got from builders' mer chants, sand and ballast merchants or educational suppliers. Because of the weight carriage is expensive so it pays to collect the sand yourself. Silver sand, obtainable from ironmongers and educational supplies, is delightful for pouring but expensive. Beware of sand from glass-works which may contain slivers of glass.

Sand has a surprising habit of disappearing! Always provide sufficient for the children to be able to pile it up and make deep holes. If you can hear a continuous scraping sound as tools scrape the base of the container, order more sand immediately.

CONTAINERS If inside keep sand in a movable container. A large surface area is important as well as depth. Commercially produced sand-trays are best. Choose one with castors because sand is very heavy. Arnold and E.S.A. make plastic containers on stands, which are equally suitable for water play and cost about £12. The same manufacturers also produce cheaper and smaller plastic sand-trays. A plastic baby bath, a zinc bath or a strong drawer lined with polythene can be used.

Contact reports on a supervisor who made a sand-tray for indoor use from an old door (see Figure 17). Build up the sides and end of the door with strips of wood 4 ins. wide, ½ in. thick so that you have a tray. Then screw a large square piece of chipboard ⅝ in. thick across the lower third of the tray. When tipped up on its enclosed end, this tray can be stored in a space only 5 ins. wide – behind a door perhaps. You can attach 'eyes' at the inside top end to attach to hook on a batten for storage. All the loose sand runs down into the 'box'. About 3 dozen 1½ in. number 8 screws should be adequate. Give the wood several coats of polyurethane varnish or deck varnish to protect it against wet sand – paint inside the chipboard before screwing it on.

To protect the floor cover with a ground sheet or large sheet of heavy-duty polythene – much larger than you would ever think necessary. The PPA film 'Children and Dry Sand' (excellent to hire for parents) shows an old candlewick bedspread which retains a great deal of spilt sand. The children should be ex-

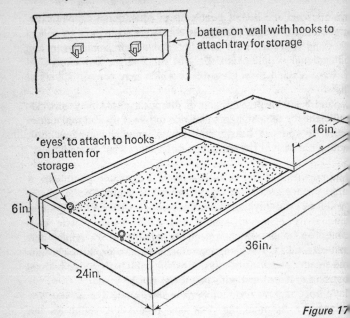

batten on wall with hooks to attach tray for storage

'eyes' to attach to hooks on batten for storage

16 in.

6 in.

36 in.

24 in.

Figure 17

pected to sweep up major spills and to learn how to rub their
hands together over the sand-tray when they have finished
playing, so that any surplus does not 'walk' across the room.
Provide a fairly small plastic dustpan (which sits firmly on the
ground) and brush by each sand container and show each child
how to use it. Give one helper responsibility for keeping an eye
on the sand, particularly if any new children are playing in it.
Sand thrown about is unpleasant as well as wasteful. Sand in
the eyes is particularly upsetting but this should rarely happen
in a well-run playgroup. Limit the number of children in the
sand at any one time. The size of the container will dictate this
but the fewer children there, the less trouble there is likely to
be. This also ensures a decent amount of sand for each child.
Make sure the children know how many are allowed in the sand
– practical number experience.

Clean out the sand regularly; it is amazing how much di-

and odds and ends accumulate there. Children with bad cuts or eczema on their hands should not play in sand.

Wet sand

This is quite different from dry sand. If you cannot manage two sand-trays, then wet sand is more important. The pouring activities which form a large part of dry sand play can to some extent be substituted in water play. Wet sand can be made into endless shapes which are easy to knock down without any bad feelings. This is very valuable for aggressive or tense children.

Sand outside

A permanent outdoor sandpit is a great asset; on p. 235 we suggest a cheap one from second-hand bricks. Galts make a wooden frame for a sandpit 4ft × 6ft – rather expensive at about £24. If you cannot afford a ready-made pit, a team of playgroup fathers may offer to make one; or ask the woodwork master at your local secondary school for help or get in touch with the local scouts and guides. Important points to remember are that all pits need a rim around the edge to prevent the sand spreading. They must also have a cover at night to keep out cats: heavy polythene anchored with bricks at each corner, or a piece of fine mesh or hardboard are all suitable. Drainage is vital to keep the sand fresh so an outdoor pit does not need a base. If possible, avoid siting the pit under a tree; falling leaves make the sand unpleasant. A pit can be improvised with old sinks or baths, the plug removed for drainage, or tractor tyres with the rubber forming comfortable seating.

SMALL EQUIPMENT TO USE WITH SAND

wooden spoons with the handles cut short to protect eyes from being poked

buckets, spades, rakes – rubber or plastic. Galts and Arnolds make good rubber sets

colanders, flour-shakers

sand sieve – Arnolds do a big one at about 47p
scales and paper bags for weighing and measuring
yogurt pots – remove broken ones, they are very sharp
wooden tools for raking and making patterns. Arnolds mak
    these for about 84p a set.
tops of plastic bottles make good funnels and tunnel support
plastic jelly moulds – real ones are best, toy ones too fiddly
cars, lorries, ships to develop imaginative play with the olde
    children. Plastic ones are best as they don't rust. Keep an
    metal ones in a special box so they don't get muddled wit
    the cleaner ones used for other activities.

'No sand allowed'

Some hall committees will not allow sand on their premises fo
fear of spoiling the gloss on their floor. Supervisors who ar
convinced of the great benefits to young children of sand-pla
should do their utmost to convince unsympathetic committee
that adequate floor-covering and proper management will pro
tect the most sensitive floors – we know this from wide ex
perience of playgroups. If they can't be persuaded then outdoo
sand play is a good and in many ways preferable alternative
For indoor use, use sawdust instead. It does not have the sam
pouring properties as dry sand but if water is added it wil
behave similarly to wet sand. You can usually get it free o
charge from builders or timber merchants. One advantage is tha
if any goes in a child's eye it is not as difficult to remove as sand

Plastic materials

Mud is a natural and very basic material of our environment
However, it can be a messy one, and many adults are unabl
to tolerate this kind of play even when a child is suitably clad
If you do have mud-play at your playgroup, and it is highl
commendable if you do, make sure the mothers understand it
value.

Clay

If you can't have mud-play, or have no outdoor play area, clay is an excellent substitute. It is in fact essential to every good playgroup. It is a natural material which children need to experiment with and learn about. They will bang, twist, punch and pummel it, often with a continuous verbal commentary. How delightful to be as aggressive and destructive as one likes! Far better, in fact, to bang around at a large lump of clay than do that to the new baby. Children who have been confused and worried by their mothers' over-strict toilet-training benefit tremendously from opportunities to play with a material which is socially acceptable and yet bears a close resemblance to their forbidden excreta. Clay provides opportunities for intellectual learning too – the children become familiar with different tensile strengths and learn that bigger lumps of clay are heavier than smaller ones.

It is far better for two children to have enough clay to experiment with – a piece about half as big as their own head – than for six children to have pieces the size of table-tennis balls. Beware also of drowning the activity in a sea of irrelevant odds and ends. The prime object of the exercise is for children to come to terms with clay, not with rolling pins or plastic knives. These may be added for older ones to renew interest, but the newer and younger children just need to be left alone to experiment at their own pace with their lump of clay. Once tins and rolling pins are provided the play is being directed – adult suggestions are being presented to the child. Make sure your helpers realize this.

If possible buy clay in large quantities and share with another playgroup. Art and craft shops, educational suppliers, sometimes pottery departments in large schools may be able to get it cheap for you.

It is very important to keep clay the right consistency: too wet and it will stick to everything, too dry and it cannot be manipulated by a young child. Ideally it should be just stiff enough to mould easily and hold its shape. Divide it into as many balls as there are to be children at the clay table. Press a

deep hole with your thumb in each ball and fill with water
Then draw the edges together to enclose the water. Wrap al
the balls in polythene and place in a plastic bucket with a well-
fitting lid. Dried-out clay can be rescued by filling the storage
bucket with water and letting the clay absorb it for a couple of
days.

SMALL EQUIPMENT If you are sure it is the children, and not
the adults, who need something to renew fresh interest in clay,
ring the changes with the following small equipment:
rollers – broom handles chopped up are cheap and adequate
pastry cutters – adult-sized ones, toy ones are too fiddly
knives – plastic or blunt tea or fish knives
forks – plastic, to make patterns
split peas, shells, buttons, lolly sticks, anything with an interesting shape.

Other plastic materials

Occasionally you may decide to provide plasticine or some
other commercial material. Many children have this kind of
thing at home, very few clay – so though these materials make
an occasional change, they are *not* a substitute for clay.

Dough

Try to dissociate dough from cooking. Let the children experiment with a large lump of their own. As with clay, it is
the pushing, pulling, poking and stretching that is valuable.
Baking activities fit better into play in the home corner (see p
267). However, because of its wholesome associations with
cooking it may be a useful material to encourage an over
fastidious child towards 'messy' play.

RECIPES – each sufficient for 4–6 children

1. 3 lb plain flour
   ½ block cooking salt
   about 1½ pints of cold water

2. 3 lb self-raising flour
   1 ¼ pints water (no salt)
   a very stretchy dough
3. 3 lb plain flour
   1 lb salt
   1 teaspoonful alum (available from chemists, makes dough keep longer)
   mixture of cooking oil and water to mix
   This dough is very good for holding its shape.

These doughs will keep for a week in a plastic bag. Food colouring can be added. This helps to get children away from simply 'baking tarts' and on to more general creative play with the material.

'Messy' play

Occasionally one finds a child who is too inhibited to play with messy materials. He shows disgust at the idea of getting his hands soiled and fears his mother's anger if his clothes are dirty. He may even dislike other children's messy play. Do not underestimate the importance of helping such children, for ironically they are in the greatest need of the more liberating types of activity. Many psychologists believe that an over-rigid toilet-training which has taught a child to feel shame and disgust at his natural bodily functions is at the root of this problem. It then follows that anything which the child (or his mother) associates with these basic functions becomes 'dirty' or 'naughty' too. A baby attempting to wipe scrambled egg through his hair is not all that different from a playgroup child squelching clay through his fingers. If mother told him not to do this kind of thing when he was in his high chair and continued saying 'no' for another two or three years, you can see why a child coming to playgroup may be just too tense and frightened to get dirty. A supervisor should fully understand and sympathize with the causes of such inhibitions. The child needs to learn that 'good' is not always synonymous with 'clean'. And it is essential that he should be able to trust the adult who is encouraging him towards what can be quite a frightening situation. As far as possible try to allocate one adult to be responsible for building up a relationship with the child. Let them talk together frequently and get used to playing together in non messy situations, perhaps with a jigsaw or looking at books.

As the child gradually gains confidence in the adult he can be very slowly moved towards more basic materials. Hasten slowly. You can undo weeks of good work by one hasty move. Try to work out a progression in the activities so that the process is slowed down for the child. For example dry sand which can be easily brushed off may be more acceptable than the stickier wet sand. Plasticine, a familiar material probably approved by mother at home, or dough with its whiteness and wholesome associations may prove more inviting initially than clay. A relaxed atmosphere in the playgroup will help. The child will learn that you do not mind the occasional spill as long as it is mopped up. In fact children often enjoy the mopping up as much as what they were doing.

To encourage the child to paint, give him a pot of white paint, or pink perhaps, to use on black paper. Introduce him to comb-painting before finger-painting. Make sure he has more than adequate protective clothing. A bowl of water, with soap and towel actually on the table you are using will be very reassuring. Above all, ensure that the other adults in the play group behave in the same way towards him. A helper who says to a child up to his elbows in clay 'You *are* dirty, aren't you dear.' even though she may smile benignly, is not very different in her reaction from the mother who scolds the child for not keeping clean.

Sometimes supervisors themselves find it difficult to accept messy play and shy away from providing it in their playgroup. While we sympathize with the difficulties of changing deeply ingrained attitudes in adults, such supervisors need to be aware of how much valuable play the children are missing. Try visiting playgroups where clay, dough and wet sand are regularly and successfully provided. Your local PPA area organizer or Infant School Advisor will supply addresses.

Imaginative play

Imaginative play allows children to play out the facts and fantasies of their everyday lives. Coming to terms with a new baby or going to hospital are obvious situations when a child needs to play through his fears and doubts. He also needs the chance to practise being a mother, a father, or to find out what it feels like to be the opposite sex, the eldest, blind, or a postman. In other words, children need to be given the chance to play out different roles from the ones they have in real life. In this way they can begin to gain insight and knowledge into human behaviour and relationships.

The home corner

Give as much space as possible to this. Screen the area off to give privacy inside the 'house'. The quieter the area, the more chance the children have to talk with each other and develop their language skills. Screens covered with painted paper or hessian or opaque curtains hung on wires are suitable. A piano or large cupboard turned at right-angles to the wall can be used to cut off another side of the area. Manufactured Wendy houses, apart from being expensive, tend to be much too small. Remember it is *inside* the house that is important – this is where most of the play takes place. Meticulously painted door knobs and bricks are irrelevant to the fantasy play which takes place behind the door.

EQUIPMENT Try to provide as many of the following as possible and have them life-size – which means looking in Woolworth's rather than toy catalogues.

dustpan and brush
duster – hung up
kettle, saucepans, frying pan
tea-set and cutlery – plastic picnic sets in different colours
    give an opportunity for learning to match up colours
telephone – ex-GPO. In many areas, these can be obtained

free of charge. Contact the local Telephone Manager's office (address at front of telephone directory).

iron and ironing board – child-size

cooker – this can be improvised and renewed frequently by painting, together with the children, a large cardboard carton. A more permanent alternative is an old bedside locker with cotton reels for switches and circular rubber mats stuck on for hotplates.

plant or vase of flowers – real not plastic. Let the children arrange flowers in a vase.

small table and chairs – adult ones with the legs shortened. Ask the PPA area organizer if you can buy second-hand infant-school furniture from your local School Supplies Depot. These depots are a great source of cheap equipment.

pram and cradle – ask mothers to provide dolls clothes and bedding. If they do any knitting, suggest they use a synthetic fibre so that the clothes will withstand children's washing at playgroup. Put an assortment of fastenings on the dolls' clothes – press-studs, hooks and eyes and buttons all large. Simplicity pattern 9137 shows how to make a set of rag dolls dressed in clothes incorporating a variety of fastenings.

talcum-powder tin, nappies, baby's bottle

rubber sheet – for dolls who wet the bed

child-sized bed and bedding – a camp bed, or discarded cot with a side removed and the legs cut down.

dolls, including teddies. Dolls can be loved or hated, depending on current needs. Boys need this kind of play as much as girls – remember the need to play out roles other than those of real life. Provide a selection of dolls – some cuddly, some washable, not only baby dolls. Include a sixteen-inch doll in the family.

Sexual curiosity

Some manufacturers, including Galts and Abbatts, are now producing boy dolls – hitherto dolls have been sexless. If you provide a boy doll it will arouse comments and curiosity about the

doll's genitals. Discussions with playgroup staff about sex education suggest that most playgroup children show surprisingly
little curiosity about the subject other than an interest in the
way their sex organs differ from those of the opposite sex.
Hospital and family play is where most of this curiosity is
worked through, and if we accept that one of the main reasons
we provide these activities is for children to learn about other
people, their differences and their similarities, then we must
accept, indeed welcome, their curiosity about each other's
bodies. Children from homes where brothers, sisters or parents
are not seen unclothed will tend to be the most curious – they
still have a lot to find out.

Supervisors should be fully accepting of children's conversation and comments on this kind of subject, no matter how
'shocking' they may be to some sensitive ears. A young child
rarely speaks to shock – he is merely using the only vocabulary
available to him, perhaps from a home where parents find it
difficult to discuss personal topics with their children. If you
also show embarrassment or squash any questions you will
not be helping. If you fear you may be imparting your own
embarrassment to the children, try imagining that you are
answering questions about another more easily discussed area
of the body – arms or ears perhaps!

Even if a supervisor is relaxed about matters of sexual curiosity, she must make sure that her helpers are too. Iron out
any opposing views at staff meetings. It is never wise to give
conflicting values to children and, whilst respecting a helper's
modesty, your first responsibility is, as always, to the children
in your care.

Dens

Most children like to feel they can escape from adult eyes for
a time. Provide a secret place where children cannot be seen or
see anyone else. A trestle table with a dark blanket draped over
it, or a cupboard under the stairs in a home playgroup, will
give great scope to the imagination.

Hospital play

This is closely linked with the home corner – a bed there may
well stimulate hospital play. Many children have to go to
hospital, and even if they do not their mothers may, which can
create equally unpleasant associations. It is helpful to let a child
come to terms with his fears through play. If you know a child
is soon to go to hospital, introduce a relevant book into the
book corner, and have a story about it such as *Zozo Goes To
Hospital* (Chatto & Windus, 90p).

EQUIPMENT Bed and bedding, bandages – strips of old
sheets; safety pins – snaplock type used for nappies, train
children to use these sensibly and effectively; stethoscope –
Galts do a good child-sized one that works, your GP may oblige
with an old one; white overall – cut down a real one for the
doctor; white masks – often the most frightening thing in hos-
pitals for younger children (make sure they don't upset a timid
newcomer); nurse's uniform; injection kit – syringe from an
icing set, or your local Child Welfare Clinic may let you have
their used disposable syringes.

Dressing up

Keep this near the home corner. All children love dressing up
and gain much from so doing. Don't keep the clothes in a
jumble – get free wire coat-hangers from dry cleaners, wrap a
little sticking pláster to blunt the end of the hook and then
hang the clothes from a strong wire which can be taken down
at the end of each session. Dressing-up clothes soon become
dirty and tattered – look upon this as a chance to involve playgroup mothers in washing, ironing and mending. Do not do
plays or acting with the children when they are dressed up. The
idea is to develop their imagination, not yours.

Try to provide a wide range of clothes including men's gar-
ments, the need for these is often overlooked. Hats are especially important – they may be enough to transform a child into

an imagined character. The following are very useful : policeman's helmet, crash helmet, bowler hats, men's caps, garden-party hats, wigs, spectacle frames, grown-up shoes – male and female, jewellery, ties, belts, large safety pins, nighties, lace curtains, bedspreads, handbags, shopping baskets, large mirror, shaving kit – without blades.

Boys who wear female clothes

Some little boys spend much of their time at playgroup dressing up in female clothes and following female pursuits such as pushing dolls prams. Don't be worried by this and always re-assure an anxious mother that it is quite common in young children. A mother may become extremely troubled if she feels her son is constantly playing at being a female, and she may fear he will develop homosexual tendencies. Your attitude to this will affect to some extent how she deals with it. Don't stop a little boy in this kind of play – he obviously needs it and, because of his mother's attitude, is unlikely to be allowed the opportunity at home. If, however, a child's behaviour is still worrying you after at least a couple of terms at playgroup, you can seek outside advice from the local Child and Family Guidance Clinic. Their specialized help and experience will re-inforce the reassurances you have given the mother and if any help is needed it can be given before the mother has had too long in which to aggravate the situation by her anxiety. Many children live in an almost totally female world, and in sorting out for themselves the interrelationships of their world need to play through the roles of the people they see around them. If most of the people they see happen to be female, it follows that their play will be on female lines.

In all this we should remember that most of what we con-sider to be male behaviour or female behaviour is not innate. It is conditioned into our behaviour as we grow up by the society we live in. When we look at the way other societies live, we often see men carrying out quite happily what we con-sider to be female occupations and vice versa. A little boy at playgroup who constantly wants to play at being a girl or woman, has not yet received enough of the conventional conditioning to have acquired the concept of maleness expected of him in our society. This may be due, for example, to his being fatherless or to having an over-dominant mother. Regular visits from men to the playgroup will go some way to helping such children.

Shops

Shopping play is an important part of pre-number experience, since shopping is a real situation in which children see numbers being used most frequently. Money is paid, change is given, goods are weighed and measured and quantities are discussed. Shopping need not be organized by the supervisor – it will evolve naturally if a shop is provided, though sometimes you may have to help decide who is to be shopkeeper. Two orange boxes sanded and painted with a plank across the top make an ideal counter with storage space below. Otherwise use two chairs facing each other frontwards so that the seats form the counter.

Avoid the temptation to organize activities for making things for the shop. This is a pleasant activity for infant schools but under-fives are rarely ready to be so specific in what they make. Instead, ask them to bring empty food packages from home. You will soon have far more than you need and any surplus can be used for junk modelling. You can also use a selection of the following: scales – balancing or spring type; small paper bags; shopping baskets and carrier bags; boxes of split peas, buttons, with a scoop for weighing; tape measure; 'open' and 'closed' signs to hang up – pre-reading experience for the older children; cash register – a strong toy one, real ones can sometimes be picked up from junk shops or auction sales; telephone – ex-GPO if possible (see p. 267); purses and money – some playgroups provide real money.

Each session a certain amount, say 10p, made up of different combinations of coins, is put out. This provides a good opportunity for children to become familiar with the names of the coins and gives valuable training in checking up and returning the right amount when it's time to clear away.

Puppets

Puppets are discussed on p. 295. Always be aware that some of the younger children may be frightened of them. It is usually best to leave them around, so that children can get used to handling them gradually at their own rate.

Dolls house

Dolls houses are not generally suitable for under-fives – more so for little girls of around six. However, you may have a few precocious girls in your playgroup who enjoy a dolls house. Remember that people are needed in the house as well as furniture. Ready-made miniature figures are very expensive – you can make your own out of pipe-cleaners and scraps of material. Galts' open-sided dolls' house is ideal as at least two children can be accommodated around it.

Cooking

This is always a popular activity, possible in home groups and those halls lucky enough to have the use of an oven. Cooking provides endless opportunities for number experiences and number language. You can take two or three children to the shops to buy the ingredients, discussing their names, weights and prices. Back at playgroup, the weighing out and mixing to different consistencies stimulates lots of good conversation and fun. You will no doubt also have some favourite recipes of your own. The following are three of ours.

GINGERBREAD MEN
(approximately 16 'men')
8 oz plain flour
1 level tsp. baking powder
1 level tsp. powdered ginger
3 oz margarine
2 oz sugar
1 level tsp. golden syrup

milk to mix
a few currants

Sieve together flour, baking powder and ginger. Rub margarine into flour. Add sugar and golden syrup. Mix till smooth with a wooden spoon. Gradually add just enough milk to make a very firm consistency. Roll out and cut with special cutter or cut around pattern made of thick card. Transfer to greased baking tin. Add currants for eyes, nose, mouth and buttons. Bake near top of hot oven (425°F., gas mark 6–7) for approximately 10 minutes.

CRISPY CRACKOLATES

1 oz sugar
1 oz butter
1 oz cocoa
1 tbs. golden syrup
1 oz cornflakes

Put butter, sugar and cocoa into a pan. Add golden syrup. Leave on low heat till all ingredients melt slowly. Remove from heat and cool slightly. Add cornflakes and stir in. When they are thoroughly coated with the mixture, spoon into small piles on to a dish or bun cases and leave to set.

PEPPERMINT CREAMS

1 lb icing sugar
1 egg white
half a lemon
peppermint essence

Sift icing sugar through a sieve into a bowl. Separate egg and put white only into the bowl with the sugar (the yolk is not needed for this recipe). Mix with a wooden spoon. Knead with hands until thoroughly blended. Squeeze lemon and add juice till mixture is bound together and not crumbly. Add peppermint essence, drop by drop, to a suitable strength. (About half a teaspoonful is right for most children.) Press out with fingers on a cold surface – a plastic table top will do. Cut into shapes if you have special cutters. If not use a knife to make squares and triangles.

Destructive play

For some children this is a stage of development which must take place before constructive play can begin. Such children may be very difficult to handle and although supervisors must ensure that other children are not hurt or their play spoiled, this often becomes the only concern so that the long-term task of trying to help a destructive child is neglected.

Sand and clay are extremely valuable here. They can be bashed and banged at will and are very satisfying emotionally. A particularly destructive child may respond to being given a few large cardboard cartons of his own each day, to do what he likes with. He may feel so delighted with this special privilege that he will stop being destructive and make something out of the boxes. See p. 182 for other ways of handling disruptive children.

Guns

Aggression is present in all young children. This is normal and natural. One of the biggest problems for a sensitive parent is how to help a child keep a balance between not being a bully and yet not being bullied. At playgroup you can try to channel a child's aggression into more socially acceptable behaviour.

The Wild West, guns and cowboys with their special suits and hats are part of our culture and we cannot, and indeed should not, rule them out altogether. However, if a few children bring their guns to playgroup and are allowed to use them, more children will bring *their* guns on subsequent days until the whole situation gets out of hand. Why not have a 'gun box' in the cloakroom? If guns are deposited on arrival gun play will die a natural death!

Some supervisors complain that the children, particularly the older boys, insist on making guns from construction sets or woodwork. If this happens a great deal, examine the quality and quantity of play you are providing in your playgroup. There is some evidence to show that aggression and gun play are at their highest where the general play environment is poor. Is there enough equipment to encourage physical play, so that the children can get rid of surplus energy? Are they able to bang a large lump of clay around, or scrub black paint over a big sheet of white paper? As always when you are worried about problem behaviour, check on what you are giving the children, rather than what they are not giving you.

Manipulative play

Children need opportunities to practise cutting, drawing, screwing, pouring and many other skills though you should be careful not to have too much of these as do some playgroups. The advantages are of course obvious – they are clean, quiet, adult-controlled and their educational values are much more immediately clear to an untrained eye than many other playgroup activities.

It is essential to provide equipment that covers a wide range of difficulty, so that a child can progress as he develops understanding and skill. If the equipment is too demanding he will become frustrated; if it is too easy, he will get bored and possibly naughty. So avoid toys which are small and fiddly – the younger the child, the larger the equipment.

Sometimes problems arise when children begin putting odd pieces of a toy in their pockets 'to take home'. The PPA Supervisors Handbook offers a delightful way of dealing with this :

> If you have a child going through a 'taking' phase, slip a piece of the puzzle and a bead or two into your own pocket and say 'I've found these in my pocket, just have a look and see if you can find any in your pockets.' The child who produces the missing piece has the satisfaction of being thanked, of helping you to complete the puzzle and of putting it away with you. His conscience is cleared, your puzzle is complete, his mother will have no cause for anxiety and the child will have received gratitude and approving attention – which was what he was needing.

Table-top toys

JIGSAWS These provide practice in hand-and-eye coordination and in recognizing shapes – a valuable pre-reading activity. Children can often do ones far more difficult than the age group stated by the manufacturer. The range should extend from picture-trays whose objects lift out through to puzzles of twenty or so pieces. Wooden puzzles are best if you can afford them. Try making an arrangement with another playgroup to exchange jigsaws say once a term. When boxes disintegrate, store puzzles in plastic bags with punched holes, tied up with a pipe-cleaner.

PEG-BOARDS Children find these very satisfying. Galts make trays of peg-board with houses, animals and trees which lift out. These can be rearranged as the child wishes to depict farms, villages. Arnolds sell packs of 100 plastic pegs in assorted colours for 26p. Children enjoy fitting these into a piece of peg-board (an off-cut is fine). The older children will progress to sorting colours, different groupings and patterns.

THREADING BEADS Cube beads are best – round ones roll about too much. The beads need to be large enough not to go up noses or in ears. Arnolds sell packets of 100, 18 mm. cubes in assorted colours for approximately £1·24. Painted cotton reels are very good. Thread on to plastic-covered wires or metal-topped laces with a very large knot at one end.

TOYS FOR MATCHING AND GRADING SIZE, SHAPE AND COLOUR There are many kinds on the market – try to provide a balance rather than random odds and ends. Make sure there are no pieces missing or the purpose of the toy is lost.
    nesting barrels or boxes
    long pegs for pyramids of graded rings
    posting box – different shapes 'posted' through matching
        cutouts in lid
    activity board – a large piece of strong wood on which are
        nailed four or five real-life objects which require skill to

work and stimulate intellectual curiosity and language. For example: zip fastener, padlock and key, bicycle bell, telephone dial, bolt, inside of clock with its winder

Matching games – picture lotto, picture dominoes, snap cards for older children

HAMMERING TOY – pegs to knock down with a wooden hammer. Reverse and knock them back again.

Construction sets

These are expensive, so it is worth discussing relative assets and snags with other playgroups. Keep to one type initially, and add to it as finances permit – it is frustrating for a child not to have enough pieces to complete what he has set out to do. Avoid sets which will make only one end product. Sets which have proved successful in many playgroups include Lego and Jumbo Lego, Fit-bits, Abbatt's 'Connector', Galts 'First Construction Set', Matador, Plastic Meccano, Bila fix.

Floor toys

These toys require careful thought concerning the layout of your room. Arrange the floor toys in bays, preferably in a far corner away from the main areas of movement so that a painstakingly built tower is not in constant danger of being knocked down by a trike or pram. Provide an area of smooth carpet so that if a tall tower does collapse, the noise is lessened.

BRICKS These are essential and will last so don't economize on quality. Many manufacturers provide duffle bags to keep them in. Ready-made beechwood bricks have the advantage of being always constructed on the same module. The children will learn, incidentally, that 'two small bricks are as long as one big brick' or that a rectangular brick is made up of four small bricks. Many other mathematical concepts and size relationships will be discovered through play and discussion with adults.

The small coloured cubes in toy shops often called 'Nursery bricks' are not suitable for playgroups on their own, their use being too limited. They can however be used in conjunction with a sack of beechwood blocks.

ROAD LAYOUTS Strips of hardboard and a traffic or train roundabout can be made quite simply from hardboard painted with white lanes (Figure 18a). Add a garage or multi-storey car park for older children; also models of trees, houses and traffic signs to stimulate further ideas. You can discuss road safety here. You will need hardboard, ½-inch thick wood and ½-inch panel pins. To make the track cut the hardboard as in diagrams A, B and C. Then make sure the pieces can be easily interchanged make a template of the interlocking shape F and draw round it for each junction. Cut carefully *on* the drawn line. To make the bridge (Figure 18b) cut two sides as on E using ½-inch planed wood, and D using hardboard. Fix D to sides E with the panel

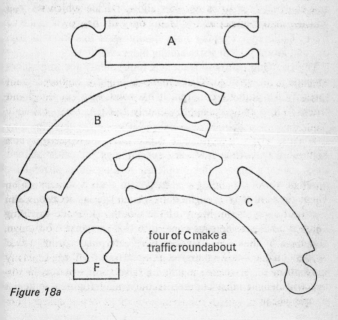

A

B

C

four of C make a
traffic roundabout

F

Figure 18a

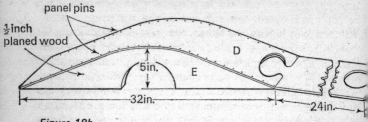

Figure 18b

pins, starting in the centre. The wider the base dimension of
the bridge, the easier the construction will be as there will be
less 'bend' on D. The track can be stored neatly inside the bridge.

TRAIN LAYOUT The 'Child Guidance' sets are plastic, reasonably priced and do not distort. The Brio miniature railway is an
excellent wooden set. Both of these are available from Arnolds
and can be added to as finances allow. Decide which set you
will use at the outset as toy trains only fit their own make of
track. Children may play individually with this kind of toy,
or good group play develop among older children.

The coupling of many train sets is too fiddly for under-fives
to cope with unaided. Galts make a brightly coloured train
specially for younger children. It has solid, easy couplings and
trucks to load and costs approximately £4·64.

GIMMICK TOYS Experienced supervisors may keep a box
hidden away with a few very special toys for using on wet
days, calming turn-taking problems, settling in a particularly
upset new child, building a relationship with a solitary child.
These toys are only brought out on such special occasions and
then put away again. Many of the clockwork 'Made in Hong-
kong' type of seaside toys come into this category. You might
also have a 'slinky' – a strange wire caterpillar spring which
'walks' unaided downstairs; a musical box; an egg-timer; a
snowstorm paperweight; a pair of false teeth – hardly a toy
but will delight most children (though may frighten some); a
jumping bean.

Woodwork

We need only remember the toddler banging a spoon on the saucepan lid to realize what pleasure children find in hammering; the problem is that some children find it *too* pleasurable and can drive an adult to distraction!

The most obvious solution to this, if you can possibly manage it, is to put the woodwork outdoors. If not, use a cloakroom, corridor or some anteroom so that it is not in the main play area. If it *has* to be with the other activities, arrange the woodwork in a corner far from the entrance – a timid child may be put off by a hammer being the first thing he sees on entering! This leads on to the question of safety. Some supervisors do not provide woodwork because they fear accidents. It is our belief that accidents occur most in playgroups where the quality of both play and supervision is poor. Undoubtedly, woodwork must be constantly supervised (though not directed). There must be one adult throughout the session responsible for keeping an eye on it. When this is coupled with a generally calm and busy atmosphere accidents rarely happen.

If you are still sceptical, limit the number of children at the bench to two until both children and adults are familiar with the tools. On introducing the activity show the children how to hold a nail when it is to be hammered, carefully pointing out the best way to avoid hammering one's fingers.

Some children will progress to the stage of making simple toys. The majority, however, will simply learn the properties of wood, the best way to cut, smooth and join it, the physical skills involved in putting in and taking out nails, the angles and surfaces which will or will not join together satisfactorily. The adult at the woodwork bench, wanting to feel 'useful', may try and persuade the children to make something. Explain to her that her role, apart from ensuring safe play, is to tread the delicate line between letting children discover at their own rate, and stepping in when a child reaches deadlock in what can be discovered through practical experience and needs a word from someone with wider knowledge.

Woodwork may provide an ideal opportunity to involve

fathers. Some men may be willing to enter the predominantly female playgroup world if it is to take part in a 'masculine' activity. The supervisor must ensure in such situations that the fathers understand the gradual way in which children learn, so that an over-enthusiastic father doesn't pressure the children into making highly complex creations! However, if it is to be a one-off visit from the father there is no harm and much to be gained by the children in watching an adult's skills being simply and clearly demonstrated.

Equipment

BENCH – most educational suppliers produce child-sized ones. They are good but very expensive, around £29. A sawn-through log of wood that does not wobble or an old infant-school table are alternatives.

FLOOR PROTECTION may be necessary – use an old piece of carpet.

WOOD – soft wood is essential, balsa is ideal. It is very frustrating and unfair to expect a child to drive a nail into a piece of hard wood. Local timber merchants will usually supply cheaply (or free, if you are lucky) sacks of offcuts. Explain that they are for young children so that there is no hard wood in the sack. If you run out of offcuts, the nails can be banged into a solid log which has been cut to sit firmly on the ground. Also supply a wide variety of odds and ends such as bottle tops. The junk table nearby may provide further material.

3–4 LB. MIXED NAILS, LARGE AND SMALL STAPLES – keep in a tin with a lid. A magnet deals with spills.

TOOLS Toy tool sets are a waste of money, use adult ones, a a child will gain far more skill and satisfaction from learning to use real tools. Check, however, that hammers in particular are not too heavy. Also include a vice, two claw-ended hammers, pincers, gimlet, small saw (no sawing unless wood is in the vice), sandpaper, small plane or surform. Children must learn respect for their tools from the outset. A piece of pegboard with the tool-shapes outlined on it is a good means of storage and helps to check what is missing when clearing up.

APRONS – not vital, but can be useful to limit the number working at the woodwork bench. Large pockets across the front of the aprons are good for storing 'important' things.

GLUE – provide small amounts of Marvin Medium or Evo-stik in a yogurt pot to join soft woods. Apply with plastic spatula, lolly stick or old toothbrush.

PAINT – need not be at the woodwork bench as its presence there may pressure some children into making things before they are ready. Should however always be available for completed toys if required.

Junk modelling

This costs virtually nothing and provides an ideal opportunity for mothers to see what children can do with junk – by looking in at playgroup and thus seeing how they could do similar things at home.

The value of junk play lies in allowing the children to experiment with the vast range of materials you provide. They will discover the best way to cut certain surfaces and the best way to join others together. It will be a long time before they begin to make specific objects. Some children may never reach that stage at playgroup, though they will reach it far quicker at school if they have had full opportunity for experimentation at playgroup. An older child may occasionally need some adult direction to be shown, for example, how and when to use a split paper-clip. This is very different from the 'this is a nice box, wouldn't it make a lovely train' variety of adult-directed creativity.

Equipment

The list of objects to collect is endless, but here is a cross-section
of the kind of things to be on the lookout for:
shoe-boxes – shoe shops are usually delighted to give these
away, egg boxes, cereal cartons, yogurt pots and lids, round
cheese boxes, matchboxes, supermarket packaging for fruit,
yogurt pots etc., apple-trays – from greengrocers, tin-foil dishes
– various shapes and sizes, corks, string, rope, raffia, wool,
broken eggshells (washed), melon seeds – dried out slowly on a
tray in the oven, spaghetti, macaroni, rice, split peas, cabbage
leaves – savoy cabbage has an interesting texture, a bag of
material scraps – varied in texture, fibre and colour, gummed
paper, cellophane, sweet papers – coloured and clear, doyleys,
corrugated paper, milk tops – washed, box of wood shavings,
box of dead matches, pipe cleaners, toilet-roll middles, buttons,
toothpaste-tube caps, cotton reels, polystyrene, slices of plastic
bottles.

New material will supply new ideas – try to provide different
combinations each day.

You will need at least one very large box to keep the materials
in. Three or four smaller containers may be better so that the
children are not perpetually rummaging around. Cheap square
washing-up bowls, three-tier vegetable racks, or supermarket
display baskets if you can get them, are good containers. Small
objects such as buttons, feathers, milk tops, can be kept separate
by storing each in a different pocket of a plastic shoe holder.
Sorting the junk into separate containers is an activity in its
own right and it is interesting to see how the children, left to
their own devices, choose to group the materials. If you have a
very wide selection of objects it may be overwhelming for the
children to have everything out at each session. The supervisor
will choose what to have.

Glue

Marvin and Multiglue (by the gallon) are similar and both are
suitable for junk play (see p. 343 for address). Both these glues

are water-soluble, so a little water can be added to make them go further. If glue gets on a child's clothing, wash off immediately with clean water. Dried-on glue will come off with Toluene available from chemists; two fluid ounces last a very long time.

If you put out too much glue, the children will use too much. Pour a little from large containers into a small yogurt pot each day. Remember to wipe the bottle top or it won't open next day! Spatulas or lollysticks are better than brushes for applying the glue – the children cannot put as much glue on a spatula. If you have to use brushes, try old toothbrushes.

Other things you will probably need are steel wool – for scraping plastic bottles and pots to be painted; split paper clips – for attaching wheels and other difficult shapes; needle and cotton – keep in a place where the children can go to get it when needed. Adults may have to give practical help when a child asks for something to be sewn. Short-arm stapler; sellotape – with a dispenser if possible; brown paper tape; scissors – these must be round-ended but sharp. Far more accidents arise in playgroups from the frustration caused by blunt scissors. Only two or three pairs are necessary. Children can share as the scissors are not likely to be needed simultaneously. Aprons provide protection from glue. They also limit the number of children taking part. Paint – a child may want to paint a completed object, but if it is not to disintegrate he will first have to leave glue to dry overnight. This may be too long for a younger child who may lose interest in the previous day's work. For those children who do need paint, mix Marvin in with it so it becomes thick enough to cover wording and plastic adequately. Litter bin or old box – place this on a chair, easily accessible for the children so that they learn to put waste straight into the bin.

Cutting out

Using scissors is a difficult skill and young children need plenty of opportunity to practise it. The scissors provided must be sharp enough to cut a variety of thicknesses, but have rounded ends. It is unfair to make a child feel he has failed simply because the scissors are too blunt. Newcomers will enjoy just cutting strips of paper – newspaper is adequate. Later they can cut out pictures from magazines or old toy catalogues – choose large, bright, clear pictures. They may then later stick what they have cut out onto large sheets of paper. Small bottles of glue made with a rubber nozzle are good for this. The children need to learn how much glue is required, that too much makes their picture dirty and too little will not stick.

For variety and cutting practice give children pieces of material of different thicknesses and textures. They can also use materials from the junk table. Older and more skilled children can then experiment with colour, shapes and texture to create patterns and even eventually picture collages, which can be glued onto large sheets of paper.

11
Language – The Most Important Skill

Language development

'We simply do not know how many people are frustrated in their lives by an inability ever to express themselves adequately; or how many may never develop intellectually because they lack the words with which to think and reason.'*

Language and speech are an important means of communication between people. We know that language is an important factor in peoples' emotional development and that poor language development may hinder their educational attainments. Recently a great deal of research has taken place into the way language skills develop and it has been found that the basis of good language development is formed in the very early years.

You will probably have noticed enormous differences in the language skills that children have when they come to playgroup. Age obviously plays a large part in this, but the most important factor is, as usual, what has been going on at home. Has a child had adequate opportunity to hear, understand, and later repeat the names of familiar objects and people? What opportunity has he had to assemble and reassemble these into thoughts and ideas? How much speaking has he heard at home? Has he grasped the fundamental notion that language is a means of communication? When learning to talk, the child echoes the speech of others and the lucky child is then rewarded with praise for the sounds he has made. Surprisingly soon, the normal child learns to use a word to get what he wants. Most mothers will remember the all-demanding baby in his highchair calling

* Ministry of Education Report of Central Advisory Council for Education (England), 'Half our Future', H.M.S.O., 1963.

for 'More, more!' His mother and other adults reinforce the child's attempts at speech and he is encouraged to practise his new-found skills, improving and increasing his understanding and use of language as he does so. The greater the variety of experiences and conversations a child has, the better his language skills will be.

Children from homes and institutions are often stunted in their language development. Because no single adult has been able to take a continuous interest in them, the gentle day-to-day talking and listening situations, practice and rewards, may not have taken place. When we consider that these children are the ones most likely to be suffering from complex emotional problems too, their double handicap becomes apparent: many fears and problems, and no words to be able to communicate them. A pathetic picture indeed.

The eldest child in a family often speaks more fluently than his brothers and sisters. His mother has probably had the time, in those vital early days, to talk with him, but there will have been less time to talk with each subsequent child. She may not have appreciated the importance of these early years because she herself was never fortunate enough to experience the rewards of verbal communication. If she cannot easily use speech to make contact with her children, they too will grow up not really understanding or relying on the value of language to communicate with other people – a short, sharp cuff around the ears may be a much more familiar experience! And as this method, no doubt, achieves the desired response, the system is perpetuated in the same way as speech is perpetuated in a more articulate home.

What can be done in a playgroup to help children who lack fluency or have difficulty in making themselves understood? First of all, ways must be found to encourage mothers to help children at home. Let a mother sit in the book corner and hear a skilled helper look through a book, talking about the illustrations. Ask her if she would like to borrow the book to look at at home with her child. If she has the time only to position her child in front of the TV set, suggest she asks him about the programme – who was on it?, where did they go?, what did they do there? Make a point of telling her of any improvements in her child's use of language so that she comes to realize that you consider this an important aspect of his development. Thank and encourage her for any attempts to carry out your suggestions at home – they will have involved her in a great deal of effort and a totally new way of thinking.

The high ratio of adults to children in playgroups (as compared with an average of 1:35 in an infant school) is an enormous asset. Remember that children learn to talk by being talked with. Convince your helpers of the vital importance of talking with young children – show them how it is related to their future educational achievement and emotional growth.

It is very easy to fall into the trap of talking more with the talkative children. An interesting comment from a child encourages an adult to continue the conversation; a dull monosyllable and an insensitive adult may drift off to seek a more responsive child. Remember which children need your help the most and why. This is not to say you should ignore highly verbal children. The point is that with the quieter ones, it is the adult who may need to be the instigator of a conversation. An occasional 'that's very nice, dear' will not help at all.

Some researchers feel that some children require an atmosphere of so-called 'verbal bombardment'. This involves thinking out and then exposing the children to a daily programme of numerous opportunities for hearing and using language. These experiences must be repeated and reinforced as often as possible. The child is in fact 'bombarded' with language in an attempt to make up for some of what he has missed in his early years at home when the foundations of good language skills should have been laid. Certainly, showing such children an object for two minutes in a large group is hardly likely to be enough. A child needs to hear new words and phrases often, preferably in a similar context each time, until he has thoroughly understood and absorbed them.

Ways to stimulate language

How can you create an environment where it is possible to use every opportunity of talking with the children? Not necessarily by a constant noisy chatter. It is only when there is a quiet, busy workroom hum or 'work murmur' that you can pay extra attention to this – when the routine side of things ticks over like clockwork and all your helpers know just what to do and when, then you are free to see just when a child is ready to be talked with.

Much skill is required in knowing when to join in a group of children and when to leave well alone. If they are deep in some fantasy play or a painting, it is best not to intrude. But you may notice a group at the woodwork bench who have reached a certain point in their activity where you might be able to extend their achievements with the right questions and encouragement. Because it is best to lead from the known to the unknown, something the child has already begun to do is the best starting point. Lead on by discussing size, shape, colour, purpose – the possibilities are endless. Apart from developing his language skills and vocabulary, the child is gaining much from this one-to-one relationship with an interested adult. He may not experience this elsewhere outside your playgroup – at home he probably has to share his mother with brothers and sisters.

Do make sure that all your helpers are aware of the importance of talking with the children. Because there is nothing tangible to show for it, some may feel it is not worthwhile. They may think you won't appreciate their efforts if there is nothing to see or show for them. Reassure them strongly on how you feel about this.

Let us now take a look at additional ways in which we can encourage children to talk.

Visits

These are an excellent way of introducing fresh stimuli to develop new areas of vocabulary and knowledge. Some children lead very humdrum lives and you can broaden their experience enormously with new and exciting situations. Do not be too ambitious with the number of children you take out. It is better to err on the small side for your group; two or three children per adult is sufficient. Amazing things happen with the best behaved children when they are in a strange situation! Your experience will grow, and you can always take a larger group next time.

Always plan any visits well ahead, making appointments wherever necessary, and check on your insurance. You may be taking only a group – probably the oldest if you're short of helpers, and this is an ideal opportunity to ask parents for their assistance. The response is usually excellent and in informal, relaxed situations, valuable links can be forged between the playgroup and the children's parents. Wherever possible, back up your visits with books and objects related to where you have been. Suitable 'reference' books really mean something in this situation. Your library should be able to help you out. Here are some suggestions for places to visit.

Infant school

It is essential that playgroup children should visit their infant school as often as possible before they are five. How often you can arrange this will depend on the head teacher. We discuss these visits on p. 147.

Library

This is obviously linked with introducing children to suitable books. If children do not feel strange and overawed by the large building and unfamiliar surroundings, they are more likely to go there themselves when they are older. Try to discourage the awe-inspired whispering that this kind of place seems to suggest. You don't want the children to rush around noisily and disturb other people, but on the other hand you should try to make them feel at home among books, not ill at ease.

Always arrange the visit with the children's librarian beforehand. She will prefer to be prepared and may suggest a quieter day for your visit. She will usually show the children round herself. You can end your visit with a look at the books individually and perhaps a story. You could follow up this visit by asking the librarian to display paintings for a week to awaken public interest in the playgroup.

The zoo

An obvious attraction. If you are lucky enough to have a children's zoo in your area, so much the better. The larger zoos are too large and spread out for children to take everything in at one visit. If it is an 'adult' zoo tell the children you are going to look at only the monkeys and the elephants today, or whatever you feel will capture their attention most. If it is a very large zoo, it is a good idea to have been yourself first, so that you do not waste time and energy getting lost with the children.

Farm

If you are in the country, or on the edge of a city, this might not be too difficult a journey. It is well worth trying because of the endless possibilities for seeing and learning and talking.

Local pet shop

This can be a substitute for an area without a zoo, or a place to visit in its own right. If you have both, you can discuss the difference between wild animals and the more domestic kinds to be found in the pet shops. Some supervisors have followed up such visits with a 'pets day' at playgroup. This takes some organizing and you must be fond of animals yourself to cope! But it can be a great success.

Local shops

As a general rule, it is best not to visit all the nearby shops. Pick out one, perhaps the greengrocer, and discuss the names of fruit and vegetables, their colours and sizes. Where do they come from? Which do we cook? Which do we eat raw? How much are the apples today? Why not buy some to munch back at playgroup? A good opportunity for some on-the-spot health education. Similar opportunities present themselves with all kinds of other local shops.

Fire station

One of our own children still remembers with great glee being allowed to ring the fire-engine bell. And if the firemen will oblige and come down the greasy pole, the children's delight knows no bounds!

Police station

A good chance to ease away any fears of policemen that some of the children may have. A turn at wearing a helmet will make any police constable a friend for life!

Museums

Many museums are unsuitable for small children, but some may have a section which will appeal to a group of rising-fives. Make sure you know your way round the building, so that they are not weary and bored by the time you arrive where you want to be. Too much too early can turn a child against the idea of visiting museums for a very long time, so keep the visit short.

Exhibitions

This idea may sound laughable but occasionally one has four-plus children in playgroup who are visually and intellectually mature enough to enjoy a short visit to certain kinds of exhibition. One playgroup took about five of its oldest children to an exhibition of kinetic art. The children loved it and were very eager to make mobiles for themselves.

Walks

Nature walks, walks to the shops, walks to the park. Most play-groups try to do this often. For city children to kick their way through heaps of autumn leaves in the parks, and for country children to travel on a bus to see a multistorey car park are simple ways to balance the children's home environment. (See section on nature study, p. 331.)

Visitors

Visitors can give a child a sense of belonging to a wider com-munity than his narrow experience of home and playgroup permits. Similarly, by bringing outsiders in to speak to the children, you are showing such people your work and aims and the way your playgroup is placed in relation to the rest of the community.

On p. 79 we discuss how seldom some children see their fathers. Shift work and office hours often mean that a young child's world is almost wholly female. One way to compensate for this is to invite males into your playgroup. Draw on the many skills represented by fathers (and mothers, too, of course). Does any of them play a musical instrument? A guitar-playing father in one playgroup we saw proved a great success with 'Polly-wolly doodle'! Another father, who was an electrician, explained and demonstrated simple circuiting to a group of older boys – no trouble from them that morning! Policemen are regular visitors to many playgroups. They may give practical talks on road safety, whilst helping to overcome fears of the police that some mothers may have given their children. Play-groups in church halls usually encourage the vicar to drop in as often as he can. Caretakers, as we have seen, can be a great source of information to children.

Of course there are many female visitors to encourage too. The local infant school head and reception class teachers are very important people for your children to meet. If they can see what the children have been doing at playgroup, while simultaneously becoming familiar to the children, a healthy link will be formed which will go a long way towards easing the path into infant school.

Some group activities are particularly good for helping language development – the home corner, hospital and shops with their verbal playing. There are, also, specific activities which will encourage the children to talk. Here are some suggestions.

Glove puppets

These are best kept for the older children. Some of the younger ones who cannot yet fully separate fact from fantasy may be frightened and in fact need protecting from other children's puppet play. If you are going to speak through a puppet, let the children see you put it on at the beginning. There is no need to buy an expensive puppet theatre. A table with a cloth over for the 'actors' to hide behind is quite sufficient or a television set made from a large cardboard carton.

Most children do not need an audience. The chance to talk through the puppet, either individually or in a small group, is quite sufficient for them. Try to choose puppets of familiar characters or animals. Unfortunately the nicer ones tend to be rather expensive – Galts make a rabbit, monkey, badger and dog at approximately £1·35 each. Some of the cheaper puppets can be very ugly and frightening. There are many cheap ways of making your own puppets – papier mâché, yogurt cups, table tennis balls can all be painted over and 'dressed'. A child who is frightened of puppets can sometimes overcome his fears when he has seen one actually being made. Ideas for making simple puppets can be found in *Play with a Purpose for Under-Sevens* by E. Matterson, Penguin, 35p.

Telephones

– are best if they are real. In many areas the GPO will oblige with obsolete models. Contact the Telephone Manager's office; his address will be given at the front of your local directory. If you can manage to get two models, all the better, then they can be fixed up properly, perhaps one in the home corner and one across the room at the shop. This job needs someone with professional skills – if necessary get in touch with the electrical engineering department of your local technical college or secondary school and ask for help. Many shy children will open up to talk through a telephone when they feel there is no pressure being put on them to speak. If you cannot get real telephones, try to buy the best imitation. Some toy ones are too small and fiddly. The bigger and more robust model you can find, the better.

Pictures

are one of the more obvious ways of encouraging language. Remember to choose ones which are large and clear and linked with reality. Avoid pictures of Father Christmas on a hot July day. Pictures, like books, can be used for reference to link up with something you have discussed recently with some of the children. Make sure all the children can see the picture when you are showing it to the group, clipping it to a painting easel will help. Then follow the pointers for a successful group time, p. 157.

Interesting objects

which may be familiar to adults, will be fresh and exciting to young children. There is no end to the variety. Show one at a time. You can leave the object at the playgroup to show different groups on consecutive days until they have all seen it. Children themselves will sometimes bring something interesting in – it can boost the ego of a new shy child tremendously if his birthday present or new toy is discussed and appreciated by the adults and children at his playgroup. Here are the sort of things you could show : magnet with examples of familiar objects some of which will magnetize and some not, snowstorm paperweight, a magnifying glass with a box of things to look at (pebbles, a piece of knitted stuff, piece of rope, an insect), a kaleidoscope (beware of turn-taking problems : a large prism may be better to show a group), a thermometer, a cactus – why does it have spikes? where and how does it grow?, a melon – look at all the seeds inside, a pineapple – cut it open and let the children eat it as a grand finale, a cabbage – show the way the leaves fold one over the other, an orange – discuss segments, pith, peel, vitamin C and pips, shells, pebbles, stones, fossils. See also nature study p. 327, science p. 334.

A colour table

Much of the teaching apparatus used in infant schools is based on colour recognition, so all children should be able to name the most common colours. You can do much to help them in incidental conversation, 'What a pretty blue dress Sarah,' 'What smart brown shoes Peter', 'Can you find a brick the same colour as your cardigan?' Some playgroups like to reinforce this by choosing a particular colour, say red, and then having a 'red table' for that week in playgroup. Cover the table with some red material and put on it red objects as varied in size, shape and purpose as you can find. Supplement by cutting out pictures to make a red book. You will find a tremendous amount of discussion evolves from this. A progression of plain colours may lead on to a 'tartan table' or a 'spotted table'. We saw a very effective table in one playgroup where the supervisor had provided a spotted tablecloth to form a background for an enormous variety of spotted objects ranging from a toy dalmatian dog to a doll with chicken pox!

The book corner

An attractive book corner is an essential to every good playgroup. Unfortunately, books often come far down on a supervisor's list of priorities; but if supervisors themselves appreciate the importance of providing suitable books for children, the book corner soon becomes a popular part of the playgroup.

Someone to read a story, or discuss the pictures with, is vital to the pleasure and the learning that the children gain from books. As we saw on p. 141, the book corner is an ideal place to use a new mother-helper. It is also a good place to place a mother settling in a new child. And once there is an adult in the book corner, children will start to drift towards her. Some children may gather around to hear a story being read, others may choose a book for themselves and sit, turning the pages – parallel reading, if you like! So much language development takes place when you are looking at books with children. You can stretch and develop their vocabulary and imagination in a relaxed natural way. A fairly new or shy child will often blossom under this intimate relationship.

A helper may sometimes feel she is wasting her time because she is not actually *doing* something; because there is no tangible end product, she may feel her hard work has been in vain. In such cases it is up to the supervisor to try to convince her of the importance of language development and the way in which books can stretch a child's imagination and his verbal and intellectual skills. Point out that the extent to which a child sees books being used and enjoyed will greatly influence his attitude to reading when he starts school. Not all children come from homes where the adults and older brothers and sisters regularly look at books; nor do they all enjoy the intimacy of a bedtime story or have a mother who helps them to find the answer to a difficult question in a book. All this is part of what has been called 'reading readiness' – a steady build-up in the child's mind that it is worth making the effort to learn to read.

You will have to change the person in the book corner – no one can read aloud for three hours non-stop! But an adult there implies that books are worthwhile; that you want the children to use the books. An empty, dreary book corner will appear to mean that books are dull and cannot supply any enjoyment. No one is tempted by a line of chairs and a few tatty annuals.

The book case

As far as possible books should be displayed frontwards rather than spine on. For this reason ordinary book cases are not usually satisfactory. If you do use them castors underneath

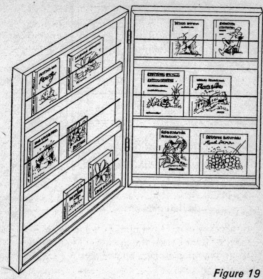

Figure 19

will facilitate moving. You can buy light-weight wire racks with a pocket to hold each book (E.S.A. and Arnolds, about £18). Another good design is Galts portable book rack which has two wings opening out to give six shelves, see Figure 19 – also about £18. You could copy the design. You can also make your own bookcase from a clothes horse, as shown in Figure 20.

Layout of the book corner

Somewhere relatively quiet and cut off is ideal, though take care that it is not so cut off no one ever goes there. A small separate room off from your main play area is a good place, but keep the door ajar so that the books are visible and tempting. Even if you have to make do with literally a corner of a large draughty hall it is still possible to create a cosy and quiet area. A piano can be turned at right-angles to the wall, as can the book case itself, to form a kind of screen. In a home playgroup, a corner of the living room, especially if this includes a settee, is suitable.

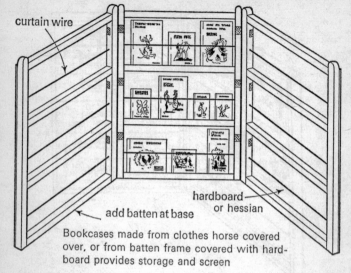

Bookcases made from clothes horse covered over, or from batten frame covered with hardboard provides storage and screen

Figure 20

Provide a child-sized table and a couple of comfortable chairs. A plant or a few flowers on the table provide a talking point and make the area look pleasant. The adult in the book corner will find it easier to communicate with the children if she sits on a child-sized chair, rather than an adult one. Do not however rush out and buy half-a-dozen small chairs. Too many may give a more formal atmosphere than necessary. Ask the school supplies officer of your local education authority if he has any old infant-school tables and chairs to sell cheaply. If your playgroup floors are cold and splintery put down a couple of rugs or cuttings from an old carpet; better still, a few cushions.

Looking after the books

Good books are expensive. It is essential, therefore, that the children learn from the beginning to treat them with care. No one wants to look at a tatty old book with the covers half gone – even two or three books looking like that will give the book corner a miserable appearance. The majority of the books should be hard, not paperbacks – this is more expensive initially, but well worth it in the long term.

Show the children how to turn over the pages. Young children usually turn over at the bottom edge of a page near the centre. A few minutes careful instruction can show them how to turn over at the outside bottom corner. You can make this point quite casually as you look through a book with a group of children. Tears and dog-eared corners will of course appear eventually. You don't want to be so meticulous that you put off the children from touching the books! But if a book is torn, take it away from the book corner until it is sellotaped together. The children will probably comment on the mended part – you can talk about why you did it, and generally explain how you care about the books. Never allow books to be thrown around or walked on. A child who drops a book should know he is expected to pick it up. Some playgroups let the children tidy the book corner each morning – there may be a special duster to dust the shelves, someone else can water the plant or flowers. By being involved in and caring for this part of your playgroup the children will be encouraged to treat the books with respect.

How many books?

Quality is more important than quantity. It is far better to have six really suitable books than twenty scruffy annuals from a jumble sale. Children who are beginning to gain pleasure from books will enjoy seeing familiar friends on the shelves, so it is best not to change the books around too often. Most playgroups consider about once every half term is sufficient. If you buy or borrow an odd book in between which links up with something you have been talking about try to find some suitable time in the morning to introduce it to at least some of the children. Usually others will gather round so that, in fact, almost everyone knows that there is a new and interesting book in the collection. You may find this is just what is needed to stimulate a renewed interest in books, if this has been flagging lately.

Using the library

Good children's books are an expensive investment. One solution is to use your local library. Many librarians will now lend a box of books – perhaps a dozen – for half a term, without tickets or fines. If you are having a battle on this topic with your local librarian, point out that other librarians report that books used in playgroups are far less worn than if they had been in and out of the library shelves over the same period of time. Ask your local PPA branch to write to the Library Committee at the Town Hall, stating the needs of playgroups. If there is no branch, write yourself and seek the help of any councillors who have shown interest in playgroups. Remember that the children's librarian has had a long training in children's books so make the most of this by seeking her help and advice when you go to make your choice.

Your own lending library

Some playgroups have started their own lending library. Children take home a book of their choice, perhaps just overnight. This can be a good link between home and playgroup, giving parents an opportunity to see suitable books for children under five. It can also provide a pleasant feeling of continuity: 'I'll bring my book next time it's a playgroup day.' You can provide tickets and a rubber stamp, getting the children to help you so that they get a feel of what a real library is like. Meanwhile, they will have gained valuable social training from 'borrowing', 'taking care of' and 'bringing back' their books, even if they have only kept them overnight.

What books to choose

Many of the stories you read aloud can be put in the book corner for the children to look at on their own. If the books have illustrations to help tell the story, the children can retell it for themselves. They will enjoy feeling they are reading. If they want to discuss one of the pictures or ask a question about it, there should be an adult close at hand.

Reference books

A book can often be used to give further information about something you have been discussing with the children. In one playgroup, Susan brought her pet rabbit for the morning. The next day, the supervisor showed the children a book about pets. The text of this book was in fact far too advanced for under-fives, but the illustrations were excellent. And because an adult was there to talk about the pictures and to translate the information into language the children could understand, the book became an enormous source of interest in the playgroup. Another bright little girl of four-and-a-half was making an elephant out of clay. It was almost finished when she began to ask questions about its tail. 'Does an elephant have a tail?' 'How long is it?', 'It's a very big animal, so it must have a big tail,' she concluded. The supervisor suggested that they went to consult the animal book in the book corner and to Sarah's delight and surprise the elephant page showed her just what she wanted to know. This child had learned not only the length of an elephant's tail – but a very important fact: books can give information as well as pleasure.

Count With Me, If I Were King, Look For Colours, When We Play, Blakeley and Witt, 'Fact and Fancy Books', A. & C. Black, 55p each.
Rain, Trees, The Sea, Dinosaurs, 'Starters', Macdonald, 35p each
  Books on nature study, science and music are given in the appropriate chapters.

Stories in pictures

The Egg and The Chicken, The Apple and The Butterfly, I. Mari, A. & C. Black, 75p each.
In The Forest, In The Village, The Three Birds, When The Sun Shines, H. Huth, Burke Publishing Co., about 50p each.
Wild Animals, Birds, Fish, Brian Wildsmith, Oxford University Press, about £1 each.

Let's Go Shopping, Let's Go On a Picnic, Young World Publications (in conjunction with the PPA), 18p each.

Ladybird Books – a complete list is available from the publishers Wills & Hepworth Ltd, Derby Square, Loughborough, Leics. Their series 'Learning With Mother' (702) and the picture book series (704) are very useful and good value at 15p each. The stories are often told in a far too complicated way for under-fives, however, so make sure these are not the only books you provide.

Books about numbers

Numbers of Things, H. Oxenbury, Heinemann, 90p
1, 2, 3, Brian Wildsmith, Oxford University Press, £1·10
Teddybears 1 to 10, S. Gretz, Benn, 95p

Story time

Story time is a happy, intimate occasion whether it is with a small group or an individual child. It's also important at playgroups as many mothers are too busy to read on demand. Storytelling can help to form and deepen good adult/child relationships. A shy child will often begin to respond for the first time when he becomes interested in a story. He forgets his shyness and joins in spontaneously 'and he *blew* the house down' – he has become part of the group, involved and participating. Children can gain enormous pleasure from the rhythm and sounds of new words. When they join in with 'millions of cats, billions of cats, millions and billions and trillions of cats' not only is their vocabulary being extended, but their feeling for language is being enriched and enlarged. And when they copy the story-teller's clear tones, they are learning, incidentally, the correct pronunciation of new words.

Stories also help a child to anticipate and understand particular fears and problems. He may soon have to go into hospital. What happens there? Can Mummy stay? Most important – Does it hurt? Will it be a long time? Your children's librarian can probably recommend suitable stories on this theme. Similarly, coming to terms with the new baby or even a trip to granny's may be helped by a relevant tale.

A wide range of stories can widen the experience and knowledge of children in a variety of ways. How many children from city slums have had the opportunity to run free in the countryside? And, for that matter, how many country children know about traffic jams or tower-blocks?

When to have story time

If your playgroup has a free morning (see p. 151) story time will arise spontaneously as the children become interested in a book. An adult always in the book corner ensures there is a story 'on demand'. A set story time creates many problems. If you are to keep the group time short enough you cannot tack a story onto the end of lunch or finger-plays. It is very tempting to do this so that all the bother of disturbing the children at play and gathering them together, yet again, may be avoided. But you gain nothing because the children, particularly the new and younger ones, will probably be very fidgety by the time you are half way through the story. The end of the morning is definitely not a good time for a story. There are usually far too many distractions and it becomes impossible to keep the children interested and concentrating.

Size of group

If you have decided by trial and error to have a set story time, then you must consider the size of the group. Generally speaking there should never be more than ten children in a group, so that a home-based playgroup is probably small enough to accommodate the needs of all the children who wish to come and listen. A hall-based group however may have so many children that it is impossible to create the right kind of atmosphere for a story. The range of comprehension over all the children will also be too large for one big story group so you should try to spare two helpers and divide the children into at least two groups. Division is usually by age, not forgetting the importance of stage. If you already have the kind of family groups recommended on p. 132, the problem will more or less resolve itself. If you are lucky enough to have a smaller room, one group can go in there while the other remains in the hall. An alternative is for each group to go in turn to the small room for their story. This room can be developed as a quiet room where the children look at books and hear stories.

Do's and don'ts in telling stories

1. Begin by telling the children 'This is a true story' or 'This is a made-up story' – this helps them to come to terms with the difference between fact and fantasy. Young children cannot make this distinction instinctively, it has to grow as their understanding of reality grows.
2. Timing. Always err on the shorter side, five minutes is ample for the under-threes. You can gradually lengthen the time for those who have been in playgroup a longer period and are used to sitting and listening. Never serialize stories; most playgroup children are not ready for the story to be finished the next day. If you cannot fit it in the time available, choose another story.
3. It is always best to tell a story that you enjoy yourself. Your enthusiasm will communicate itself to the children. If you know the story well – and that means having read it through at least once before – you can highlight the best parts and give the right emphasis where needed. If the story amuses you or you like the illustrations, show this to the children.
4. The skill of story-telling comes much more easily to some than to others, but it does develop and improve with prac- tice. Some playgroup staff find they become very embarrassed if another adult is within earshot so try to arrange matters so that the group and their story-teller are in an area by themselves.
5. Sit with the children, on the floor if you can, but always among the group, preferably on a child-sized chair. Never tell a story across a desk or table.
6. Speak slowly and distinctly. Make sure you can be heard by

all the group but avoid shouting at all costs – if you are having to shout stop and examine what is wrong. Make each
point clearly and wait for it to be digested. Explain any new
words.

7. If you are showing illustrations make sure every child can
see. You can show them from left to right and right to left
alternately so that everyone has a chance of seeing them
first. Otherwise save all the pictures till the end.

What stories to read

It is important to have a high standard in the stories you read.
Always go to a book shop rather than a toy shop to buy books.
Ask the advice of the assistants and order what you want if
it is not in stock.

If there is no decent bookshop in your area or the children's
librarian says 'They don't need books until they can read,' join
'Books for Your Children', 100 Church Lane East, Aldershot.
This is a pressure group concerned with many aspects of children's literature, including making good books more widely
obtainable. We suggest you also buy 'Reading for enjoyment
with 2–5-year-olds', Moss, 15p, from Children's Book Centre
Ltd, 140 Kensington Church Street, London, W.8.

Repetitive stories

Young children love repetition, whether it is joining in with
an often repeated chorus such as 'He huffed and he puffed and
he *blew* the house down', or a cumulative story like *Chicken
Licken* when more and more characters are added. Children
will often ask for this kind of story again and again, and woe
betide the story-teller who changes one word from the original
version!

Stories with a chorus

Millions of Cats, Wanda Gag, Faber, 70p. *The Gingerbread Man*,
Barbara Ireson, Faber, 20p. *The Three Bears*, W. Stobbs, Puffin,
22p. Know your children well for these, some may find them
frightening.

Cumulative stories

Chicken Licken, *The Rain Puddle*, Adelaide Holl, Bodley Head,
90p. *Little Red Hen*, Ladybird Easy Reading Book, Wills &
Hepworth, 15p. *The Tale of a Turnip*, Anita Hewett, Bodley
Head, 70p.

Fairy stories

As a general rule, these are unsuitable for under-fives. They are
often far too long and the plots too complicated. To appreciate
fairy stories, children need to have a firm grasp of what is fact
and what is fantasy. The reward of marrying a handsome prince
does not mean very much to a three-year-old! Fairy stories
tend to have clear moral values – good is rewarded and bad is
punished. But they also tend to suggest that good is beautiful
and bad is ugly – doubtful values to be presenting to children.
Beware, too, of the wicked stepmother. Under-fives just cannot
cope with this. They are still far too concerned with the basic
need for reassurance that their mother will come back and still
love them.

Similarly, many of Enid Blyton's stories may prove unsuitable
for playgroup children. The plots are often too complex, the
characters conforming to crude stereotypes and the moral values
oversimplified. Some supervisors argue that the children 'love'
Enid Blyton. We would reply that children love toffees too,
but adults with their experience of children should see themselves as there to guide them to a wider and healthier diet. It
is generally unwise to ban Noddy and his ilk completely, however. An element of forbidden fruits may creep in and do more
damage than the odd tale of Dame Crosseyes unobtrusively
read between stories of a higher standard.

Comics

Similar arguments apply to comics. There is no doubt that children of all ages enjoy looking through comics and if we ban them, they will get hold of them for themselves somehow. The main appeal of comics is the ease with which they can be browsed through. The pictures are usually self-explanatory and little or no reading skill is required. But all these things apply to well-chosen books, too.

There is now an increasing variety of comics specially designed for young children. Some of these are quite good. They may for example have a pleasant 'Nature Study' photograph which you can use for discussion with a group of children. If you decide to go on the mailing list for any of these comics, they will ensure that some fresh reading matter comes into the playgroup each week, but do make sure new books come too.

Making up stories

Sometimes you may be unable to find a story to fit the point you want to make. Or perhaps some of the younger children are not yet ready for a five-minute listening time. The best solution may then be to make up your own story. Many playgroup staff are amazed at their skills in this sphere, and children seem to particularly enjoy a story which they know you have created specially for them. Your voice and facial expressions can provide all the illustrations necessary. Keep the plot very simple and give names to the children taking part. Here is a simple example of the home-made variety.

One day it was very sunny. Mummy said to David and Susan, 'Let's go to the zoo.' When they got there, they saw a man washing the elephant with a bucket of water. The elephant made a big shower with his trunk. 'I expect he's feeling much cooler now,' said Mummy.

Then they saw the lion eating a big piece of raw meat. 'He looks very fierce,' said Susan, 'I'm glad he's locked up in his cage.' 'So am I,' said David.

Suddenly the wind blew round and round just where they wer standing. And what do you think? It lifted up David's cap righ off his head and carried it along the ground into the monkey' cage. 'Oh, dear,' said David. 'Oh, dear,' said Susan, 'What shall w do? The wind has blown away David's hat.' 'Don't worry', sai Mummy. 'We'll ask the zoo keeper to get it for us.' Just as sh was going to find the zoo keeper, what do you think happened One of the little monkeys pushed his tiny pink hand through th bars of his cage and held out David's hat. What a surprise Mummy very carefully reached up and took the cap and put back on David's head. 'Oh, thank you monkey,' said David, am glad to have my hat back again.' – 'So am I,' said Mummy 'Wasn't he a kind monkey?'

Here is a list of stories which have proved successful in man playgroups with children from widely differing backgrounds.

Time For A Story, Tell Me A Story, Tell Me Another Story E. Colwell, Young Puffin, 20p

Lucky Dip, Ruth Ainsworth, Puffin, 25p. Stories and verse from 'Listen With Mother'

Little Pete Stories, Leila Berg, Puffin, 30p

Stories with good illustrations

Miffy and Snuffy series by Dick Bruna, Methuen, 45p each. Bol clear illustrations, simple text.

Snippy and Snappy, Millions of Cats, Wanda Gag, Faber, 20 and 70p. Unusual black-and-white illustrations, good repet tive chorus.

'Topsy and Tim' series, J. and G. Adamson, Blackie. Very goo value; bright illustrations about a pair of twins who hav simple plausible adventures.

'Papa Small' series, L. Lenski, Oxford University Pres 45p.

'Angus' series, M. Flack, Bodley Head, 60p. The adventures a small scottie dog.

'Mouse Looks For A House', H. Piers, Methuen, 37½p. Goc coloured photos; stimulates a lot of discussion.

A Baby Sister For Frances, Bedtime For Frances, R. Hoban, Fabe

25p. A little badger who has very human problems to over-
come.
Rosie's Walk, P. Hutchins, Puffin, 20p.
Thomas Has A Bath, R. Wolde, Brockhampton Press, 30p.
Boy On A Hilltop, Kotataniuchi and Blakely, Black, 80p.
Young Puffins are always of good standard and reasonably
priced. Get their regular catalogue from Young Puffins, Penguin
Books Ltd, Harmondsworth, Middlesex. Faber paperbacks are
well chosen, though most of this series are rather too old for
playgroup children. Write for their catalogue to Faber and
Faber Ltd, 3 Queen Square, London WC1.

Funny books

Dr Seuss series, Collins 60p each. Some are too long for play-
group children, but try the 'Beginner' books – *Foot Book, Eye
Book, Ear Book, Inside, Outside, Upsidedown*. Also *Put Me
In The Zoo* and *Ten Apples Up On Top*.
'Nippers', edited by Leila Berg, published by Macmillan, help
city children identify with their surroundings – try *Fish
and Chips For Supper, A Day Out, The Jumble Sale*.
The ones with a red or orange symbol on the back are
simplest.
Harry The Dirty Dog, G. Zion, Puffin, 25p

Stories from TV programmes

These can be a valuable bridge to the world of books.
'Magic Roundabout' series, Hamlyn, 55p
'Andy Pandy' series, Brockhampton Press, 10p, 20p
'Mary, Mungo and Midge' series, Hamlyn, 30p

Nursery rhymes

Although some of the words and phrases in nursery rhymes are
difficult for under-fives the rhythms are usually good and very
attractive to young children – this is their first introduction to
poetry. If a child has learnt nursery rhymes at home he will be

delighted to find that you can say them too! There are many selections available in the shops. Some have dozens of verses most of which it is best to ignore. The Ladybird collections are cheap and good. If a book has good illustrations put it in the book corner – some of the older children will get very good pre-reading experience from finding that they can interpret the symbols on the page into words they know.

The Puffin Book of Nursery Rhymes, I. and P. Opie, Puffin, 25p. A large and varied anthology suitable for the supervisor's own bookshelf.

Lavender's Blue, Oxford University Press, £2

Mother Goose Lost, Nicholas Tucker, Hamish Hamilton, £1·25p

Mother Goose, illustrated by Brian Wildsmith, Oxford University Press, £1·75

I Saw A Ship A-Sailing, B. Montresor, Collins, 80p

Rhymes, jingles, and finger plays

These can be great fun for young children and are very helpful in developing a good relationship within a group. Young children are fascinated by strong verbal rhymes and the repetition of sounds as well as words. Rhymes and fingerplays are also very useful for filling odd gaps such as when you are waiting for the last few mothers to come at the end of playgroup or as a distraction in times of trouble. Visits to other playgroups may give you new ideas for new rhymes and fingerplays – write down any particularly good ones you come across so that you gradually build up an anthology. Lend this to new helpers to start them off with their own collection.

This Little Puffin, E. Matterson, Young Puffin, 25p. An essential for every playgroup.

Forty Action Songs, Forty Fingerplays, Bath and District branch of PPA, available from PPA head office, address p. 342.

One, Two, Three, Four, Grice and Wrigley, Warne, £1.65. Number rhymes and finger games.

Acting Rhymes, Book 1, ed. Sansom, Black, 20p

Reading and writing?

Older children who are about to go to infant school, especially boys, are often troublesome in playgroup. This is usually because they are bored. Some may have been attending playgroup for two years, seeing the same equipment every day. Remember what we have said throughout this book about watching children to see when they are ready for new ideas and activities. Read and discuss new books with them, carry out simple experiments together, visit new places outside. Older children often like more responsibility – let them help tidy up, look after younger children, mend small breakages. Reassure them that you value them as much as the younger more dependent children.

What about reading and writing? This is not the answer – they both require special teaching skills and should be left till infant school. You can, however, provide a rich atmosphere of reading and number 'readiness': label all equipment containers; give children good jigsaws and a wide range of books and stories; introduce weighing and measuring into play; take time to talk to children individually using quantitative terms such as 'as big as', 'as tall as', 'whose shoe is the biggest?'.

Occasionally a child is so eager to read that it would seem stupid to hold him back. Ask your local infant head or nursery school supervisor for advice on the best teaching methods. Make sure you teach the child individually so that other children are not pressured into reading. Many parents want their children to learn to read as young as possible and will be worried if they know that you are teaching reading but that their child is not being taught. If this happens you must be firm and explain the needs of pre-school children: namely, that an environment rich in stimulating play and language, coupled with good parents who attempt to provide a similar environment at home, is the best possible basis for later achievements at school.

12
Music, Nature Study, Science

Making music

Many playgroups shamefully neglect music, being terrified of it or feeling that it should be left to the experts. We have written this section for people who have little or no musical education, hoping to show how easy it is to give children a wide and happy experience of music. There are three aims in a child's musical education: one, to help him enjoy music; two, to encourage him to make music; three, of equal importance, to teach him to listen to music. Music is also another form of communication – when you give a child an instrument, you give him a tool, a way of expressing himself in another language. Sometimes he may be surprised at the effect music has on him. A timid child may feel a surge of power as he beats a drum. A tough tearabout may listen with an awakening sense of beauty to the sound of a bell.

Singing

Everyone has one instrument easily available – their voice. It doesn't matter if you are weak and wobbly or even tone-deaf. Children are the kindest critics and would as much think of commenting on the way you sing as on the way you speak. Once you have overcome your initial nervousness you will be surprised how much you and the children enjoy singing.

What should you sing and when? We personally value a helper who sings in a casual way, perhaps as she pins up fresh paper on the easels or tidies the dressing-up clothes. Spon taneous singing can add to a child's pleasure in an activity or avert a crisis. For instance, a squabble was developing on a climbing-frame and a shy mother-helper too uncertain of herself to intervene (or was she being clever?) began to sing 'See-saw, Marjorie Daw' to two other children on a seesaw. The squabblers stopped to listen and when the song was over, the child who had shouted the loudest said, 'Sing it again.' It would seem that music really does 'soothe the savage breast'!

Keep a few of your favourite songs for moments such as this, and add to them from time to time by learning new ones – we have a rich heritage of nursery rhymes and after a time you will be surprised how many you know, whether songs, jingles, rhymes or finger-plays. There is a list of useful books, some cheap, some expensive, at the end of this section (p. 326). As soon as you can, buy some of the more expensive and count it a good investment.

Does it matter that many traditional songs are rooted in rural living and have words and concepts that are meaningless to largely urban-dwelling children? We think not. A song is valuable not merely because it has been sung for two hundred years, but the fact that it has lasted so well may indicate that it has something which appeals to children. In a society which is changing so quickly, there is some merit in keeping a thread of continuity in children's singing games. Many of our traditional rhymes have a long and fascinating history, often with political origins. Anyone interested in how nursery rhymes began might like to read *The Oxford Dictionary of Nursery Rhymes* or *The Lore and Language of Schoolchildren* by Peter and Iona Opie.* The latter may give you ideas for more up-to-date songs.

What is the best way to sing with young children? Sometimes a group will gather naturally in the music corner, and you can join it if the children seem ready for you to sing with them, for five to seven minutes. Don't be disappointed if they sing out of tune, this is very common with such young children. Help

*Oxford University Press, 1967

them by singing very slowly and if they are joining in with you, reduce the pace still more. Even if singing is quite a new experience to some of them they will learn from listening to you. They will of course have different musical backgrounds. Some come to playgroup knowing many traditional songs, others know little else than advertiser's jingles, so that the nursery rhymes you know inside out may be as novel and difficult to them as some opera might be to you. So start off with some very well-known rhymes, say 'Humpty Dumpty' which has a most dramatic ending, or as a contrast 'Baa Baa black sheep' with its pathos in the last line. Have a programme of different rhythms and subjects. Introduce a less well-known tune amongst the familiar ones, for example 'Dance for your daddy, my little laddie' (*Oxford Book of Nursery Rhymes*). Sing it twice, the second time letting your fingers dance on your lap at the appropriate time. Then unless it is requested again, leave it for another day. As long as you are interested in the songs the children will pick up catchy tunes and words with startling speed and will soon have a large repertoire. They may even want to invent simple songs for themselves.

Young children are helped to listen by the use of hand and body actions – many of these are suggested in the books listed at the end of this section. Older children enjoy hearing you sing ballads, such as 'Oh soldier, soldier, won't you marry me' or 'London Bridge is broken down'. Don't feel you must sing *every* verse. Watch audience reaction and bring the song to a close if you feel you are becoming a bore.

Include a number of songs with contrasted rhythms and volume, so that the children have to listen to the music and adapt their movements accordingly. For instance, use 'I went to school one morning' (*This Little Puffin*) with the singing accompaniment reinforced by a small drum, beating out the different rhythms. Or try 'Can you walk on tiptoe as softly as a cat?' (*Forty Action Songs*) which has both a varied rhythm and volume. Incidentally, this last-named book is printed without written music, so that each supervisor can use her own favourite tune or make one up. If you need help with this and have a set of fixed chime bars (or alto xylophone), ask a musical friend to write out some tunes like this:

     G   G   G B D B B A D B A G
Can you walk on tiptoe, as softly as a cat?

  G   G   G B D D B   A   A   B A G
Can you stamp along the road, stamp, stamp, just like that.

Instruments

So far we have talked mainly about using your voice but it can be interesting to accompany singing. Pianos are of little use unless you are a contortionist and can play without looking at all at the keys – your face must be towards the children, so they can gain from watching you and you can see what their reaction is. It isn't any better to stand up and peer over the top of the piano – this only makes a barrier between you and the children and hampers your involvement with them.

If you can play the guitar, this can be ideal to use occasionally. The chords are usually simple and as you sing the tune you can see the response of the children. Some children will join in with your singing, others will prefer to just listen. Accept this difference – children should be encouraged to take part in musical activities, but certainly not forced to do so, nor even jollied into it. If it is to achieve anything, the singing must be enjoyed by the children for its own sake and not to please the adult. Usually after a term or so, even a silent child will be joining in and sometimes those that rarely talk.

Music and movement

A child's immediate response to music is movement, especially at this pre-school age when he is intensely aware of rhythm. Most children instinctively sway to 'I saw three ships come sailing by' or clap their hands to the strong beat of 'Old King Cole'. They respond with enthusiasm to action songs, which can be a useful way of letting off steam, if your group has been cooped up for ages with wet weather or you have no outside play space. Have a collection of these (see *This Little Puffin*) and adapt them as necessary. If you are singing and acting 'Here we go round the Mulberry Bush' with an energetic group, use words like 'This is the way we dig up the road', '... chop down the tree', '... push the road roller'. With a quieter group use a more domesticated and traditional theme, 'This is the way we sweep the floor', '... iron the clothes', and so on.

Try to be totally involved with the children during these action songs. Young children are great imitators and if your movements are half-hearted, then so will theirs. Your antics may make the milkman peer through the window in amazement but as they follow your example, the children will enter into the spirit of the game with gusto. Be careful, though, to let the children interpret the music freely – sometimes let them lead and you follow.

Instruments for children to use

What should they be and how can the children best use them? As with other activities, we suggest that you have a low table with instruments available for the children to play experimentally. It may be the first time that a child has had the opportunity to touch an instrument and he will need to handle it – to shake, beat or bang it, to see what sound it makes. Such experiments won't lead to bedlam if you have a well-organized playgroup with enough things to do. Children go to work at the music table with as much discrimination and concentration as they do at any other activity.

Good musical instruments are expensive but you must look on them not only as an investment but as a necessity. Many children hear so much music distorted by poor-quality transistors that you must counteract this by giving musical sounds of a high quality. It is much better to have one good musical instrument with a few replaceable home-made ones than a dozen second-hand toy instruments.

Tone instruments

If you ever have a windfall buy a set of *chime bars*. They make a very pleasant sound – one of the few noises bearable even before breakfast – and seem to keep a pure pitch. If you are leading a hand-to-mouth existence buy two or three chimes at a time (Galts, about £1, or from your local music shop if your PPA branch has negotiated a discount). The beaters are easily broken if stepped on, so tie them to the main body of the chime bar.

ALTO XYLOPHONES are expensive – they cost about as much as a good sand or water tray – but they are one of the best instruments for under-fives, having enough resonance to be audible in a group of children, but not enough to disturb others (which can be the hazard with chime bars). The small soprano xylophone sounds higher than children's voices, so will not help them to sing as the alto does. It is also a little harder to play, having smaller notes. New Era produce a playgroup-proof alto xylophone: You can make your own but don't expect it to sound like one of these beautiful instruments. Instructions are given in *Musical Instruments to Make and Play* by Ronald Roberts, Dryad Press, £1.50.

Rhythm instruments

DRUMS Good drums are very expensive – Arnolds' approximately £11.35. Some chain stores sell imported cheaper ones for about 35p with a plastic skin which make a pleasant sound. Never buy tin drums as they are very harsh on the ear. Remember also that if you want to move with your instruments small children may find shop drums very cumbersome – you may prefer tambours (tambourines without the jingles).

TAMBOURINES A useful instrument though expensive (£2.50 Arnolds), as it can be used a great deal in musical games.

TRIANGLES are of limited use, but good ones have a nice sound (Galts, 36p).

JINGLES AND BELLS are often unsatisfactory because the metal shapes from which they are made come apart. Look for large, strong ones cast in one piece such as those recently imported by Woolworths. Indian bells are well made with a lovely sound. They are easier to handle than triangles, especially when played with a six-inch nail.

MARACCAS are fun to use. A good pair costs about £1·32 (Galts). Avoid plastic ones as they are dangerous if broken and home-made ones sound just as good (see p. 322).

Improvised instruments

If you are just starting a playgroup and have to postpone buying the expensive items listed above you can improvise to a certain extent, even with tone instruments. We have already mentioned *Musical Instruments To Make and To Play* by Ronald Roberts (Dryad). This gives clear instructions with diagrams on how to make glockenspiels and many other high-quality instruments. You do need a certain degree of skill in carpentry, patience and a good ear for tuning. The Nursery School Association, 89 Stamford Street, London sell a useful pamphlet called 'Making Musical Apparatus and Instruments' by Kathleen Blocksidge (15p) and their instructions can be followed by most practical people.

Buy some aluminium strips sawn into different lengths and drill holes, so that tape can be threaded to suspend them. The tubes will give random notes; to make a tuned scale requires a good deal of patient filing. Wooden spoons or lengths of dowel rod with padded heads of rags covered with chamois leather make good beaters.

BELLS Handicraft shops and pet shops often sell small bells; Arnolds have them at about 3p. Sew these loosely onto a strip of leather or loop them onto hooped wire glued into a three-inch piece of bamboo, which is used as a handle. Bind the bamboo with ribbon or braid to make a gay and comfortable grip (see Figure 21).

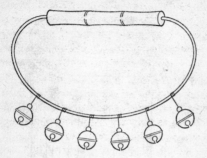

Figure 21

DRUMS Drums are very expensive. You can make reasonably satisfactory ones from rubber inner tubes stretched over a hollow container, for instance a biscuit tin. Cut the bottom of the tin out with a safety tin-opener, filing away sharp edges, stretch the rubber over each end, lacing them together tightly (see Figure 22).

If you have no storage problem, home-made tom-toms are great fun (Figure 23). Get a potato barrel from your green-

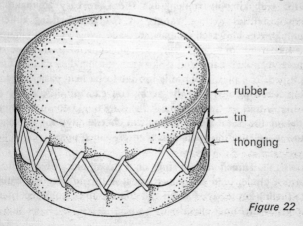

← rubber

← tin

← thonging

Figure 22

grocer, sandpaper it thoroughly and glosspaint it. Cover the open end with stretched rubber, securing this with a cord tied under the top rim.

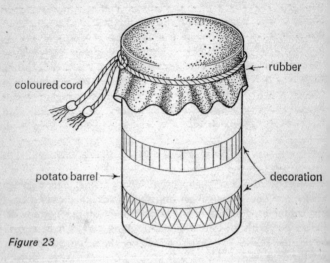

Figure 23

SHAKERS Young children enjoy following the rhythm of music with a shaking instrument and these are easy to make. Fill plastic bottles with a variety of contents making different sounds, e.g. bird seed (sounds soft and swishy), rice (sharper) ball bearings or gravel (very sharp). Remember the size of a three-year-old's hand and make sure the handles can be firmly grasped. If a plastic bottle is too fat to be held easily, attach a dowel rod pushed into the neck. You can fill almost any container – and let the children help; they ought to know what is making the noise. Be careful not to choose anything poisonous and make sure the opening is securely taped up.

JINGLES Thread curtain rings on a strong piece of wire shaped into a circle, bind the joined ends or thread through bamboo to form a protective handle and add a trail of coloured ribbon to give a streamer effect.

Group times

Small groups of children can sometimes play their instruments while you play the piano, a gramophone record or tape-recorder. Some of them have a good sense of rhythm and keep in time, others will get just as much pleasure from random playing. As long as they are all listening and enjoying themselves the time will be well spent. Some supervisors gather all their children together for music at the end of the morning with one adult in charge while the other helpers help clear away. Finger-plays or listening to records keep the children occupied for an awkward ten minutes.

Musical games

Instead of using your voice, use a tambourine to suggest to the children what to do. Beat out different rhythms for marching, skipping, hopping or jumping – remembering that skipping and hopping are difficult movements for young children. Clap your hands, or beat out on a tambourine the rhythm of a child's name, asking the children to guess what it is. You will have to provide the answers at first until they get the hang of it. Make echoes – clap a rhythm or tap it out on a tambourine, the children then echo it by clapping, tapping on the floor or using their instruments. Make up two sets of matchboxes containing a bell, some rice, some paperclips. Hold one set of boxes, put the others on a table. You shake a box and the child has to find the box containing the matching sounds.

Question-and-answer songs

For example, the children sing 'Pussycat, pussycat where have you been.' The adult answers, 'I've been up to London to visit the Queen.' At first the adult will have to sing both question and answer until a bright four-year-old takes up the lead. This is a form of training, for the child learns to wait for the answer before asking the next question, or vice versa.

If you have an instrument like a piano, tell a story interspersing words and music. Choose a simple theme, a family going on a picnic for instance. The father will walk with slow heavy steps in the low register, the mother in the middle of the keyboard, and the children skipping up higher. They could have a dog with them who would dash about all over the keyboard. The family could climb a hill (notes ascending) and the children could roll down the other side (notes descending). They could cross a stream and after eating their picnic (quieter, restful music for this) walk slowly home, tired after their day out. You don't have to be a skilled pianist to do this sort of thing: modern music has made most of our ears attuned to strange chords, and almost any combination of notes plonked down any old way will be acceptable in a story-telling context. You still need to face the children, so you are unlikely to be able to choose your notes with care. If you do find these sounds unbearably harsh use the black keys – they cannot sound unpleasant. Use the sustaining (right-hand side) pedal freely to merge the sounds, and the result will be positively professional even if you have never touched a piano before in your life!

Tape-recorders

If you have the use of a tape-recorder, you will find it very helpful. You can have a rich medley of music, a mixture of your favourite pop groups and classical composers in three to five minute sections, just long enough to hold the children's interests. You can record some favourite television signature tunes, to link home and playgroup. (Note: if you are recording from your radio or television, you must only use these tapes in your own home or playgroup, otherwise you will be infringing the laws governing copyright).

You can tape the children's own voices to amaze and delight them, sometimes recording their instrument playing. Tapes are a great asset for music and movement sessions; you can choose a simple theme and incorporate all sorts of sound effects – a bicycle bell, a revving motor-cycle engine, half coconut shells for galloping horses hooves. Make sure that what you tape is repetitive and distinctive enough for the children to be able to recognize the sounds and enjoy them. The BBC programme 'Music and Movement' is aimed at the five-plus child, but can sometimes be used in playgroups for short periods – five to seven minutes is usually enough. Be prepared for the children to move, or not to move, to play instruments or to ignore completely what you have recorded. They may want the music repeated or to record something themselves. A tape-recorder on which you can edit tapes to suit their needs is a godsend here. New tape-recorders are of course beyond the pocket of most playgroups but more and more people are buying them, so you may be able to borrow one.

Visiting musician

If you have a friend who can play an instrument, do invite him to your playgroup. Before he comes try to find a book with a good illustration of his instrument. When he arrives ask him to play some familiar music with one short unfamiliar piece. If you have a tape-recorder, ask if you can record him, so that you can use the tapes on future occasions. Be sure to ask beforehand whether the children will be able to touch or try to play the instrument – this can save great disappointment at the time of the visit. If you have no musical friends, contact the Salvation Army and ask them to visit, they usually have the best tubas in town. The local secondary-school music staff might be willing to lend you a senior pupil-musician. Get in touch with the local Education Authority's Musical Advisor, as long as he is familiar with the needs of your age group.

Records

Be sure that you have heard any record you plan to use often enough to be very familiar with it. Then you can add to the children's enjoyment and help them to listen more carefully by saying something like, 'We are going to hear a high "whistley instrument" called a piccolo. Look, here is a picture of it,' or 'In a minute you will hear a very big drum, much bigger than ours.'

Remember that the children will not want to sit and listen

for long, so if you buy long-playing records they will have to be played in short snatches. Expect to move with the children while they listen. They are not yet at the Junior stage where they will enjoy sitting still to concentrate on the sound. Their reaction will depend on the mood of the music. Quiet music may leave them sitting or lying on the floor. Anything more lively is likely to make them fidgety if they have to sit still. As basic principles to guide you in buying records, we suggest that you choose vocal records in which the words are clear and suited to the children's needs. For orchestral or single instruments choose recordings with a strong beat which the children could follow with their own instruments, such as Sousa's marches.

Some playgroups play their records as background music claiming that it creates a pleasant atmosphere for the morning. However, we feel that children are already bombarded with a great deal of background music from radios and television at home and in stores. One of our aims in writing this chapter is to encourage you to help your children to concentrate on listening and that to provide music merely as a background is contrary to these aims.

This list is intended to give an idea of the sort of things you might look out for. We have included only one selection of nursery rhymes as these are best sung live.

Children's Favourites, Music for Pleasure, Mono 1175, 80p. Medley of nursery songs.

Tunes for Children, arranged by Roger Fiske, EMI, 7EG 8575, 75p. A lovely hotchpotch of classical and traditional tunes.

Peter and the Wolf, Prokofiev, HMV XLP30064, £1·50. Too long for most children to sit through but fun for moving around to. The text is published by Faber at 25p.

The World of Christmas, King's College Choir, Decca, SPAA 104, 99p

Books

This Little Puffin, E. Matterson, Puffin, 25p. A comprehensive collection of musical games, fingerplays and songs which no playgroup should be without.

Mary Had a Little Lamb, H. E. Rey, Puffin, 12½p. Small illustrated book with very familiar songs.

Faber Book of Nursery Songs, £2·25. Very good collection of songs and games, illustrated.

Forty Action Songs, Forty Fingerplays, 15p from the PPA (see p. 342).

Oxford Nursery Song Book, Percy Buck, Oxford University Press, 45p.

Fifty Nursery Songs, Kodaly, Boosey and Hawkes, 40p

Ladybird Book of Instruments, useful for the book corner.

Starting on science

Nature study

If you work in a hall-based group, where every item you use has to be unpacked and packed away every day, it is easy to say that trying to do nature study is too difficult or not worth the effort. If this is your attitude we hope that after reading this chapter you will change your mind. Our children are increasingly forced to live away from nature and it is all the more important that we give them a chance to come into contact with living things. If we teach them to look after living things, perhaps they will be more likely to develop into caring adults who are concerned about the quality of life itself. The prerequisite for all this teaching is to have in your group someone who is prepared to say 'How much interest can I achieve under these conditions?' rather than 'I can't encourage any interest in nature in this grim hall.' We shall try to show you here simple ways of growing things which you can do throughout the year in the most unpromising conditions.

The nature table

A good place to site the nature table is somewhere near the door so that all parents and children are bound to see it when they come in. It should be low enough for the children to see its contents easily and preferably look down on it.

You may find it convenient to have a three-sided box for exhibits. This might fit easily on top of a cupboard; if it just has to be lifted down and freshened up each day, it is more likely to be used by other helpers when the nature enthusiast is away. If you don't have to pack everything away each day, as in a home group, then your work is so much the easier.

Some things can stay on the table for several weeks – an onion growing in water or slowly developing tadpoles. However, be sure to change some of the contents each week, following as near as possible a seasonal pattern, so that there is always something fresh to look at. This won't happen unless it is someone's specific responsibility and it is only fair to take turns. It is not easy for a group of helpers who live in towerblock flats and you must be prepared to feed in new ideas from magazines and books – we give a list at the end of this section, p. 334.

Keep a good quality magnifying glass on the table; this costs about £1 (Galts or local opticians) but it is well worth it, as it adds immeasurably to the interest of examining things. Attach it to the box or table, otherwise it may get lost. You can also leave a box on the nature table with pictures of some of the things you are displaying. One can often find excellent illustrations in books for older children – ask your librarian for help in obtaining these. There is a list of Ladybird books at the end of this section, which are cheap and small enough to fit on the table.

PLANTS Always try to have something growing on the nature table so that children can begin to get some idea of development by watching shoots and roots appear. Here is a list of suitable plants to grow, with brief notes on how to care for them.

Cut off about half-an-inch off the top of a carrot, stand it in a container with a little water which must be kept topped up, a saucer is ideal. After about a week, the leaves will start shooting again. Turnips do just as well, or the top of a pineapple.

Always let the children help you plant bulbs in the autumn, as early in September as possible. Use plenty of newspaper to protect the tables and floor and aprons for yourself and the children. Have a washing-up bowl and towel close by for immediate hand-washing. Hyacinths are usually most successful. Plant them in single pots, water well and put them in sealed plastic bags with about two inches of air space. Keep them in a cold place, not freezing, for three weeks before bringing them into a warm atmosphere. You should have blooms within a month. One of the nicest presents a child can take home for his family at Christmas is a growing bulb. In September, plant crocus in any plastic container (cress containers or yoghurt pots with holes made in the bottom are ideal), labelling each pot with a lollipop stick giving the child's name. Keep in the dark until shoots appear, then bring into the light. These should bloom at Christmas. Grow some hyacinths over water. You can buy special jars in coloured plastic for this, or use an old pickle jar. Don't let the bulb touch the water or it will rot, and put a small piece of charcoal in to keep the water sweet (the peat you planted your bulbs in will have small lumps of charcoal in or it can be bought at gardening shops). Often mothers catch the idea of indoor bulb planting and experiment at home. We heard of one mother in a poor area, who was asked to care for the playgroup's developing bulbs over the Christmas break. She could hardly bear to part with them when the holiday was over and vowed she would 'have a go next year'.

Buy from a seed shop beans or peas. Partly line the sides of a glass jar with dampened blotting paper or several layers of kitchen paper and place three or so beans or peas in between the paper and the side of the glass. Keep in a dark place to hasten growth. When shoot and root appear, bring onto nature table. Point out to the children how the root stays white and the shoot turns green. Put a thin bamboo stick in the jar to support the plant and keep watering.

Acorns, chestnuts or sycamore seeds will grow indoors; plant them in moist peat, put into small plant pots and keep in the dark until the shoot appears.

All these plants take time to grow and you will have to help the children learn patience in waiting for them to come up. Mustard and cress seeds, however, germinate with satisfying speed. They will grow on almost any material which holds moisture – blotting paper, flannel or sponge. Try wetting shapes on a piece of lint, a circle or a triangle, and place soaked cress seeds on this – shaped 'forests' will appear.

If you can get into the country in spring, bring back hazel catkins, pussy willows and horse chestnuts whose fat sticky buds unfold into leaves of soft green. If you have a warm place in January bring in branches of forsythia or flowering black-currant which will come out six weeks before their time. Con-tinue to bring in twigs with leaves on; let the children stroke the silky hairs on the back of a beech leaf, encourage them to find as many different shapes and colours of leaves as they can. During autumn try to get into the country to collect chestnuts, acorns, beech nuts and talk about these fruits in relation to the sticky horse chestnut buds and other twigs you had in spring. Many of the children will not remember but a few may, and begin to have a realization of the continuing life cycle of nature.

If you can provide one, a garden is very worthwhile. The children will be inexpert, but will gain a great deal from the experience. It pays to invest in real tools, long-handled trowels with matching forks, perhaps second-hand, are a good buy and really do the job. Plant quick-germinating seeds – radishes are very obliging. Choose flowers which are long-suffering and will grow under difficult conditions – marigolds, nasturtiums or pansies, usually thrive. Forget-me-nots, love-in-the-mist are self-seeding. Try to choose flowers of different sizes, everything from low-growing aubretia to hollyhocks. Have you got room for sunflowers? Their seeds are large and easy for children to handle and their height is very impressive.

Let the children examine the various forms of seed pods, show them how immaculately the seeds are packed away. Get some peas and beans in their pods, most families have frozen peas these days. Let the children pop open the pods to admire the way the peas and beans are arranged; let them stroke the delicate lining of a bean pod – more interesting than any plastic bag. If there is a grub in the pea – out with your nature viewer or magnifying glass.

Try to grow an abundance of flowers so that the children can cut some to decorate the playroom and if possible occasionally take some home. If it is impossible to have a garden, maybe you can have a window box, or at least a large pot for growing things outside.

If your hall committee will not allow you a small patch of ground, you could take small groups of older children to a park or better still a piece of waste ground. Count how many flowers you can find. Turn over stones to see what is living underneath. Touch the bark of different trees and notice the variations in texture. Look out for a wide variety of grass seeds in late June and July. Let the children feel the stubbly stiffness of wild barley and contrast it with the feathery grace of Yorkshire fog or any other types of grass which grow in your area.

ANIMALS An aquarium can be a very simple affair – a large jar or a flat dish with tadpoles or goldfish. You will need a collection of pond weed to oxygenate the water (duckweed or American pond weed). Your local pet shop will give you further advice.

If you cannot have a permanent aquarium, you could occasionally bring in a jar containing something live. Put caterpillars or snails in a glass jar with some suitable food. Cover with net or perforated paper, and tie down securely, otherwise the creature will escape. Introduce this to any child who lives in a concrete world with care. It is fascinating to see a snail with his horns out, but it might seem menacing. Tell the children how you found the snail in the long grass and how you picked it up very gently and put it in a jar so they could see. Then produce the jar out of your pocket, or buy a nature viewer (32p) from a local optician or most educational suppliers such as Galts. These tubes of plastic have a compartment in which you can put small insects – a ladybird or an ant. You then look at them through a double lens which magnifies several times. Put a few grains of sugar in first so that the children can see how strong the magnification is, because, again, an ant several times enlarged can be a horrifying sight.

If you curl up in horror at the sight of a worm, be very, very careful not to communicate your feelings; it is unforgivable to pass on phobias to a child. If you cannot control yourself, keep out of the way and let some other helper cope. You may even, through working in a playgroup, learn to overcome your antipathy to creepy-crawlies.

If possible bring a pet to playgroup, provided it can be stroked and handled by the children. Guinea pigs are delightfully tame and don't seem to mind being stroked and held; hamsters and gerbils are less reliable and it may be better for an adult to handle them or leave them in their cage. One group we know borrowed a litter of kittens and showed them to a group of flat-dwelling children. It was easy to see how much they enjoyed handling the warm soft animals.

Be sure to safeguard the animal's wellbeing. Don't let too many children crowd around, make certain each child appreciates the need to be careful. This contact with animals should not only widen a child's experience of life, but also help him to see that other creatures have needs and rights which must be understood and safeguarded. If you are lucky enough to have a resident pet – easy if you have a home-based playgroup – show children that keeping an animal is a responsibility as well as fun.

If you possibly can, find a friendly farmer and take the older children to visit a farm. Look at pictures of the animals before you go, and talk about their size relative to the childrens' (one four-year-old we knew fled weeping from a very gentle cow, protesting 'It's too big!'). Many groups we know visit zoos, but the smaller ones which cage up large animals seem to us to be sad and smelly places and better avoided.

Can you encourage birds to come to your playgroup? A bird table, so constructed that it will not allow cats or rats to climb, is ideal. A pamphlet entitled 'Garden Friends' issued by the RSPCA, The Manor House, Horsham, Sussex, gives instructions on how to make one. Site your table where it can be easily seen from a window. Let the children help make every bird's favourite pudding which consists of stale cheese, fried bacon rind, sultanas, apple, sunflower seeds, peanuts and a large hand-full of corn. Let the children cut all this into small pieces with scissors, then pour over the mixture some cheap dripping (we use old chip fat). Pour into any sort of mould. Turn out when set and watch the birds come flocking. If you are not allowed a bird table, you may be able to use a window sill. It is wise not to leave birds pudding out overnight, though, as this can encourage rats.

Sometimes, in dreary February when your bulbs become covered with a strange fungi and flu runs rife through the helpers, you may wonder what to put on your nature table. On these occasions you can exhibit things you have collected throughout the year. Various stones and pebbles (these look better in a shallow dish of water or painted with Marvin Glue) collections of shells, dried seedheads. Go to a seed merchant and ask for small samples of oats, barley and corn. Soak some of it in water and put it in your airing cupboard at home. With luck it may germinate. If all else fails, you can always grow some more cress! Or raid your vegetable basket to bring a collection of vegetables to cut open and examine under the magnifying glass. Think of the complicated way a cabbage grows or the neat way an apple is constructed, which is clearly seen when sliced straight through.

If you can dig up some worms, bring a bucket of earth, some dried leaves (the worm's food) and a glass jar, to the playgroup. Put the worms and earth in the jar, with a layer of silver sand over the earth's surface. On top of this put the dried leaves. Tie brown paper round the jar to darken it. After about a week, you should be able to see silver sand tracks in the earth where the worms have gone to the surface to drag down the leaves.

As a final point, always encourage the children to make contributions to the nature table. You may be taken aback, as one country supervisor was, by the gift of a dead hedgehog, but you may be delighted by the loan of some coral, strange shells or a potato which has grown to look like a duck.

Book list

On The Farm ('Pigs', 'Cows', 'Horses', 'Farm Birds'), BBC Publications, 20p each. Strongly made board books, clearly illustrated suitable for very young children.

Book of Pets, The Farm, The Zoo, Puppies and Kittens, Wills and Hepworth, 'Ladybird Books', 15p each

The Seashore and Seashore Life, What To Look for in the Spring (also *Summer, Autumn* and *Winter*), *Plants and How They Grow*, Wills and Hepworth, 'Ladybird Books', 15p each. Rather too old but useful to adults as a source of ideas and have suitable illustrations for children.

Eggs, Frogs, Trees, Dinosaurs, Macmillan 'Starters' series, 35p each. (Clear illustrations and simple text.)

Zoo on Your Window Ledge, Joy Sporynska, Muller. How to keep slow-worms, ants, etc. Mainly for playgroups who do not have to pack away.

'Nature Study With Children Under Seven and Concrete Yard Gardening', Nancy Quayle. An excellent pamphlet available from M. J. Wootton, 44 Claremont Gardens, Upminster, Essex, 15p including postage.

The beginnings of science

Much of our modern world is dependent on technology and it is likely that many of our children, whether girls or boys, will grow up to be involved either directly or indirectly with machines. It is important therefore to encourage children to take an interest in the scientific world, to be curious about what makes things work and not take them for granted. Your approach here should be the same as we have suggested throughout this book; that is, you introduce the material to the children, stand by to ask and answer questions, but in the main let them play at their own level. By its very nature, and because some of it is expensive, the equipment should be carefully supervised. You can keep everything in a large box, say an old drawer, securing some of the more fragile pieces of equipment with a chain to stop them being broken or mislaid. If you screw eyelets into the side of the box, breakable objects can be clipped on with a spring clip (such as is used to fasten a dog's lead). Then if the child has permission to take, say, a magnifying glass to the other side of the room he can unclip it, returning it to the box when he has finished. In addition you are more likely to notice that something is missing at clearing-up time.

MAGNIFYING GLASSES of high quality (approximately £1, Galts or a local optician) with a variety of objects of very different textures, e.g. a piece of wood, knitted square, pebble, piece of sandpaper. Encourage the children to look at their skin, nails, clothes and hair; use the word 'magnify' – to make bigger. Never say it's magic because it isn't: magnification is a scientific fact. We have already mentioned nature viewers (p. 331); Arnolds also have a good twin-lensed magnifying glass (25p).

MAGNETS Try to get powerful magnets – they are really fun to use. The physics department at your local secondary school should be able to help you acquire them or your television dealer (old-fashioned television sets used to have circular magnets which spring together with a satisfying 'glunk'). When working with strong magnets, take off your watch, so as not to affect its mechanism. Galts have a magnet set, consisting of different shaped magnets with small iron bars, balls and cylinders: a very interesting toy for older children. Train the children to take special care of this piece of equipment as the little balls are easily lost.

Provide a variety of things for the children to try to magnetize, some of which will be attracted by the magnet and some of which won't, e.g. paper clips, hair-slides, nails, drawing pins, brass screws and iron filings (obtainable from the metal workshop of your local secondary school). Put some of the things on top of a piece of cardboard, and move the magnet about underneath. The children will be fascinated to see that some things move, the magnet being powerful enough to attract them through the cardboard.

We saw an ingenious use of the magnetic sealing strip taken out of an old fridge door. It had been cut into lengths of three, six, nine and twelve inches, and was used with the solid metal side of an old gas stove. The different-sized strips stuck easily to the large surface to make patterns and provide a variety of mathematical experiences – counting, size relationships and fractions. This piece of equipment would cost you nothing but a journey to a junk yard, but it is bulky to store. The Ladybird book *Magnets, Bulbs and Batteries* gives an account of other simple experiments. Remember that as well as attracting each other, magnets repel. Many a playgroup adult only learns this principle of repulsion after playing with magnets.

ELECTRIC CIRCUITS (see Figure 24) Find a piece of pegboard (offcuts from do-it-yourself shops) approximately twelve by eighteen inches. Attach to it as shown below several feet of plastic-covered wire, a torch bulb holder, torch bulb, bicycle lamp battery, bolts for terminals and switch – about 50p altogether. This piece of equipment is a clear example of cause and effect: if the circuit isn't complete, that is if the wires are not in contact with the terminals and battery, the bulb with not light.

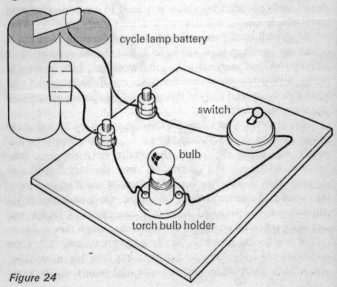

cycle lamp battery

switch

bulb

torch bulb holder

Figure 24

TORCHES – Take a torch to pieces, show how the bulb will not light up unless all the bits are in the right place. Show the effect of shining the light through different materials, some lacey, some thick, or how the light changes colour if you cover the head of the torch with different coloured cellophane.

INSIDE A PIANO – Would you be allowed to take the lid off to show the children the hammers striking the strings? Let the children try for themselves, insisting that they press the keys gently.

GEARS – play an important part in our lives: in bicycles, cars, clocks and watches, and you should give the children an opportunity to understand the principle whereby energy is transferred from one place to another, e.g. you turn a small wheel and this moves a large one. Gears are supplied in Plastic Meccano and in the Child Guidance Plastic Railway. You also may find a good example in an old clock. Have you got an old rotary egg beater? Again this shows the way gears work and a child can make bubbles galore if you put a little washing-up liquid in a bowl of warm water.

TELEVISION SETS, WIRELESSES AND CLOCKS – Ask a trained electrical engineer to remove the cathode ray tube and the mains lead from an old TV set and then let the children dismantle the remainder. Take out the valves from wirelesses and clock faces and let the children have what's left. You may be amazed at the skill and ingenuity they show in taking these to pieces. Save the bits taken off for use in woodwork or for the junk modelling collection.

OLD TYPEWRITERS, SEWING-MACHINES AND CAMERAS – You may find one of these in a jumble sale and the children will enjoy playing with them and coming to terms with the principles they incorporate.

THINGS TO SMELL – To encourage children to use their noses, collect any small containers – matchboxes with small holes punched in them will do – and place in them things which smell very differently. If you have a garden, this will be easy in summer, when you can get petals from roses, stocks, lavender, carnations as well as strong-smelling herbs – mint, rosemary, thyme or chives. Without a garden, you could rummage through your food cupboard. Take some orange peel, a piece of cheese, dried bay leaves, some cinnamon or a few drops of vanilla essence sprinkled on a tissue. Play a game with the children, giving them a box to smell and identify.

Simple experiments

Remember how limited the pre-school child's concentration is, and keep your activities short.

1. Siphon off the cream from two pints of milk into a screw-cap plastic jar, to which you have added three washed marbles (these are not essential, but hasten the process of churning) and a pinch of salt. Shake the jar vigorously for ten to fifteen minutes: you should then find yourself with about an ounce of butter. This is quite hard work, but several children can take turns. They will be fascinated to see small globules of butter forming which eventually turn into one lump. Spread the butter on some bread and see what comments you get.

2. Take a variety of similar cooking substances – salt, sugar and flour for instance. Put a little in three separate dishes and let the children add water to see which dissolves and which doesn't. Suggest that they taste each solution and ask them which they prefer. You may be surprised at their choice. We listened to a talented supervisor talk to a mature three-and-a-half about the similar shapes of a goldfish and a dead mackerel. Nearby were some garden pinks. The supervisor suggested he smelt both the flowers and the fish and asked him which he preferred. He chose the fish!

3. Try and mix a little cooking oil with water. Will it mix together? Will milk and water? Orange squash and water? Encourage the child to touch, taste and smell – you may have a scientist in the making.

As we have suggested before, don't be afraid of using correct words in connection with these happenings. For instance, some groups will only need to be told that 'the little lumps of butter stick together to make one big lump'. Others, who have been used to conversation with adults and had a rich diet of stories and rhymes, may be ready for more exact language, 'the little lumps of butter coagulate to make one big lump'. Try to have one or two such ideas up your sleeve if you feel a child is at a loose end and needs this sort of adult stimulation. But always remember that your children will achieve the most satisfaction, and the most learning, through play. So don't let scientific enthusiasm run away with you!

Conclusion

This book has attempted to show that there is a growing need for pre-school education and that this need is not being met by the State.

Whilst welcoming the Government White Paper on Education 'A Framework For Expansion' which gives local authorities the go-ahead to submit proposals for nursery expansion in their area, we feel this may lead to marked regional differences in the State provision of pre-school education. The danger is that the provision, rather than being a direct reflection of need in a particular area, may reflect the priorities of local policy-makers, who may well be middle-aged men, far removed from the needs of young families. Consequently, there is a continuing need for those of us involved in this field to be watch-dogs and to form pressure groups at a local level. We hope this book will give much-needed support to playgroup staff and help them in this, perhaps unexpected, aspect of their work.

The White Paper acknowledges that in areas of 'social deprivation' there may be a special need for full-time pre-school education, but also states:

Authorities should consider carefully the role of voluntary playgroups. Many thousands of mothers devote considerable time and energy to running and organizing such groups, which make an important contribution, providing for over a quarter of a million children under five. The Government have substantially increased their financial support for the playgroup movement. They hope that the development of playgroups will continue, particularly among socially deprived children, and that local authorities will consider how the best use can be made of them. Some playgroups, if provided with better equipment and qualified staff, could become maintained nursery classes: part of the primary school but on a separate site. Playgroups will continue to have a distinct and valuable role to play alongside an expanding system of nursery education. These voluntary groups may be assisted by local authorities in their various capacities, by cash grants, the loan of equipment, or the advice of the authority's nursery and infant specialists. They may be associated with a local primary school, and so enjoy the support of qualified teachers.*

Again, we would plead that in these areas efforts be made to build on, rather than supplant, the role of parents (as has been the traditional nursery-school approach). Here we feel playgroups offer the radical new thinking which is needed to justify the financial investment proposed. We strongly welcome the government's acceptance of 'a diversity of provision' and recommendations for continuing research into the effects of varying types of pre-school education.

We are also concerned that because of the falling birth rate, there may be a tendency in some areas to absorb under-fives into emptying infant school classrooms without the necessary trained nursery-school teachers or ancillary staff. Again a careful watch must be kept to see that administrators' statistics showing numbers of children receiving nursery education are not in fact reflecting, yet again, education on the cheap. In such circumstances parents may understandably remove their children from a good, but fee-paying playgroup to a free but possibly less effective local authority nursery class. It is only by continuing adequate financial help to playgroups that this situation can be resolved.

The playgroup movement has shown that not only is there a need for pre-school education, but that the majority of parents, given the chance, are willing and capable of being involved in their children's education. Local authorities should be sufficiently enlightened to harness the contribution of those who have formed themselves into a quite remarkable pressure group to protect one of the most vulnerable sections of our society – the under-fives.

* 'A Framework for Expansion', HMSO, December 1972.

Appendix

Useful addresses

Pre-School Playgroups Association (PPA)
Alford House
Aveline Street
London SE11
or
304 Maryhill Road
Glasgow NW
Membership open to all playgroups and interested people. £3.50 per year gives you membership at local and national level, monthly journal *Contact*, insurance scheme, discounts, etc. Send stamped addressed envelope for list of very useful publications on many aspects of playgroup work.

The Advisory Centre for Education (ACE)
Fitzwilliam House, Trumpington Street,
Cambridge
Provides information on all aspects of education for parents and teachers. Publishes the magazine *Where*.

Nursery School Association (NSA),
89 Stamford Street,
London, SE1
Campaigns for increased nursery school provision and publishes pamphlets on all aspects of nursery school education.

The National Campaign for Nursery Education. Details from Anlaby Lodge, Teddington, Middlesex.
Presses for increased provision of education and play facilities for young children, especially nursery schools.

National Playing Fields Association,
57b Catherine Place,
London, SW1
Can advise on improving local facilities for playgroups or outdoor playing space.

National Children's Bureau
8 Weakley Street
London EC1

Manufacturers of playgroup equipment

Abbatts
328 Kennington Lane
London SE11

Adventure Playthings
Queensway
Glenrothes
Fife, Scotland

E. J. Arnold & Son Ltd
12 Butterley Road
Leeds 10

Community Playthings
Darvell Community
Robertsbridge
Sussex

Educational Supplies
Association
P.O. Box 22
Pinnacles
Harlow, Middlesex

Galts
P.O. Box No. 2
Cheadle, Cheshire

Goodwood Toys (Lavant) Ltd
Chichester, Sussex

Berol Ltd
Old Medow Road
King's Lynn
Norfolk
(for Margros glue and Marvin medium)

Philip & Tacey Ltd
Northway
Andover, Hants

Reeves
Lincoln's Inn Road
Enfield, Middlesex

Thomas Little
(Rose & Crown)
Rose and Crown Street
Warrington, Lancs.

Toy and Furniture Workshop
Church Hill
Totland Bay
Isle of Wight
(this firm gives two-year guarantee)

Reading list

LADY ALLEN of Hurtwood, *Planning for Play*, Thames & Hudson

BLACKSTONE, T., *A Fair Start*, Allen Lane

BOWLBY, J., *Maternal Care and Mental Health*, Schocken Books Inc.

BOWLBY, J., *Attachment and Loss*, Pelican

EYKEN, W. van der, *The Pre-School Years*, Penguin

FLETCHER, R., *Family and Marriage in Britain*, Pelican

GAHAGAN, D. M. & G. A., *Talk Reform*, Routledge

GESELL, A., *The First Five Years of Life*, Methuen

HADFIELD, J. A., *Childhood and Adolescence*, Pelican

ISAACS, S., *Social Development in Young Children*, Routledge

ISAACS, S., *The Nursery Years*, Routledge

LAWTON, D., *Social Class, Language and Education*, Routledge

LEWIS, M. M., *Language, Thought and Personality*, Harrap

MATTERSON, E., *Play With a Purpose for Under-Sevens*, Penguin

MILLAR, S., *The Psychology of Play*, Pelican

NEWSON, J. & E., *Four Years Old In an Urban Community*, Pelican

NEWSON, J. & E., *Patterns of Infant Care in an Urban Community*, Pelican

PIAGET, J., *Language and Thought of the Child*, Routledge

QUAYLE, N., *Nature Study with Children Under Seven*, School Natural Science Society, No. 13, 1967

SANDSTRÖM, C. I., *The Psychology of Childhood and Adolescence*, Pelican

SPOCK, B., *Baby and Child Care*, Four Square Books

WALL, W. D., *The Enrichment of Childhood*, Nursery School Association

WEBB, LESLEY, *Children with Special Needs in the Infant School*, Fontana

WINNICOTT, D. W., *The Child, the Family and the Outside World*, Pelican

YOUNG, M. & WILLMOTT, P., *Family and Kinship in East London*, Pelican

YOUNG, M., *Innovation and Research in Education*, Routledge

YUDKIN, S., 0–5: *A Report on the Care of Pre-school Children*, Allen & Unwin

Acts enabling local authorities to support playgroups

1937 – Physical Training and Recreation Act, 4–(1)
1946 – National Health Service Act, 22–(1), (5)
1948 – Children Act, 46–(2)
1948 – Local Government Act, 136
1957 – Housing Act, 93–(1)
1962 – Education (Scotland) Act, 25–(6)
1963 – Children and Young Persons Act, Part I, 1 (1), 2, 3
Ministry of Health Circulars 36/38 and 37/68

Index